Who are the Celtic Saints?

Cover of the Gospel Book of St Molaise

Who are the Celtic Saints?

Kathleen Jones

Maps by Nick Bradshaw

CANTERBURY
PRESS
Norwich

© Kathleen Jones 2002

First published in 2002 by the Canterbury Press Norwich
(a publishing imprint of Hymns Ancient &
Modern Limited, a registered charity)
St Mary's Works, St Mary's Plain
Norwich, Norfolk, NR3 3BH

The author asserts her moral right under the
Copyright, Design and Patents Act, to be
identified as the Author of this Work

British Library Cataloguing in Publication Data

A catalogue record for this book is available
from the British Library

ISBN 1-85311-493-6

Typeset by Regent Typesetting, London
and printed in Great Britain by
Biddles Ltd, Guildford and King's Lynn

Contents

Maps

Illustrations

The cover design represents St Samson and his monks on their way from Cornwall to Brittany, and is taken from a thirteenth century stained glass window in the cathedral at Dol-de-Bretagne, where he founded his monastery.

Plate Section

A Prayer from the Western Isles

Helmsman: Blest be the boat.
Crew: God the Father bless her.

Helmsman: Blest be the boat.
Crew: God the Son bless her.

Helmsman: Blest be the boat.
Crew: God the Spirit bless her.

All: God the Father,
            God the Son,
            God the Spirit,
            Bless the boat.

            The God of the elements,
            The King of the elements,
            The Spirit of the elements,
            Close over us
            Eternally.

                 – *Carmina Gadelica*

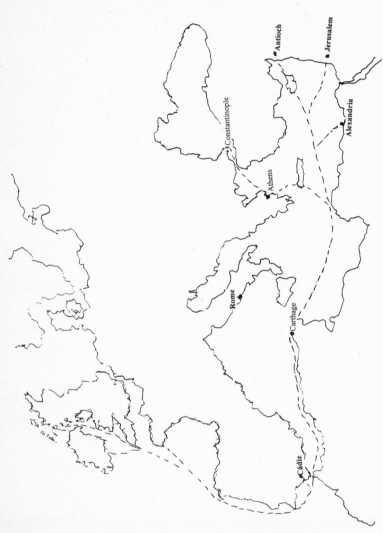

Western Sea Routes from the Middle East

Preface

In recent years, there has been a considerable revival of interest in Celtic spirituality, and stories of the holy men and women of the Celtic lands have been re-told, often festooned with quaint and charming legends and scraps of folklore. Dragons are tamed, saints float across the sea on millstones, the dead are miraculously revived, the wicked are spectacularly punished by thunderbolts or convulsions, and choirs of angels hover over births, ordinations and deathbeds. It is all mildly comic, and quite unbelievable.

The Celtic saints deserve better treatment than this: they are men and women who witnessed to the Christian faith with great courage and steadfastness in a very harsh world of war and plague and famine. It is no service to their memory if we repeat and multiply improbabilities. This account of their lives and ministry is an attempt to assess the reality of their experience, to shake it free of the cobwebs of fantasy, to set it against the historical background of their time, and to make sense of some very tangled records.

The life of the Celtic Church was largely determined by geography, for geography shaped its history. The British Isles are tilted towards Europe. The fertile lowlands of the south and east are easily accessible to invaders from the Continent, but rugged mountains and scattered islands to the north and west long kept them at bay. Until the time of the Norman Conquest, invading armies tended to be halted by natural barriers: the Scottish Border country, the Welsh mountains, Dartmoor and Exmoor, and the Irish Sea.

For some four hundred years, the lowland areas became a Roman province called Britannia; and when the Roman legions withdrew early in the fifth century, there was a descent into what are called 'the Dark Ages', when civilization decayed, and religion and learning were lost. Modern historians take a much less drastic view of this process than many of their predecessors; but if it is even partially true of what became England, it is not true of the Celtic fringe. In Ireland, in the mountainous areas of Scotland and Wales, in Cornwall and Brittany, in the islands between, and for a time in Northumbria and the Midlands, the flame of faith burned brightly, and a distinctive kind of spirituality developed.

In the eighth and ninth centuries, the Celtic Church gradually became assimilated to the organizational patterns of Western Christendom, but its heritage lingered on in remote rural areas. It has never been entirely forgotten. In our own time, it has been widely recognized as an authentic gift of the Holy Spirit from which all Christians can learn.

The people beyond the boundaries of Roman Britannia, generally called the Celts, seem, from the evidence of archaeology, to have been of a common Iron Age culture with the inhabitants of the rest of Britain before the Romans came. They lived in tribal societies, with petty kings, powerful landowners, and warriors who defended land and cattle from the depredations of other tribes. Their craftsmen produced remarkably intricate ornaments, weapons and stone carvings which show a high order of artistic skill. The Roman historian Tacitus commented that they seemed to be of two kinds: the tall, muscular red-haired people who had been driven north-west, and a darker, curly-haired breed to the south-west, whom he thought came from the Iberian peninsula. Modern scholars make a distinction between the *Goidelic* culture of the people of northern Ireland, western Scotland and North Wales, and the *Brythonic* culture of the people of southern Ireland, South Wales, Cornwall and Brittany.

Julius Caesar's two invasions of south-east Britain in 55 and 54 BC were only exploratory; but the Roman military machine which came with the Emperor Claudius and his elephants in AD 43 went on to conquer the Lowlands, and to make some inroads into Wales through the valleys and coastal strips. The Roman army included architects, engineers, builders and craftsmen, all travelling with the legions. Roman roads and Roman forts kept their conquests secure. Fine cities, luxurious villas, and a Romano-British class which had all but forgotten its Celtic heritage developed under Pax Romana. The Romans were never troubled by consideration for the culture of those they conquered. They spoke of themselves without hesitation as the *superiori*. Those they conquered were assimilated into the Roman way of life. Those beyond the frontiers were barbarians, lesser breeds, *inferiori*.

Among the many faiths which swirled around the Roman Empire and reached Britannia was Christianity. Bishops from Britannia attended the Council of Nicaea in 324–5, and the Council of Arles in 347, and the British Church is mentioned by a number of Eastern Mediterranean historians of the fourth and fifth century: Theodoret, Sozomen, Socrates Scholasticus, Palladius; but Rome's hold over the outposts of empire was crumbling. In 410, the remaining Roman legions were withdrawn from Britannia, because Rome itself was under attack from Huns and Vandals. Christian culture gradually disintegrated as the Romano-British class lost its old protectors and faced new pagan enemies, the Norsemen who were attacking their coasts.

Paradoxically, it was in this period that Christianity developed a new strength in the parts of the British Isles which had never been Romanized, and where a common culture had been established along the western seaways. Celtic Christianity was different from Roman Christianity because it did not come by land routes across the former Roman Empire. It came by sea, and looked not to Rome, but to the Church in the Eastern Mediterranean: Jerusalem, Constantinople, Antioch, Alexandria.

Professor E. G. Bowen's seminal study *Saints, Seaways and Settlements in the Celtic Lands* (1969), based on the mapping of archaeological finds and sites, has had a profound effect on studies of the Celtic Church. It drew on a series of studies in historical geography which highlighted the basic distinction between Lowland and Highland Britain. We now understand, as earlier generations of writers on the Celtic saints did not, that the gap between Roman culture and Celtic culture was a very wide one. The Romans were land-lubbers: the legions were a formidable fighting force, covering vast distances across Europe in forced marches; but though they had sea transports for their troops, Rome was not primarily a naval power. The Celts were island dwellers, used to the sea, and making their contacts across the water.

Even in the Bronze Age, six or eight centuries before Christ, trading ships had come from the Middle East in search of tin, which is a necessary constituent of bronze. The shipping routes ran from Constantinople and Alexandria along the coast of North Africa, through the Straits of Gibraltar to Cadiz, the first large harbour on the Atlantic coast of Iberia; thence to Gaul, the coast of Brittany, via the Channel Isles to Cornwall, and up through the islands of the Irish Sea between Wales and Ireland to the Clyde valley, making use of rivers and inlets and islands. Nearly all of the bases of the Celtic Church were on estuaries or on rivers, not in the inhospitable mountains or the marshes.

The great Celtic monasteries which developed in the sixth century drew less on the experience of the Church of Rome, increasingly involved with the decaying Roman Empire, than on the inspiration of the great Eastern ascetics of the fourth century – Antony and the Desert Fathers, Basil of Caesarea and John Chrysostom. When they learned from the Continental Church, it was primarily from an unusual bishop, Martin of Tours, and his successors. Tours could be reached by boat along the river Loire, without the need to travel overland through dangerous Frankish territory.

Martin (*c.* 316–97) was a Roman citizen, but he was born in Pannonia, now part of Hungary, where his father was an officer in the Roman legions. He became an officer in the Imperial Guard himself, but resigned his commission to follow the way of the Desert Fathers of Egypt, taking the gospel to the country people or *pagani* with scant regard for the territorial claims of neighbouring bishops. *Ninian of Scotland may have studied under him, and he inspired much devotion and many Celtic church dedications. In early Celtic martyrologies, the list of departed saints recited on main feasts was commonly headed by Martin's name. If there was an element of resistance against Roman control in the Celtic Church, this much-loved ascetic, with his Eastern ways, was a focus for it.

The Celtic Christians resembled the Eastern Christians in many ways: their asceticism, their penitential rules, their distinctive calculations for the date of Easter, and their tonsure. The tonsure was the most obvious sign of their differences from Rome. While Latin monks wore their hair cropped into a decent bob, and shaved the crown in memory of Christ's circle of thorns, neither Greek nor Celtic monks followed this practice. Some writers say that they shaved their hair in front of a line running from ear to ear over the crown, others that they had a small semi-circular half tonsure, possibly with a fringe at the front if their hair had not receded. In either case, they let it grow long at the back, and Latin monks were shocked at the sight of these unkempt 'half-bald' men.

From the early fifth century, the Church in Celtic lands developed its own traditions, its own saints, its own patterns of worship enriched with bardic poetry and song, and a faith remarkably close to that of the Apostles. It was based, not on a framework of bishops and dioceses, but on monasteries. The Celtic lands had no large cities, and few roads. Much of the land was bog or mountain, so they never developed the Roman pattern of administration by diocese and parish. It was this basic difference of organization, rather than the much disputed issue of 'the correct date of Easter' (an arcane calculation, see Chapter 10) which made them reluctant to accept the jurisdiction of the Roman Church. Continental clergy, with their clear line of authority to Rome, their fluent Latin and their neat tonsures, found them baffling, their customs incomprehensible and their names unpronounceable. They often concluded that they were unlettered and probably heretical; but Celtic Christianity was firmly based on the Nicene Creed. It seems to have been unaffected by any of the unorthodox beliefs which troubled the Continental Church. The Celtic monasteries were centres of sound theological study where libraries were built up, and ties of affection and respect bound teacher and student.

Their faith and their learning spread from Ireland eastwards to Iona, and from Iona to Scotland and Northumbria. From Wales, groups of emigrants took it south to Cornwall and on to the Welsh colonies in Brittany; but its distinctive character was not to last. As the other great Mediterranean bastions of Christianity were

threatened, and began to fall to Asiatic invaders, the bishops of
Rome claimed supremacy over the whole Church. This claim was
resisted by the Celtic Church leaders, as it was by the patriarchs of
Eastern Christendom. The Celtic lands had never been part of the
Roman Empire, and they were opposed to what they saw as a
second and more extensive Roman invasion, this time ecclesiastical
rather than military in character.

Eastern influence in the Celtic Church was so strong that, at the
Synod of Whitby in 664, when Celtic and Roman ecclesiastics
argued out their respective positions, Abbot Colman of Lindisfarne
based his defence of the independence of the Celtic Church on the
writings of the patriarch Anatolius of Constantinople, who had
similarly resisted papal control. The Celts lost their case; but when
Pope Vitalian came to appoint an archbishop of Canterbury two
years later to reconcile the two parties, it is significant that he chose
a Greek monk-scholar, Theodore of Tarsus in Asia Minor. Before
taking up his new office in Canterbury, Greek Theodore was forced
to wait in Rome until his front hair grew, so that he could have a
Latin tonsure.

Though the Celtic Church eventually lost its independence,
Celtic spirituality has remained as an inspiration to all the
Christian Churches; but centuries later, the sources of information
on its work and its leaders are difficult to handle: scattered, patchy,
and often positively misleading. The ancient Lives of the saints are
not biographies. They are accounts of an individual's holy acts and
virtues, written to instruct the faithful in piety, not for information.
Historians become understandably irritated by their lack of dates
and reference to identifiable events, and deterred by the frequent
recounting of improbable miracles. They are also deterred by the
partial nature of the evidence available. Many records were lost
through the sackings and burnings of the monasteries, and more
through damp, decay and bigotry in the succeeding centuries.
There are great gaps in the evidence. Some saints greatly revered in
their own tradition have almost disappeared from sight through
the accidents of history, while others may have gained in reputation through the survival of manuscripts.

Many of the Lives of the Celtic saints were re-written by twelfth

century Norman monk-chroniclers in an attempt to prove conti-
nuity between the Celtic Church and the Roman Church, and to
boost the claims of their own newly instituted dioceses. Conse-
quently, the sources have to be treated with great caution (see
Notes on Sources). The ancient Lives present a series of fascinating
intellectual puzzles which theologians and historians are still
endeavouring to solve. Much effort has gone into identifying
individual saints. Continuing efforts are being made to quantify
numbers and to date events by cross-reference.

In the past century, new insights have come from other academic
disciplines. There are some physical remains – ruins, wells and stone
crosses, identified as traditional pilgrimage sites right through the
Middle Ages. Archaeological excavations have revealed the ground
plans of oratories and monastic communities, and helped to reconstruct the daily lives of the people who used them. Linguists have
added much from their knowledge of the Celtic languages.
Historical geographers have continued to trace patterns of missionary journeys and migration along the sea-routes.

Many of the Celtic saints have slipped into the shadows of
history; but if we cannot reach across the centuries and discover the
whole truth about their lives, we can at least get closer to it by re-
examining the records and defining more clearly those whose
memories have been preserved. They are unusual people: dedicated,
and full of the Holy Spirit. They are also sometimes anti-social,
quirky, and plain obstinate. They love remote islands, where they
can contemplate the Creator through the creation – sun, moon and
stars, winds and frost, mountains and seas and forests, birds and
fish and great seals. They bless freely, and they curse freely. They
live plainly, and pray much. Though the outlines of their story are
blurred by time or distorted by inaccurate reportage, it is often in
the details of their lives that we can make direct contact with them.
When we read of Brigid companiably sharing a bacon sandwich
with Bishop Ibar while her nuns disapproved, of David's voice
ringing out 'like a trumpet' at the Synod of Brefi, of St Neot, who
was a very small man, having to climb on a stool in order to reach
the altar and say Mass, of King Oswin of Northumbria warming
himself by the fire and mulling over the gentle reproaches of his

friend Aidan, we touch the reality of their experience. This really happened, this is how it was. In learning about the Celtic saints as individuals, we can begin to reconstruct the world in which they lived.

Notes

1. Celtic saints are holy men or women who were commemorated in the Celtic liturgies and listed in Celtic calendars. They have not necessarily been through the formal process of canonization by the Roman Catholic Church, which is of much later origin.
2. The ancient Lives of the Celtic saints are distinguished by a capital 'L'.
3. An asterisk before the name of a saint denotes that there is a separate entry elsewhere in this study. The saints are grouped according to the country in which their main ministry took place, and can be located through the alphabetical index.
4. A single date after a saint's name is the date of death. Many dates, particularly in the fifth and sixth centuries, are only approximate. The date is followed by the saint's traditional feast day where this is known, as an aid to identification.

Palladius and Patrick

The earliest Christian communities in Ireland were probably groups of traders who had come by sea from Gaul or the Mediterranean, and settled in the south of the country. They may have been there for a century or two before Pope Celestine I sent a bishop named Palladius to visit them in 431. His mission was *ad Scottos in Christum credentes* – to the Scots who believe in Christ. The name of Palladius, the date, and the pope's letter, reported by Prosper Tiro, bishop of Aquitaine and later a papal secretary, provide a reliable starting-point for enquiry. Papal records at this time described Ireland as *Scotia maior* and present-day Scotland as *Scotia minor*.

The word *credentes* (present tense) makes it clear that the 'Scots' in Ireland were already believers. At this time, the Roman Church did not undertake missionary activities among the barbarians outside the Roman Empire. The main concern of successive popes was to regulate the Church within the boundaries of empire, not to breach those boundaries and convert pagans; but as the imperial boundaries crumbled, Pope Celestine, whose pontificate lasted from 422 to 432, initiated efforts to strengthen papal control in the outlying territories where the secular power of Rome was declining, and to root out unorthodox beliefs. He had particular trouble with the Gallic bishops, who were inclined to go their own way, and many of whom were Pelagians.

In order to understand the purpose of Palladius's mission to Ireland, it is necessary to know something about Pelagius, and about the Pelagian 'heresy' in what is now south-eastern England. Pelagius opposed St Augustine's extreme view of original sin, holding that human beings had free will, and possessed the capacity to

Iona

Moville

Derry

Bennchorr

Dromore

Clonbroney

Tuam

River
Shannon

Clonard

Clonmacnoise　　Tallaght

Enda

Clonenagh　Timahoe

Glendalough

Scattery
Island

Killaloe

St. Mullins
on the
Barrow

Beggary
Island

Ballyvourney

∧　**Mountains**

50 km

Ireland

do good. Though this is now theologically acceptable, he was accused of heresy in Jerusalem, and condemned for his beliefs in Carthage in North Africa (where Augustine had been a student) in 415. His tenets had spread to south-east Britannia (what we would now call Kent and the Home Counties), and Bishop Germanus of Auxerre was commissioned to make two short visits in about 429 and 445 to assist the local clergy in rooting out Pelagian beliefs.

Latin chroniclers after the Norman Conquest often asserted that Celtic monks in the fifth and sixth centuries went to study in Auxerre rather than in Tours, but it is extremely unlikely that Germanus had any contact with the Celtic lands, or that Celtic monks, who were sea-farers, subsequently went in any numbers to Auxerre. As early as 1864, the eminent Victorian historians Haddan and Stubbs dismissed the Auxerre assertion as unhistorical, 'legend mixed up with evident fiction'. The main reasons for it seem to have been first, the fact that Martin of Tours, with his unortho-dox practices, was none too popular in Rome, while Germanus and Auxerre were highly regarded; and second, a confusion of Germanus of Auxerre with other saints of the same name, which was not an uncommon one (see *Germanus of Man and *German of Cornwall); but there is a third reason which is less well known. Pelagius died in about 420, and Palladius would have known about him. He is often described as 'a British monk', and he may have been of Celtic stock. Pelagius is the Greek form of his name: the original form was Morgan, which means 'sea-borne', and he could have been a Brython from Wales. Though Pelagius spent most of his active life on the Continent, and probably picked up his unorthodox ideas there, the suspicion of Pelagianism may have been a reason for the mission of Palladius, who may have accom-panied Germanus on his first visit to south-east Britannia, and the accusation of Pelagianism subsequently provided a useful stick with which to beat the Celtic Church. There is no evidence that Pelagianism was ever found in the Celtic lands. The strength of the Irish penitential discipline suggests a firm belief in original sin.

Though a good deal has been written about Palladius and his 'mission to Ireland', it was not a missionary visit in the usual sense of the term. It was a pastoral visit to existing Christian settlements.

He arrived late in 431, probably landing in southern Ireland at Arklow or Wicklow, convenient points on the sea-route from Gaul, but he was not with the Irish Christians for very long. In the following year, he either died in Ireland or set out for Rome on the death of Pope Celestine, and died on the way there. Some commentators have judged his Irish visit to be 'unsuccessful', comparing it with Patrick's mission, but this is to misunderstand its purpose. Palladius was making a short-term visit to a rather dubious outpost in order to examine the orthodoxy of its beliefs, to set up a diocesan structure and to report back to the pope. It was no part of his remit to make converts.

Palladius would not have travelled alone. By the fifth century, bishops of the Roman Church moved about the Roman world surrounded by attendant clergy, and the consecration of a new bishop required the laying on of hands by three bishops. If Palladius went to Ireland to regularize the life of the Church, this would have required the consecration of at least three new local bishops, almost certainly by three existing bishops. On his way to Ireland, he may have been joined by two colleagues from Gaul for this purpose.

Southern Irish tradition, based on the Life of Declan of Ardmore, says that when Patrick reached Ireland, there were four bishops already in office: *Ailbe, *Ibar, *Declan and *Ciaran of Saighir. The four are known as 'the Palladian bishops', and they all worked in the south of Ireland: Ailbe in Meath, Ibar in Wexford, Declan in Waterford and Ciaran in West Cork; but what is known of their Lives suggests that they lived and worked some decades after the visit of Palladius. They are unlikely to have been the original bishops consecrated by Palladius and his fellow-bishops in 431 or 432, though they may have been active during Patrick's mission.

Patrick (fifth century: dates usually given as *c.* 390–461), 17 March, has become the patron saint of Ireland. His mission had an entirely different origin from that of Palladius. He reached Ireland not from Rome, but from one of the Romanized cities on the west coast of Britannia. He went as a missionary, and to northern Ireland, working largely in the areas of Ulster, Leinster and

Munster. The chief evidence for his life and work consists of two long documents which he wrote towards the end of his ministry – the *Confessio* and the *Letter to the Soldiers of Coroticus*. Though many other writings have been attributed to him, and some, such as the Celtic hymn known as 'St Patrick's Breastplate', may be based on his prayers and teaching, only these two are now accepted as authentic. His mission in Ireland probably began twenty years or more after the visit of Palladius to the south.

The issues of when Patrick lived and when he commenced his Irish mission have been hotly debated, and beset by political and religious arguments which are often still tenaciously held. Did he reach northern Ireland in the 430s, soon after the mission of Palladius to the south? Did he arrive at some time in the 450s, which fits better with the dates assigned to people said to have been his followers or co-workers? Were there *two* St Patricks, of whom the elder *might* have been Palladius under another name if he did not die when we think he did, and stayed in Ireland? It has even been suggested that 'Patrick' was a local name for Palladius, and that they were the same person. No theory seems too outlandish to attract adherents. From the time of St Augustine's mission in 597, scribes and scholars have been hard at work on the issues, and it seems that the more Patrick is studied, the less we know about him. A great deal of misinformation has had to be cleared away to establish what we do know.

Patrick himself is no help at all. He makes it clear that his purpose in writing the *Confessio* was to defend himself against charges made against him by a unspecified group of 'elders', but he does not say who the 'elders' were, or what charges were made. His purpose in writing the *Letter to the Soldiers of Coroticus* was to try to secure the release of Christians who had been taken captive by a raiding chief, probably from Dumbarton in the Clyde estuary. In neither case does he quote place-names, apart from one which has proved unidentifiable, or the names of his fellow-workers, and he gives no dates. Presumably these details were well known at the time, but since these two documents are the only contemporary evidence on his life and work, they are now susceptible to widely differing interpretations.

We do not know where Patrick was born, though it is generally agreed that it must have been somewhere on the west coast of Britannia, and not in Wales. The Clyde valley, Carlisle and Bristol have all laid claim to him. Of these, Dumbarton or Carlisle seem the most likely. *Ninian, the apostle of Galloway, came from an international trading settlement along the Clyde, and Dumbarton may have been the headquarters of Coroticus and his soldiers, whom Patrick seems to have known. Carlisle was a large and fortified Roman city guarding the northern borders of Britannia, and likely to retain its Roman character long after the Romans withdrew their legions. Both were on a short sea-route to Ulster, protected by many small islands. A mission from Bristol is much less likely. The shortest sea-route from Bristol would have taken the missionaries to the south of Ireland, and we know that Patrick landed in the north.

Wherever it was, Patrick's home was still a centre of Roman culture and Christian worship after the departure of the legions. His father, Calpurnius, was a city councillor and a deacon of the Church. His grandfather, Potitus, was a priest. Both were evidently married. Though Rome advocated celibacy for the priesthood, the rule was not always kept in the remoter parts of the Empire. The Armagh copy of the *Confessio* has a marginal note to the effect that Potitus's father was also a deacon, which suggests a clerical dynasty. Patrick had a Roman name (though he does not say what it was, and we have to wait for an eighth century Life by a monk-chronicler named Murchiu, who worked on material now lost, to tell us that it was Magnus Sucatus Patricius). The family was evidently wealthy. They lived in the city, but had a country villa at a place named Bannaventa Burniae. This is the only place-name which Patrick provides, and exhaustive research has failed to identify it. When he was 'almost sixteen', he was captured there with some of his family's slaves by Irish raiders, and taken to Ulster as a slave himself.

Patrick was a nominal Christian, but he says that up to this time, he had given little thought to his faith. He was 'like a stone in deep mud' when he first encountered God in his captivity; but he found himself praying, 'in a single day up to a hundred prayers, and in a night nearly the same'. He was in Ireland for six years. He tells us nothing of his circumstances, except that he was 'pasturing domestic animals daily' on the mountain and in the forests. It has been suggested, largely because of his later knowledge of Druidic rites, that he may have been attached to a Druid's household. We know very little about Druidic practice in the fifth century, because the Druids kept no written records and had no temples: they worshipped in the open air, in sacred groves or at springs. Though latter-day Druids and New Age followers have romanticized their practices, they may have practised human sacrifice, and their rituals involved wizards and warlocks, spells and incantations. Possibly this experience strengthened Patrick's Christian faith. We do not know whether he was well or badly treated, but eventually he was inspired by a dream to escape. He travelled something like 'two hundred thousand double paces' (estimated at two hundred miles, which is practically the length of Ireland) and found a ship. The ship's captain was surly, and did not want to take him as a passenger, though he had money for his passage. We are not told how a runaway slave acquired it. However, when he turned away, disheartened, some of the crew called him back. Whether they were sorry for him, wanted his passage money, or intended to sell him as a slave at the next port, is not clear.

After this, the record becomes even more obscure. Many speculations have been made about the ship's course. At one point, Patrick says, they unloaded their cargo and took it overland for some time. This was a common procedure for cargo boats: currents could be dangerous round a peninsula, and the boat would be easier to handle without a shifting load. They may have crossed Cornwall, avoiding Land's End, or a spur of Brittany, avoiding Finistère. While they were on land, he says that they crossed a 'desert', a statement which has sent some enquirers in the direction of North Africa; but in the Irish language, *disaert* or *disert* meant simply a deserted place, without habitations, where a hermit might go to be away from the world: it did not require sand (cp. the *Disert Coemgen*, *Kevin's rocky place of sanctuary). The land party probably avoided settlements, for fear of being robbed of its cargo. They must have encountered at least one band of raiders, because Patrick was either captured or sold by the crew, and became a slave again. After sixty days, he tells us, he managed to escape with some others from this second captivity.

After that, he spent 'a few years in the Britains', a term which he does not explain. He could mean Wales, the land of the Brythons, or possibly Brittany, referred to as Little Britain, where the Welsh had settlements. We do not know how he lived or what he did. He does say that he 'suffered great tribulations', as a runaway slave might, but there is no foundation for the repeated assertions that he studied at Lérins, the celebrated monastery off the Mediterranean coast of France, or in Auxerre with St Germanus. In the *Confessio*, written towards the end of his life, he repeatedly bewails the fact that he is 'unlearned'. He begins, '*Ego, Patricius, peccator et rusticissimus*' – 'I, Patrick, a sinner and very uneducated'. He would not have been *rusticissimus* if he had trained in the great schools of Lérins or Auxerre; and he would have written in good classical Latin. His Latin was fluent enough, but he expressed himself awkwardly, like the provincial he was. In his Romano-British home, colloquial Latin would have been his first language, but it was not the Latin of the Augustan age or the Latin of the monks of his day.

When he finally reached home, his family was thankful to see him again. He does not say what he did on his return, only that he dreamed of a man named Victoricus, who called him back to Ireland: 'We request you, holy boy, that you come and walk farther among us.' And he was 'stabbed at heart', and knew that he must go back to the land where he had been a slave to convert the people. He did not do so until 'after many years'. At some point, he must have trained for the priesthood, but we do not know where, who his teachers were, where he was ordained, or where or when or even if he was consecrated.

These sparse facts have left room for endless conjecture. Did he prepare for the priesthood in Britain, perhaps in his own remote home town? Was he tutored by some rather limited local theologians? Did he serve as a priest in his home area before he went back to Ireland? He went to Ireland with a party of missioners, which suggests that the senior clergy in his own city knew of his enterprise and approved it. He had funds for his mission: he says he sold his patrimony to pay for it. He makes it clear in the *Letter to the Soldiers of Coroticus* that he paid his own way, and refused to accept the many gifts which were later piled on his altars.

Was he consecrated as a missionary bishop before he left home for Ireland, or did his consecration come later? Was he consecrated at all? For generations, his *Confessio* has been published as *The Confession of St Patrick the Bishop*, but there is no evidence that a consecration actually took place. The suggestion that he went to Rome and was consecrated by the pope as the successor to Palladius did not arise until many centuries later, when commentators began to look for a way of establishing a smooth transfer of authority from one to the other. It is unlikely, because in his claims to divine authority for his mission, he always appeals to God directly: 'Was it without God or according to the flesh that I came to Ireland? Who compelled me? Men look askance at me. What shall I do, O Lord? I am exceedingly despised.' He would not have written in this vein if he had believed in the supreme authority of the pope, and had been commissioned in Rome.

Patrick sailed up the Boyne when he reached Ireland, and his early ministry centred on Armagh. He says in the *Confessio* that he made a practice of going straight to the clan chief or petty king in each area to convert him and his court, but he makes no mention of one of the best-known stories about his ministry, a dramatic confrontation with the High King at Tara. This story occurs in Murchiu's Life, written between 680 and 700 for the bishop of Sletty. The purpose was to advance the claims of the bishops of Armagh to be primates of Ireland, with authority over the other bishops. The story of a direct confrontation between Patrick, the missionary saint of Ulster, and the High King of Tara made the point very clear. In Murchiu's account, Patrick went to Tara, the holy place of the Druids, 'the capital of all paganism and idolatry'. All the fires had been extinguished in preparation for a Druidic festival. The first new fire for the festival had to be lighted in the king's house, and all the nobles and important people, 'not to mention the wizards, enchanters, soothsayers and devizers, and teachers of every art and deceit', had gathered at Tara for the occasion. By coincidence, it was Easter Eve. Patrick climbed the nearby hill of Fiace (Slane) and lit his Paschal fire in a cemetery. It was 'very bright and blessed, and as it gleamed in the darkness, it was seen of all the inhabitants of the flat plain'. The king, infuriated, gathered twenty-seven chariots, and set off with his wizards and warlocks to punish the perpetrator of this sacrilege; but Patrick performed several miracles, and left the king 'terrified and shaken at heart, and the whole city with him'.

Unfortunately, this splendid story of Murchiu's is now generally discounted as sheer invention. Patrick never claimed that he could perform miracles; and the ceremony of the Paschal fire did not develop until the eighth century. It was not practised in the Church of Patrick's time.

Patrick's life was a very hazardous one. He speaks in the *Confessio* of 'twelve dangers', of many other trials, of poverty and calamity, of imprisonment in irons, and of the fear of death; but he gives no details, nor does he name any of his colleagues. In his *Letter to the Soldiers of Coroticus*, he lists his achievements: he says that he has baptized 'thousands on thousands' in Ireland; that the sons and daughters of the petty kings have come in 'countless numbers' to be monks and virgins at his call; that 'pious women' threw their jewellery on the altar to support his cause; and that he converted a 'beautiful princess' (some writers later tried to identify her with *Brigid). He may have exaggerated a little in order to impress Coroticus. He does not mention a confrontation with the High King of Tara, which would certainly have impressed the robber king from the Clyde valley; but he must have had many confrontations of a less dramatic nature.

As far as we can tell, Patrick was not a great ecclesiastical organizer. He was essentially a missioner with a roving commission. He negotiated, he preached, he exhorted, he baptized, he ordained Irish clergy. He claims that he went to parts of Ireland where Christianity was unknown, but nowhere does he claim that in his day it was unknown throughout the whole country. There is no record of how or where he died. It seems that he was not regarded as an outstanding figure in Ireland immediately after his death; and there was evidently no knowledge of his burial place.

His tomb would have been a valuable asset to support the claims
of the Armagh diocese in the eighth century, if it could have been
found. Though the *Book of Durrow* (late seventh century) mentions
him, he is listed as a priest, not as a bishop. *Adamnan notes in his
Life of *Columba, written about 690, that Mochta (*Mochua?)
was a disciple of Patrick, but makes no other reference to him. In
Northumbria, Bede records the mission of Palladius, but does not
mention Patrick at all. Some recent commentators have suggested
that, if it were not for his *Confessio* and the *Letter to Coroticus*,
Patrick would be unknown today. These two documents somehow
survived all the hazards of tribal warfare, Viking attacks, a damp
climate and later conquest.

Both historians and theological writers have been contemptuous
about the 'mass of rubbish' which has subsequently been written
about Patrick, but it should not be used to detract from his achievements. Murchiu complained that even in his day, many had
attempted to record Patrick's life, but that 'because of differing
opinions and numerous persons' numerous conjectures', they had
'never succeeded in reaching the one sure path of historical fact'.
The opinions and the numerous persons' numerous conjectures
have gone on multiplying ever since; but when all the legends and
the accretions to his story have been set aside, Patrick is still an
outstanding figure. The strength of his faith and the personal
commitment which come through his writing contributed greatly
to the rich and sudden flowering of Celtic Christianity in Ireland.

Early saints who may have been associated with Patrick:

Asicus (*c.* 470), 27 April, was a disciple of *Patrick, a married man
and a metal-worker. He may have accompanied Patrick on his
mission from Britain, for his name is a Romanized one, though he
is sometimes called Tassach. He subsequently became a priest.
*Oengus the Culdee calls him 'the royal bishop', and describes him
giving Holy Communion to Patrick. Patrick is said to have left
Asicus in charge of a church at Elphin. Asicus sought the solitary
life, and became a hermit on an island in Donegal Bay. His monks

wanted him to return to the monastery in his old age, and came to take him back again, but he died at Ballantrae on the way.

Attracta (Athract, Araght, Taraghata) (dates unknown), 9 February, is reputed to have been a consecrated virgin whom Patrick* instituted in the religious life. She founded a hospice for travellers by Lough Gara in Connaught (west of Boyle in County Sligo), and became skilled in herbal medicine. The *History of Sligo* records that the hospice still existed as a 'hospital or religious house' in 1692, and was called Termon Killeracht. The place is still known as Killaraght (Araght's cell or oratory).

Attracta's half-brother Conall, who had a church at Drum, near Boyle, refused to let her settle near him because he had resolved to avoid the company of women. She is said, in the fashion of strong-minded sisters, to have cursed him 'in robust terms', and expressed the hope that his foundation would fail. While they both have a place in Irish martyrologies, Araght also figures in the Roman Martyrology of Cardinal Baronius (1596), but Conall does not.

Gobnet (fifth century), 11 February, was a virgin from County Clare who fled her home because of a family feud. It is not clear whether she ran away to avoid an arranged marriage, or whether her immediate family was killed in some clan conflict. She wandered for a time, and was apparently told in a vision that she must settle where she would find nine white deer grazing. She found them at Ballyvourney, near a spring on a hillside, close to a coppice, which meant that she had fresh water and wood for a fire. There was a monastery nearby, where the monks would have helped her with supplies, and offered her some protection. She is said to have kept bees, though the traditional story of how bees were introduced into Ireland relates to *Modomnoc, who brought them from Wales in the sixth century. She was under the spiritual direction of a saint named Abban (there were several of this name). Other women came to join her, and a religious community developed. There is a stone with a cross in her valley, known as St Gobnet's stone. Excavations on the site of her community in 1931 produced finds suggesting that the community kept cattle and sheep, gathered hazelnuts, grew grain and wove cloth. The place of her settlement became a place of pilgrimage in medieval times, and her feast day a holiday. There was a special Mass and a 'round' or procession round the site, with a special prayer for her favour: 'May God hail you, holy Gobnet. May Mary hail you, and I salute you myself. I come to you complaining about my affairs, and seeking my cure of you through God.'

She became one of the best-loved saints of Ireland.

Loman (*c.* 450), 17 February. The Life of *Patrick compiled by Goscelin of Furness in the twelfth century says that he was the son of Patrick's sister, whose name was Tigris. *The Tripartite Life* of St Patrick says only that he was a disciple of Patrick, and went to Ireland with him. He was left with a group of clergy to look after the boat and take it up the River Boyne while Patrick began his mission. He developed a mission of his own, and made contact with the wife of the chieftain of Trim, who was a Brython from Wales. She welcomed the clergy. The chieftain's eldest son was converted, and Loman was given land for a church. Later, the chieftain was converted, and Loman is sometimes described as the bishop of Trim.

Macanissey (Oengus MacNisse, Macanasius) (*c.* 514), 3 September, is reputed to have been a disciple of *Patrick. Very little is known about him for certain, though he has been identified with a boy described in *The Tripartite Life of St Patrick* who carried Patrick's books. One legend is that he had such a great respect for the Scriptures that he would not carry them in a satchel, but proceeded on all fours so that he could carry them on his back. Latin Lives say that Patrick consecrated him a bishop, that he went to Rome, that he went on pilgrimage to the Holy Land, and that he was the founder of the monastery at Kells, but none of these claims can be confirmed.

Macarten (Aedh MacCairthinn) (*c.* 505–6), 24 March, is said to have been an associate of *St Patrick, and consecrated by him as bishop of Clogher. The Lives are fragmentary, but they include the only liturgical Office to survive from this period except one of Patrick's. Macarten's grave was at Clogher. A reliquary, 'the Great Shrine of St MacCairthinn', reputed to have contained a fragment of the True Cross, is known as the *Domnach Airgid*.

Mel (Maol) (*c.* 487), 6 February, was a Briton, a disciple of *Patrick, and probably a relative. It is he, not Patrick, who is reputed to have 'given *Brigid the veil'. The procedure for clothing a nun had not been developed at this time, but he may have confirmed her in a consecrated life as a virgin. *The Irish Saints* says that he came over to Ireland with Patrick, and *The Tripartite Life* of Patrick claims that Patrick consecrated him, though most sources now doubt whether he was a bishop. His work was centred in Ardagh and district (Ulster), where he founded a monastery and a church about 454.

Mel lived with his aunt, who acted as his housekeeper, but 'slanderous tongues spread serious accusations against them'. According to one legend, Patrick went himself to investigate the gossip, but they were both cleared of the charges, though Patrick advised Mel to be more circumspect in future.

The *Annals of Ulster* record Mel's death as occurring in 487. He is also mentioned in the *Félire* of *Oengus and the *Martyrology of Tallaght*. He is a patron of Limerick. References to him in the Life of Brigid by Cogitosus suggest that he may have had a brother named Melchus, but most modern writers have concluded that 'Melchus' is merely the Latin form of Mel's own name. There is no extant separate Life of Mel, but he is frequently mentioned in the Lives of Patrick and Brigid.

Mochta (Mo-Chuta) (?535 or 537), 19 August, is said to have been a Briton and a disciple of *Patrick. He may have been one of Patrick's original companions from Britannia, though the name we have for him is Irish. He was the first bishop of Louth, and there is a story that he and Patrick had an agreement that if one of them died, the other would look after both communities. Other stories about Mochta (that he had 200 bishops among his disciples, that an angel taught him how to write on a tablet, that he was conse-crated in Rome) can safely be dismissed as later inventions designed to emphasize his importance, or to confusion with one of the many other Mochtas. He is said to have had the impertinence to question the biblical account of the age of the patriarchs, whereupon Patrick sentenced him to an unusually long life. One account says that he lived to the age of 300, but another says that he died at 90. John Cumming in *Butler 2000* describes Mochta's Life as 'moderately entertaining' and 'highly fabulous'. However, there seems no doubt that he is a real person. The *Annals of Ulster* record his death in January 535, and add that he wrote in a letter, 'Mauchteus, a sinner, priest, disciple of St Patrick, sends greetings in the Lord'.

He may be the Mochta mentioned by *Adamnan in his Life of *Columba as 'a pilgrim from Britain, a holy disciple of the holy bishop Patrick', who is said to have prophesied the birth of Columba.

The 'Twelve Apostles of Patrick': traditionally, these are *Ciaran of Saighir, *Ciaran of Clonmacnoise, *Columba, *Brendan of Birr, *Brendan of Clonfert, Colum of Tir da Glas, *Molaise of Devenish, *Cainnech (the navigator), *Ruadhan of Lorrha, Mobi of Glasnevin, Sinell of Cleenish, and Ninnid of Inismacsaint (Lough Erne); but there is no evidence that any of them actually lived in Patrick's time.

The Tara Brooch

2

Ireland: the Monastic Founders

Traditional accounts of the sixth century Irish Church assumed that there was a continuous line of authority from Rome from Palladius to *Patrick, though recent Roman Catholic writers have been much more cautious about this claim. Other recent writers, mainly from the Free Churches, have tended to focus on Patrick as the charismatic leader; but the ecclesiastical structure which developed after Patrick's time does not in fact fit closely with the activities of either Palladius or Patrick. It was neither a structure of dioceses nor an association of freely operating missionaries. It was based on monasteries, religious communities which combined learning and piety with the traditional functions of the Irish bards and chroniclers. There was no central authority. Each monastery was independent and self-governing under its abbot.

Among the famous early foundations were *Ciaran's Clonmacnoise, *Comgall's Bennchorr (Bangor), *Finnian's Clonard, *Mo-Chuta's Lismore, *Declan's Ardmore and *Ailbe's Imlech or Emly (see map, p. 2). The traditions of these founder-abbots were carefully preserved and much honoured. The historians Myles Dillon and Nora Chadwick comment in *The Celtic Realms* that the system was 'in some respects comparable to that introduced by St Martin of Tours' and that it 'had its origin in the ascetics of the Eastern deserts, Egypt, Syria and Mesopotamia'. Monasteries were usually sited on or near the coast. On the west coast of Ireland, where there were few trees, they were made of stone, and the remains of some of these monasteries survive to the present day; but most were less permanent, being constructed of timber frames with wattle-and-daub walls, and thatched with reeds. Collections of these round 'beehive' huts, surrounded by a wall or a trench, closely resembled Celtic villages.

The distinction between a monastery and a village was often not very clear, for a monastery might house lay people as well as monks: people who came for instruction or healing, and whole families, probably of the same clan. In a clan-based society, land could only be granted for a monastery with the agreement of the clan leaders, and grants were seldom made to members of other clans. Sometimes the monks led a detached life, building their own monastery and farming for themselves; but often there were families already living on the estate. The men of such families were often semi-attached to the monastery and were termed *manaig*. They lived with their wives and children (but were allowed only one wife: pre-Christian Irish society was polygamous, but monastic authorities were strict about monogamy). They would go to church services in the monastery, bring their children to be baptized and their dead to be buried, and their sons would go to the monastery school. One or more of the monks would act as their parish priest, making pastoral visits to their homes. The inclusion of *manaig* and their families in the figures given for the population of monasteries may account for the very large numbers claimed for some monasteries. These figures represented the total number of people living on the monastery's lands, but they were not all monks in the strict sense of the term.

The monks proper lived in the monastery. Some, but not all, would be priests, and some, but not all in most monasteries, would be ascetics who had deliberately chosen a life of hardship and penance. The abbot was often the son of a king or a powerful landowner. Though there are cases of abbots with more humble origins, like Ciaran of Clonmacnoise, the son of a cartwright, they were sufficiently rare to be notable. In some cases, the position of abbot was hereditary within particular noble families. The abbot combined the functions of a spiritual director and an estate administrator. Large monasteries had one or more bishops attached to them. Bishops had distinct liturgical functions in ordaining the clergy, and taking part in the consecration of other bishops, but they were missionaries, subject to their abbot's authority when they returned to their parent community.

Occasionally the two roles were combined, but the installation of an abbot, with the consent and loyalty of the community, was an even more important ceremony than the consecration of a bishop. Bishops had no territorial jurisdiction, no cathedral seat, and no diocese: they were not bishops *of* a defined area, but merely bishops *in* that area, travelling from one village to another, founding churches and monasteries, preaching, converting, baptizing and ordaining, inspiring isolated groups of Christians.

Observers from the more highly organized Latin Church found it difficult to understand this pattern of administration, and perhaps not many of them tried. They repeatedly commented adversely on the Celtic lack of inter-monastery organization of the kind which developed in Europe, and the failure of the Irish clergy to establish dioceses. They appear not to have understood that the lack of roads and cities dictated a different form of ecclesiastical structure. At a time when the Continental monasteries were growing wealthy and powerful, the Celtic monks' poverty, simplicity and humility, combined with a frequently alarming asceticism, stood out in sharp contrast. Continental observers suspected unorthodoxy in belief, but could not find it. The Celtic faith was strictly Trinitarian, following the Nicene Creed; but it was all very informal, very irregular, very *Irish*.

The modern Catholic historian David Hugh Farmer comments in his introduction to *The Age of Bede* that:

Irish monasticism was a movement of great interest and significance. Its dependence on Eastern régimes as well as the unusual circumstances of Irish society combined to give it a character of its own. This was in many ways unlike that of most Benedictine monasteries in the West.

Benedict of Nursia (*c.* 480–550) founded a monastic system which was adopted all over Europe; but its principles included the complete rejection of home and family. Irish monasteries, by contrast, were almost extended families, often composed of members of the same extended family group. Their relations with each other were warm and affectionate. They commonly spoke of their abbot or their teacher as their father (often using the word *papa* in their chronicles, which led to further misunderstandings, since Roman clergy assumed that this word referred to the pope of Rome). Many of the Irish saints have names beginning with 'Mo-', which means 'My', followed by a diminutive. Laserian became 'My Laise' and so *Molaise, Aed became Mo-aed-og or *Maedoc, Carthach became *Mo-Chuta, Lugaid became *Molua. The chroniclers write of the saints not only as figures to be respected, but as personal friends, and this affection became part of the tradition.

Most of the monasteries practised subsistence agriculture. The staple food was corn, baked into loaves or eaten in a thin gruel with milk. (There were of course no potatoes, later the staple food of the Irish peasantry. The Spaniards imported them from the Americas at the end of the sixteenth century.) Dairy farming was important, and only the more ascetic abbots like *Comgall or *Fintan of Clonenagh tried to deprive their monks of milk and butter. The virgin *Gobnet may have been the first to set up beehives (though later a counter-claim was made for *Modomnoc), and honey must have been a very welcome addition to the diet, since there was no sugar. Apart from the ascetics, the monks were regular meat-eaters except during the periods of fasting prescribed by Church practice. The weight of bullock bones discovered in archaeological digs on monastic sites is remarkable. They also kept pigs and hens (eggs were greatly prized), and sometimes there would be venison or wild boar, perhaps the gift of a nobleman after a hunt. They also ate fish: there was Irish salmon in the rivers, and monastic sites on estuaries or coast meant access to an abundance of fish from the sea. The monks grew their own vegetables and apples, and gathered nuts. The usual drink was milk, beer or water, though monasteries near trading centres may sometimes have had wine from the Mediterranean countries for meals, as well as the necessary wine for the Eucharist.

This sounds like an attractive and well-balanced diet, but in practice the standard of living varied a great deal from monastery to monastery, and the agricultural economy was always precarious. Cattle disease or the failure of a harvest spelled disaster. Food might be plentiful in the summer and autumn, but stocks of grain would run low by Christmas, and in the spring months, the only

meat available might be salt pork. Salt for preserving meat was a
rare commodity: a lump of salt was a much-appreciated gift, and
salt often had to be secured from the evaporation of sea-water, or
a paste made from the ashes of burned seaweed. There was real
hardship in the winters on the off-shore islands, where rough seas
would prevent the delivery of supplies from the mainland. Even on
the mainland, supplies stopped altogether in times of inter-clan
wars, lengthy famines, and plague. Some monasteries failed
because the monks could not feed themselves, and it was not
unknown for monks to starve to death.

Life was always lived on the edge. The rhythm of the Church's
year, the fasting of Lent, seedtime and harvest, reflected the periods
of dearth and plenty, and the extreme penances of some of the
ascetics, who made a virtue of austerity, have to be viewed against
this uncertain background.

Many stories are told about the monks' reverence for creation,
their love of the natural world, and their ability to communicate
with animals. Many of the animal stories, such as those told of
*Cainnech and the two Ciarans, are probably apocryphal, but they
speak eloquently of a gentle culture in which the monks were
friends with the lesser creation, and lived at peace with it. In Helen
Waddell's resonant phrase in *Beasts and Saints* (1940), they are
reminders of 'the mutual charities between monks and beasts . . .
the untroubled acceptance of an ancient understanding'.

Once the monasteries were established, they became centres of
learning, enriched with a Celtic gift for song and poetry, the
heritage of the bards. There was an intense respect for monastic
training and education. Chroniclers would recite the clan status of
their saints in great detail, but they were also careful to mention the
monasteries where their saints trained, much as Victorians would
note whether a man was at Eton or Harrow, Oxford or Cambridge.

It was the custom for children of noble families to be fostered,
and then sent young to the monastery, where they would live in the
abbot's household, and be taught in Latin. Many of them stayed on
to become monks themselves. Monastic life was the only means of
education and spiritual understanding, and it offered an escape
from a life of continual clan warfare. The Lives of the saints

contain many stories of men whose warrior fathers opposed their intention to enter the Church. The sons were the 'new men' of their day, who saw something better and finer in human life than the ritual spilling of blood. Their fathers' habit of marching back from a victory with the heads of their opponents fixed on their spears must have appalled and distressed them. They were not weaklings: they were prepared for martyrdom – and one of the perpetual embarrassments of the Irish monks was that they had no opportunity to give their lives for their faith, like the early Christians. So they spoke of three kinds of martyrdom: the 'red martyrdom' which meant facing death for Christ's sake; the 'blue martyrdom' which involved freeing oneself from evil desires by fasting, penance, hard labour and sleep deprivation; and the 'white martyrdom' which meant abandoning everything they held dear. These beliefs explain both the severity of their penances and their practice of 'exile for Christ': leaving the land they loved for alien countries and alien peoples.

There are repeated references in the literature to 'plagues' and 'leprosy' affecting the Irish monasteries. Some writers have assumed the epidemics to have been an early arrival in the West of bubonic plague: there must have been rats in plenty, and trading ships could have brought it from the Middle East. Others have suggested that that the main recurrent plague was smallpox; but there are no records of pock-marks, and in the Life of Mo-Chuta, abbot of Rahan, it is recorded that those whom the plague attacked 'first changed their colour to yellow', which suggests some kind of liver disorder. This links with the Yellow Pestilence which is recorded in more detail in seventh century Wales (see Chapter 5). It is likely that there was more than one epidemic disease. As we gain a fuller understanding of the extent of travel between the Celtic lands, it is not difficult to imagine how crowded conditions on board ship might lead to the transmission of disease – and how it would spread among people whose resistance must have been very low in the monastic settlements.

Several of the Irish saints are said to have suffered from 'leprosy', but this is almost certainly an anachronism. The Norman scribes who later wrote or revised the chronicles and the Lives of the saints were very familiar with the effects of leprosy in their own society: the Crusaders brought it to Europe in the early eleventh century; but the Irish word which they translated as 'leprosy' merely meant 'infirmity' (see *Finan Lobur). It is unlikely that leprosy existed in Ireland on any scale in the preceding centuries. However, there must have been many other kinds of infirmity. The spartan conditions under which the monks lived probably encouraged scurvy and other skin diseases caused by a restricted diet. The penitential practice of wearing an iron belt next to the skin would have caused festering wounds; and it would not be surprising if there were many cases of severe rheumatism and arthritis. The Desert Fathers, whose practices the Irish monks emulated, had at least the advantage of a warm, dry Egyptian climate. They did not live in damp, rainy Ireland.

Most of the Lives of the Irish saints refer to men living in community. The only women's communities which are known to have become established are those of *Brigid at Kildare, *Ita at Killeedy, *Monnena at Kileevy and *Samthann at Clonbroney. We know far less about the women. A basic reason for this is that under the Irish system of inheritance, a woman could only gain a life interest in land which she inherited. She could not leave it to a community, because on her death it reverted to her male kin. There may have been many small houses for women, but they would usually have been broken up on the death of the superior.

Women were virtually invisible in the male-dominated monastic culture, where many monks regarded them as a source of temptation to be avoided, rather than as co-workers for God. The women did not always accept this quietly: *Attracta seems to have made her views clear to her brother, and there is the early story of a woman who made a spirited theological defence of her position when *Senan tried to send her away from Scattery Island.

Misogyny was common, but not universal. *Bishop Ibar counselled Brigid and Monnena, *Ciaran of Saighir welcomed a small community of women led by his mother, *Liadain, and both Brigid and Ita had groups of clerics who supported their monasteries. But we can also see the beginnings of the problems of women in the religious life – living unprotected in a dangerous and divided society, supporting themselves economically, doing heavy manual work. They probably had very little education. There are few monastic records, no annals, few entries in martyrologies for the women. In all probability, most of them could neither read nor write, and they must have recited the Scriptures and the liturgies from memory. Despite Patrick's claim that he had consecrated many virgins, only a few were remembered.

After all the intervening centuries of destruction and neglect, we can still find some tangible evidence of how the Irish saints lived: archaeological excavations have revealed settlements where the lay-out of living space, church, well, cemetery, look-out tower, and embankments against outside attack can still be traced; and Irish museums preserve monastery bells and what are often labelled as bishops' croziers. The bells are usually abbatial bells. The abbot would summon monks to their regular offices by a single stroke, and if the bell rang three times, it meant that there was a call to a community meeting for some special purpose. Many of these bells do not have clappers: they were designed to be struck on the outside with a piece of metal. The 'bishops' croziers' are pastoral staffs – originally simple shepherds' crooks which would help a missioner in his journey across rough country, and be used for denouncing and cursing the ungodly. The practice of lowering the staff and pointing it at the miscreant while the curse was recited was much feared. Such a staff, known as a *bachall* or *bachuill* (Latin *baculatum*), was a monk's prized possession – often the only thing he owned apart from his Gospel and his service book. The staffs of great abbots and teachers were preserved with a special reverence. After the Norman Conquest, they were often enriched with gold and jewels in the mistaken belief that they represented the power and jurisdiction of a diocesan bishop; but these adornments were often lost as a result of later despoliation, so that the staffs returned to their original simplicity.

Men and women alike, the monastery founders lived hard and worked hard. One gets the impression of immense activity and immense industry, as their foundations were constructed, and the task of learning and teaching the faith was set in motion.

Ailbe of Emly (Ailbhe, Albeus) (?534), 12 September, was a travelling evangelist in southern Ireland, and is frequently named as one of the four 'Palladian bishops', the friend and colleague of *Declan. He was the founder of the monastery of Imlech or Emly, now the name of a diocese in County Tipperary. He must have been one of the very early teachers, because his tomb, long forgotten, was discovered at Cashel during the inauguration of the king by *Brendan of Birr about 580 in very dramatic circumstances. The legend was that he had been converted 'many years before *Patrick' by a British missionary priest, after marvelling at the glories of nature and wondering if there was a Creator.

It is said that Ailbe taught *Enda, and asked Oengus, king of Munster, to send the younger priest to the Arran Islands, to the west of Ireland. The monastic Rule of Ailbe at Emly (Imlech) is thought to represent his teaching and his monastic system, though the form in which it is now preserved dates from after his time. It consists of 56 verses in Irish, including the following injunctions to a monk:

> Let him be steady, let him not be restless, let him be wise, learned, pious; let him be vigilant; let him be a slave; let him be humble, kindly.

> Let him be gentle, close, and zealous, let him be modest, generous and gracious; against the torrent of the world, let him be watchful, let him not be reproachful; against the brood of the world, let him be warlike.

> The jewel of baptism and communion, let him receive it.

> Let him be constant at prayer, his canonical hours let him not forget; his mind let him bow it down without insolence or contention.

> A hundred genuflections for him at the Beata at the beginning of the day . . . thrice fifty psalms with a hundred genuflections every hour of vespers.

> A genuflection thrice, earnestly, after going in past the altar rail, without frivolity and without excitement, going into the presence of the king of the angels.

A clean house for the guests and a big fire, washing and bathing
for them, and a couch without sorrow.

The Rule mentions dry bread and cress as 'pure food for sages', but
salt meat, mead, curds and warm milk were allowed on occasion.
There is mention of 'a generous cook with a well-stored pantry' to
provide hospitality for guests, but women and warriors were
strictly forbidden to enter the monastery. This detailed Rule suggests a well-developed monastic system at a very early date.

Ailbe was known in South Wales, and is said to have baptized
*David.

Brigid (Bridget, Bride, Brigida) (*c*. 452–524), 1 February, is the
principal woman saint and patron of Ireland, second only to
*Patrick. Her fame was taken across western Europe by travelling
Irish monks. There were church dedications to Brigid in the Low
Countries, in the Rhine valley, in Brittany, and in Piacenza in Italy,
where there was an Irish bishop in the ninth century.

'Brigid, excellent woman, golden flame' says the poet-chronicler
*Oengus, and she is frequently celebrated as 'Mary of the Gael', an
Irish version of the Blessed Virgin Mary. Legends say that Brigid
was the daughter of a tribal king, and that she received the veil
from Patrick himself. Some writers have identified her with the
'beautiful princess' whom Patrick mentions in his *Letter to the
Soldiers of Coroticus*. Other accounts even credit her with becoming a female bishop (see *Conleth); but like Patrick, Brigid has
suffered from the myth-makers, and it is necessary to rescue her
from the myths in order to see her more clearly.

She was born in Leinster, but it is unlikely that she knew Patrick.
If their usually accepted dates are correct, she was only a child
when Patrick died. Her father, Dubthach, was a major landowner
of royal blood, but not the king of Leinster. Her mother was his
bondmaid and concubine – a fact not mentioned in Brigid's eighth
century Life, written by a monk named Cogitosus, and subsequently hotly denied by many chroniclers writing in a tradition
which required that all saints should have a holy birth and devoted
parents as well as a holy life and a holy death. Dubthach sold the

mother and kept the daughter, as he was entitled to do in a society where slavery was an accepted fact of life. When she grew up, she proved to be comely and spirited, and in his mind over-generous to the wretched peasants and slaves of his estates. Dubthach tried to sell her to the king of Leinster, because he 'liked not his cattle and wealth to be dealt out to the poor'. The king was astonished that Dubthach should want to sell his own daughter, and said that he would not bargain for her, because 'her merit was higher before God than before men'. Somewhat abashed, Dubthach gave the girl her freedom, and tried to arrange a good marriage for her. Illegitimacy was not of great importance in a predominantly pagan society, where legitimate and illegimate sons inherited equally, and good marriages were often arranged for illegitimate daughters. She steadfastly refused to be married off, and eventually Dubthach agreed to let her go to see the aged bishop *Mel in Ardagh, who is said to have been a disciple of Patrick. Mel accepted her dedication to the religious life.

A small community of women gathered round her in a settlement named Cill Dara (Kildare). Their chief support came from a priest named Conleth, who was then living as a hermit at Old Connell. Brigid asked him to be the pastor and confessor for her community. Conleth was a metal-worker, and he made sacred vessels for them. No doubt other monks came to join him, and they may have assisted the women, and turned to Brigid for guidance; but it is very unlikely that she headed a double monastery. This practice, in which a noblewoman was the superior of a monastery where she and her Sisters were enclosed, and priest-monks were responsible for liturgical services and external relations (see *Hilda of Whitby), did not develop until the sixth century, and was never adopted in patriarchal Ireland.

The many stories which still circulate in Ireland about Brigid support the view that she lived a simple, pastoral life. She was not an enclosed nun of the later medieval pattern, but more like a modern missionary sister, driving her chariot about the neighbour-hood to serve the community. Irish horses were already famous, and a chariot was a useful way of getting about over bogs and brushland. Brigid spoke freely to both rich and poor, finding out about their troubles. She visited the homes of the poor, and gave them a blessing. She treated the sick, and prayed with them for healing. She reconciled the unhappily married, and told fighting men in no uncertain terms to cease their petty conflicts. She is always associated with cows. She looked after her own herd, and sang runes to the cows to increase their milk yield. There are prayers to Brigid, asking her to help other people's cows to give milk, or to ease their calving. She was homely and kind and compassionate, a saint of the people, and this accounts for the great affection in which the Irish people have held her through the centuries.

Some writers have found it remarkable that a woman saint who left no writings, knew no famous ecclesiastics, held no power, made no journeys to Rome or Jerusalem and has no relics, achieved such great and lasting fame. One reason may be that she fitted into Irish tradition, both pagan and Christian. There was a Celtic goddess named Brigg. Her feast day was 1 February, the time of the spring ploughing, and this is also Brigid's feast day. Brigg was the goddess of knowledge and wisdom and fire. The nuns of Kildare kept a perpetual fire burning in the abbey for centuries in Brigid's memory, and her emblem includes a flame. As so often occurs in rural areas, the old ways and the new Christian ways became fused: Pope Gregory the Great instructed Augustine of Canterbury that he should not try to break down existing patterns of devotion, but build on them where this was practicable, turning temples into churches and giving a Christian meaning to festivals. So Brigid the Christian saint acquired some of the mystical characteristics of Brigg, the Celtic goddess, in the minds of the people.

Even more remarkable in this coincidence of names and traditions is the fact that when the Vikings began to make settlements on the Irish coast, they brought with them a goddess of their own, named Brigantia. Brigg–Brigid–Brigantia became an Irish icon, a composite character; but it says much for the real Brigid that through all these attributions, the distinctive personality of the bond-maid's daughter who was remembered for her kindness and mercy to the poor makes its mark. These are Christian virtues not associated with the Druidic or Viking cultures. The four-armed cross of reeds or straw, the *Crosóg Brigde*, was believed to protect houses from burning down. These crosses are still made in Ireland, and displayed on the eve of her feast. The Lives of Brigid are of relatively late composition, and many folk-tales became interwoven with oral traditions stemming from Druidic and Norse mythology, as well as from Christian records.

Many miracles are attributed to her. St Bride's church, Fleet Street, known as 'the journalists' church', is dedicated in her name.

Buite of Monasterboice (?519 or 523), 7 December. Monasterboice is west of the main Dublin–Belfast road, north of Drogheda. There are two Latin Lives of Buite, but they are of late compilation, and dubious accuracy. One says that he studied in 'Italia', but this is either a copyist's error or an attempt to strengthen links between Ireland and Rome. He is known to have studied in Wales (Walia), under *Teilo of Llandaff. His people came from the Louth area. He returned to Ireland to found what became a great monastery. The Book of Leinster lists 'Thrice fifty pilgrims across the sea with Buite the bishop, and ten holy virgins with the grace of God'. The celebrated High Crosses of Monasterboice, north of Dublin, may still be visited, but they are thought to date from a later period, probably the eighth or ninth century.

Buite is said in the *Annals of Ulster* to have died on the day on which *Columba was born.

Ciaran (Kieran) of Clonmacnoise (*c.* 512–58), 9 September, was the son of a travelling chariot-maker or cartwright. He went to study under *Finnian of Clonard, taking with him his favourite cow, which was all that his family could spare as a fee for his education. It seems to have been a common practice for poor scholars to take a cow with them when they commenced their studies: the monastery could profit from the milk and butter, the calves, the meat and ultimately the parchment from the skin; but the Life of Ciaran says that the cow's hide was preserved in his memory. 'It remains honourably in the city, and miracles are performed upon it.' Later, Ciaran went to learn from *Enda on 'Arran of the saints'. Enda ordained him, and he spent some time with *Senan on Scattery Island.

Ciaran, who became known as Ciaran the Younger to distinguish him from *Ciaran of Saighir, founded a monastery on the Shannon at Clonmacnoise (Cluain Mocca Nois) with about ten monks, working with them to raise the timbers and thatch the roofs. King Diarmaid Mac Corbaill, who gave him the land, drove in the first stake for the wooden church, placing Ciaran's hand over his own as he did so as a gesture of royal favour and support. This support, and Ciaran's great learning and piety, brought him much hostility and envy because of his humble origins. Some monks in neighbouring monasteries were said to be so jealous of him that they fasted and prayed that he might die young. Perhaps he was already a sick man, for he died at the age of 33, according to the *Annals of Ulster*. *Oengus, the ninth century poet of Tallaght, calls him 'The wright's son beyond kings'.

There are many stories about Ciaran's love of animals – including one about a pet fox which used to fetch his writings, 'until it was old enough to eat the satchel'. Clonmacnoise became a celebrated monastery which survived Viking raids and Norman wars, and lasted until 1552. The Clonmacnoise crozier, said to be Ciaran's, is in the National Museum at Dublin.

Ciaran of Saighir (Kieran, Ciaranus, sometimes called 'of Ossory') (?fifth to sixth century), 5 March, was born at Cape Clear in West Cork, where a ruined church and a well survive from this period at his birthplace. He is thought to have gone to Europe, probably Gaul, as a young man, and was baptized and ordained there. He is known as Sean Chiaran (Ciaran the Senior), and is credited with being one of the first apostles in Ireland, consecrated by Palladius. His medieval Lives, both Irish and Latin, go back to an earlier common source written by a monk of Saighir, but contain little biographical material, being preoccupied with animal stories and reputed marvels. He is said to have had a wild boar to help him build his monastery. The boar cut down trees, dragged timber and levelled the ground for him. A badger, a wolf and a fox came to do him service, and when the fox, reverting to type, stole Ciaran's shoes, the badger chased it, and brought it back to be reprimanded and instructed how to live a godly life.

Closer examination of the Lives suggests that these delightful stories do not represent a realistic picture of Ciaran's work. He had no serfs or labourers, but the work of raising the monastery buildings was carried out by his monks, not by animals. Ciaran attracted so many monks that the monastery became known as 'Saighir the hostful', that is, the populous, and 'Saighir the wealthy'. In a society where wealth was reckoned by heads of cattle, the monastery was outstanding. Ciaran had 'ten doors to the shed of his kine; and ten stalls to every door; and ten calves in every stall; and ten cows with every calf'. *Oengus writes of 'the victorious tumult of great Clonmacnoise', but if it was a celebrated centre of learning and piety, it was also a very successful business enterprise.

Ciaran's mother, *Liadain, brought a community of women to live near Saighir, and built a church for them. His monastery became the burial place of the kings of Ossory, and there are ruins of a high cross.

Though Ciaran of Saighir is commonly listed as one of the Twelve Apostles of *Patrick, and named in the Life of *Declan as one of the four 'Palladian bishops', the chronology suggests that these claims are unfounded. A confusion by John of Tynmouth is responsible for the story that Ciaran went to Cornwall (see *Perran).

Colman of Dromore (Mo Cholmoc of Druim Mor) (early sixth century), 7 June, was born in Ulster, but 'of the blood of the kings of Cashel'. He became a disciple of *Ailbe, founded a monastery by the river Lagan, near Dromore, probably about 514, and became abbot and bishop. *Finnian of Moville was one of his monks in what became a famous monastery. Colman is thought to have died about the middle of the sixth century. There is an Irish Life, but it is almost entirely confined to unlikely miracles and marvels. There are accounts purporting to be of his life in the *Aberdeen Breviary* and *Kalendars of Scottish Saints*, but these may refer to another Colman. They give a different feast day, 20 November, and there are many Colmans among the Irish saints.

Comgall (?520–602), 10 May, was the founder and abbot of the great monastery of Bennchorr (Bangor) and the Life of *Columbanus, one of his pupils, by Jonas, says that he was 'the outstanding father of the monks of Ireland'.

Comgall's father was not of noble blood. He was a free warrior, and expected his son to follow his example; but Comgall refused a military career, and studied for the priesthood. He was at one of the celebrated monastic schools, either with *Fintan of Clonenagh or with *Finnian of Moville. After he was ordained, he lived as a hermit for a time, and made a foundation on Lough Erne, Ely Island, before founding Bennchorr or Bangor on the south side of Belfast Lough. This monastery was sited at a strategic point for contacts with *Ninian's *Candida Casa* in Galloway and what was later known as Bangor Fawr in Wales. From the Irish Bangor, missionaries went out to Iona, the Isles, northern Scotland and the Continent. *Columba taught there before going to Iona. *Cainnech, *Brendan the Navigator, *Gall, *Columbanus, *Moluag and *Maelrubba were among the many students. Comgall is mentioned by *Adamnan in his Life of Columba, and two versions of a Latin Life of Comgall seem to be based on a lost original from Bangor.

The Litany of Irish Saints speaks of 'four thousand monks with the grace of God under the yoke of Comgall of Bennchorr'. It is not clear whether this is the tally of all the people living on the monastery's land, or the total of all the monks Comgall taught during his time as abbot: it can hardly represent those present at any one time. The Rule of Bangor instructs the monk to 'love Christ, hate wealth', to show 'piety toward the king of the sun and smoothness toward men'. He is told, 'These are your three rules, have nothing else dearer: patience, humility, and the love of the Lord in your heart.' The régime was one of great application in study and strict discipline, with an emphasis on obedience and silence. 'Let him come tired out to bed,' is the injunction for the student monk, 'and sleep on his feet, and be made to get up before he has had his sleep out.' The monastery of Bennchorr was no place for weaklings.

The *Antiphonary of Bangor*, which has been dated to 680–91,

less than a century after Comgall's death, is thought to be faithful
to his teaching. It sets out three night Offices, Vespers, Vigils and
Lauds, and three day Offices, Terce, Sext and Nones. Prime and
Compline were added later. The *Martyrology of Donegal* says that
Comgall 'kindled in the hearts of men an unquenchable fire of the
love of God'. The Mass and the Sacrament were central to his
teaching. One of his prayers reads:

> Come, you who are holy,
> Receive the Body of Christ,
> Drinking the holy Blood,
> By which you are redeemed.

Comgall visited Iona, and made a foundation there for a time,
but this did not prosper. He accompanied Columba on his visit to
King Brude at Inverness. He made a foundation on the isle of Tiree,
and had a farm there. He is reputed to have scared off pirates when
he challenged them on Tiree, because he was carrying a box
containing a pyx which they took to be magic. When Finnian of
Moville, who may have been his former teacher, was a very old
man, he visited Bennchorr, and advised Comgall to let the monks
drink milk, because their diet was very poor. Comgall did so, but
continued to drink only water himself. His shrine at Bennchorr was
desecrated by Viking raiders in 822.

Comgall's death is listed in the *Annals of Ulster* as occurring in
601 or 602, and his birth date was entered retrospectively as 516 or
520. The *Martyrology of Tallaght* adds that he died in his ninety-
first year, and that he had been abbot of Bennchorr for fifty years,
three months and ten days.

Conleth (Conlaed) (*c.* 520), 3 May, previously 10 May, was an
Irish monk, possibly an abbot or bishop, in Kildare. The Life of
*Brigid by Cogitosus, written between 830 and 835, says that he
was a hermit who lived at Old Connell (Co. Kildare) and a skilled
metal-worker. Brigid invited him to make sacred vessels, and to be
priest and confessor for her community. After the death of *Mel,
he became Brigid's principal spiritual adviser, and was devoted to

her. Conleth is said to have made the pastoral staff of *Finbar, now in the Royal Irish Academy; but if the dates are approximately correct, this cannot be the case, since Finbar, himself the son of a metal-worker, was not born until about 560.

According to Cogitosus, Conleth was buried near Brigid in her splendid church, the effigies of both wearing crowns. This was the Eastern fashion for abbots and abbesses, and may be why Brigid was later mistakenly reported to have become a female bishop. A curious story which appears in an Irish Life (not in a later Latin one) is that Conleth set out for Rome, and was devoured by wolves on the way. This story may have been suggested by his name: *coin* means 'to wolves', and *leth* means 'half'.

Declan of Ardmore (Declanus) (? 600–50), 24 July, came from the Deisi clan of Waterford in southern Ireland, and was said to be of the blood of the kings of Cashel. He is listed as one of the four 'Palladian bishops', and there are stories which emphasize both his links with *Patrick and his royal connections. It is said that he and Patrick met, and made a compact, Patrick saying that 'Declan is the Patrick of the Deisi'. It is also said that Edban, king of Cashel, refused to be baptized by Declan, temporizing and saying that he would wait for the arrival of Patrick; but when Patrick arrived, he still refused to accept the Christian faith. There was a revolt among the Deisi, and Declan confronted them, saying 'I am your lord', and appointing one of his own relatives to rule over them.

These stories are evidently later fabrications, together with accounts which refer to Declan as *sanctus pontifex Declanus*. He was said to have visited Rome 'many times', to have been consecrated by the pope; and to have met both Patrick and *David in Rome. Such accretions are fairly easy to identify.

Declan's early religious education was undertaken by priests in Ireland. When he was old enough, he went abroad, and studied either in Wales or in Gaul. Wales is the more likely, because the Deisi already had extensive settlements there. He worked in Lismore and Waterford, and was closely associated with the ministry of *Ailbe of Emly. Ailbe and Declan 'especially loved one another as if they were brothers, so that, on account of their mutual affection, they did not like to be separated from one another – except for something arising out of duty to their followers'. The two of them 'made a bond of friendship, and a league amongst themselves and their spiritual posterity in heaven and on earth for ever'.

Declan is reputed to have been exceptionally kind and generous: paupers, pilgrims and beggars followed him wherever he went. In his last days, he took refuge from them in 'a small venerable cell' in 'a narrow place on the brink of the sea', whence he 'went with the angels to heaven on the ninth day of the kalends of August'. *Oengus writes of him:

> If you have a right, O Erin,
> to a champion of battle to aid you,
> you have the head of a hundred thousands,
> Declan of Ardmore.

Even if some of the legends which developed around Declan's name are a product of local affection – or of distrust for anything coming from Armagh – he has been long remembered in Waterford. There are the ruins of his oratory, a round look-out tower thirty metres high, and a well at the site of his monastery at Ardmore, and 'St Declan's stone' is on the beach. It is said that only those who are in a state of grace are able to crawl under the boulder through a shallow pool to the other side, and perhaps not many now attempt it. The parish church is dedicated in Declan's name. There is also a small black stone with a cross inscribed on it which has attracted much devotion through the centuries. It measures about two and a half inches by one and a half, and is about half an inch thick, and may have been used as an altar cross. The Celtic saints used small portable altars of stone or wood, and this stone, known as the *Duibhin*, may have been designed to stand on such an altar as a focus for worship. It may be a genuine relic of Declan's ministry.

Enda (*c.* 530), 21 March, is another of the very early Irish saints. He succeeded his father as the ruler of a small kingdom in Meath, and had to defend it against raids from neighbouring clans. He was on his way back from a successful engagement, flushed with victory, when he passed the hermitage of his sister Fanchea, who was in charge of a small community of consecrated women. He was attracted to one of her young virgins, and would have carried the girl off if Fanchea had not prevented him from doing so, and subsequently converted him. He went off to study with *Ailbe of Emly, and founded monasteries in the Boyne valley. At some point, he again became involved in fighting, and Fanchea suggested that he should go to *Ninian's *Candida Casa*, then a celebrated monastery in Galloway. There he was ordained. When he returned to Ireland, his brother-in-law the king of Munster gave him land on the largest of the Arran islands, and he founded a monastery at Killeany (Cell Enda), digging the first deep trench round the monastery with his own hands. Later, he founded churches on a number of neighbouring islands. *Ciaran of Clonmacnoise was one of his disciples.

Towards the end of his life, Enda prayed that every contrite person who desired to be buried in his monastery cemetery should not find 'the mouth of hell closed upon him'. This prayer later attracted criticism from some Catholic theologians on the grounds that it was unorthodox not to wish the dead to suffer the pains of purgatory.

Enda's reputation in Ireland became so great that *Brendan the Navigator was said to have discovered him (long after his death) on the Isles of the Blest. *The Oxford Dictionary of Saints* rates Enda as 'the earliest organizer of Irish monasticism', but is dubious about the influence of Fanchea. There are no biographical details available about Fanchea and her possible claim to sainthood. Part of Enda's church on Taglach Enda, including the staff of a cross and the remains of a round tower, are still visible, though now half covered in sand.

Erc of Slane (512), 2 November: the name of Erc occurs in several Irish martyrologies. He is reputed to have come from Tara in Armagh. In the *Martyrology of Tigernach*, probably written in the ninth century, he is described as a bishop, and there is a quatrain of considerable antiquity (though probably not, as has been claimed, the work of St *Patrick):

> Bishop Erc
> Whatever he judged was rightly judged.
> Whosoever gives a just judgement
> Shall receive the blessing of Bishop Erc.

There are references to Bishop Erc in the Lives of other Irish saints. In particular, there is a story in the Life of *Brendan of Birr that he was the priest or bishop who discovered the infant Brendan. He saw the Northern Lights, and not realizing that this was a natural phenomenon, thought it presaged the birth of a wonderful child. He made enquiries, and came upon the mother and baby, taking the child to be cared for by his sister *Ita with her other fosterlings.

Finnian of Clonard (Fintan, Finden, Vennianus) (539), 12 December, was a distinguished scholar, known as 'the tutor of the saints of Ireland'. He was baptized by a St Abba (there are many of this name), who taught him 'the Psalms and the Ecclesiast-ical Order' - that is, the Liturgy. He made three foundations at Roscarra, Drumfea and Kilmaglush, then went to Wales, where he studied with *David, *Cadoc, *Barry and *Gildas, and is men-tioned in their Lives. He lived very austerely, usually on bread and water: on feast days, he is said to have celebrated with fried salmon and beer, but he would not touch meat or wine. His great founda-tion was at Cluan Iraird or Clonard, said to have 3,000 monks. Finnian had a great reputation for his knowledge of the Scriptures, and Clonard became a centre of Bible studies. According to the Book of Lismore, his monks were sent out with a Gospel book, a pastoral staff and a reliquary, and many of them made their own foundations. Kenney notes that 'almost every saint living within a century of his time is represented to have been a pupil of the founder of Clonard'. He is said to have died of the plague ('the yellow pest', according to an Irish Life).

The *Penitential of Finnian (Poenitentiale Vinniai)* is thought to be his. This document shows wide learning, partly based on such authorities as St Jerome (*c.* 341–420), who moved from Rome to Jerusalem, and St John Cassian (*c.* 369–533), who is regarded as a transmitter of the culture of the Desert Fathers of Egypt to the West. Finnian may have learned about both in Wales, but much of his work is thought to be original. He laid down penances for the sinful, chiefly consisting of abstinence from wine and meat or a bread and water diet, frequently for periods of forty days. For gross sins, the period of fasting might run to three years or longer. Penalties were notably heavier for the clergy than for the laity: for instance, a cleric who struck or killed his neighbour would be sentenced to 'bread and water for half a year, and a whole year without wine and meats', while the direction for a layman committing the same sin was: 'He shall do penance for a week, since he is a man of this world, and his guilt is lighter in this world, and his reward less in the world to come.' Killing among the laity was regarded comparatively lightly. Most of the sins listed are sins of the flesh, and all the penalties prescribed are for men. Women are not considered at all, except as objects of temptation for men. For monks, any relationship with a woman, however innocent, was assumed to be carnal in intent, and dealt with severely. The least penalty was 'forty days on bread and water without receiving Holy Communion . . . until he cut out of his heart his fellowship with the woman'.

After Finnian's time, Clonard continued as an outstanding Celtic monastery, in spite of ravages from the invading Danes. In the thirteenth century, it was taken over by the Augustinians.

Finnian of Moville (Finbar) (579), 10 September, came of the royal house of Dal Fitach (Down and Antrim). He was educated at *Colman of Dromore's monastery in County Louth, and then went to *Ninian's *Candida Casa* in Scotland, at Whithorn, which was based on Continental monasticism. He travelled on the Continent, and brought back some dubious relics, including a lock of the Virgin Mary's hair and one of St Martin's ankle-bones; but he also brought with him a precious biblical manuscript, part of St Jerome's celebrated translation of the Scriptures. *Patrick must have known of this translation, for he quoted from it in his

Confession; but the possession of a copy of the manuscript would have meant a great deal to an Irish monastery. Finnian's monastery was founded at Moville at the head of Strangford Lough in Co. Down, and he later founded another at Dromin, Co. Louth. *Oengus refers to Finnian as *súr*, a wise man.

Fintan of Clonenagh (603), 17 February, was born in Leinster. He is said to have been educated by St Colum of Tir-da-Glas (Terryglass). He founded the monastery at Clonenagh, which had a reputation for great austerity. The *Litany of Irish Saints* says that the monks 'fed on nothing but herbs of the earth and water'. Fintan himself existed on 'bread of woody barley and clayey water of clay' according to *Oengus. The community did not own even one cow, and both milk and butter were forbidden. The monks complained that they could not undertake the heavy labour required of them on such a meagre diet, and the local clergy were so concerned that they sent a deputation headed by *Cainnech to urge him to improve it. Fintan agreed as far as the monks were concerned, but kept to his own diet of barley bread and clay-ey water. In spite of the hardships of monastic life at Clonenagh, the monastery had 'so many monks that there is not room to enumerate them because of their multitude'.

According to a Life compiled at Ferns (see *Maedoc), *Columba described Fintan to a young monk from Leinster named Colman as 'a holy and beautiful man of your race, ruddy of face with bright eyes, little hair, and that white'.

On one occasion, a group of armed men came to Clonenagh after a battle, bearing the severed heads of their enemies. Fintan had the heads interred in the monastery cemetery, saying that he hoped that they would profit from generations of monastic prayer by the Day of Judgement.

Ibar (Ybarus, Iubar) (500 or 501), 23 April. *The Irish Saints* says that 'he is always coupled with the other pre-Patrician saints, and appears in their Lives'. He is said to have been one of the four 'Palladian bishops', the oldest of the four, though *Ailbe was their leader. The Life of *Declan says that Ibar was the one most opposed to *Patrick, chiefly on the grounds that he was a foreigner and not an Irishman. However, the *Annals of Ulster* record his date of death as 500 or 501, and the *Annals of Innisfallen* give it as 499. Assuming that he had a normal life-span, he is unlikely to have been much more than eighty when he died, which would mean that he was born about 420. He could hardly have been a senior bishop in 431 or even 451. The ancient Irish Lives often credited their saints with a remarkable longevity, claiming that they lived for two or three hundred years, which was a convenient way of covering such contradictions. It is possible that Ibar met *Patrick, though not when he himself was an old man.

According to an Irish Life, Ibar was the brother of Milla, wife of the king of Leinster. When her child was about to be born, she called for him:

> Bishop Iubar to my aid,
> It is he who knows my secrets,
> Let him ask forgiveness of my sins.
> Sharp pains have overtaken me.

Ibar went at once to be with his sister, and assured her:

> Bishop Iubar is before thee.
> Sharp pains have overtaken thee.
> Thou shalt bear a noble, wondrous son,
> May the King of the elements aid thee.

Her child, Abban, also grew up to be a saint, though little is known about his life. Ibar is said to have had 'many a saintly pupil, and many a noble church', and he taught Abban in his monastery on Beg-Eire (Beggary Island) in Wexford Harbour. The site is now reclaimed land, but was then an island with tidal channels flowing round it. Sea links with Wales and Gaul would have been excellent, and this may have been one of the earliest settlements of Christians from the Continent. The *Litany of Irish Saints* records 'three fifties of true monks under the yoke of Bishop Ibar'.

*Oengus speaks of:

> The light of Bishop Ibar,
> who has smote heresy's head,
> a splendid flame over a sparkling wave.

There is an agreeable (though perhaps apocryphal) story in Cogitosus' Life of *Brigid. The two could have met, for she was born about 452. Brigid went to see the old bishop, but he lived very simply, and 'had no food for the arrival of the guest but dry bread and the flesh of a pig'. Lacking any more suitable food, bishop and abbess sat down and ate bread and bacon, though it was 'during the Lenten feast before Easter'. Brigid's two accompanying nuns were shocked, and refused to eat meat. Their portions were changed into snakes as a sign of 'the sinfulness of their rigorous attitude'. Possibly the bacon was many days old, and the 'snakes' were maggots; but the point of the story is that Ibar rated hospitality and rejoicing at the arrival of fellow Christians more highly than the letter of the Rule. In addition to giving counsel to Brigid, Ibar also advised *Monnena and her nuns.

The monastery at Beg-Eire was plundered by Norsemen on a number of occasions, notably in 813, and none of its documents have survived.

Ita or Mo Ide (?569), 15 January, is the patroness of Munster, and ranks as the second woman saint of Ireland, next to *Brigid. She came of the royal family of the Deisi of Waterford, refused to take part in an arranged marriage, and became a consecrated virgin about the same time as Brigid. Other women joined her, and they settled five miles south of Newcastle West, in the foothills of the Sliab Luachra, in the south of Co. Limerick. The place is called Killeedy (Ita's cell). She became known as 'Foster mother of the saints of Ireland'. *Brendan of Birr is said to be her most famous fosterling – though *The Irish Saints* suggests that they were too close in age to make this probable.

Ita seems to have been a natural organizer: she travelled about the district, taking part in the affairs of her clan, and she bred horses. In addition to running a small school for girls and young boys, she saw that her nuns became skilled in herbal medicine, and visited the sick. They led a life of prayer and penance, spending much time in contemplation of the Holy Trinity. Killeedy was known as *Cluain Chredal*, the holy meadow, and they made another foundation called Kilmeedy (from Mo Ita). There are many legends about Ita, and *Oengus calls her 'the white sun of the women of Munster'. Her feast day is traditionally a day of family reunion, and girl children in the area round her foundations are still given her name.

Jarlath of Tuam (*c.* 550), 6 June, was born in Galway, where his father was the local chieftain. He is said to have been a disciple of *Enda, and he founded a monastery at Tuam which developed a high reputation. He trained *Brendan the Navigator and *Colman of Cloyne among others. There is a high cross in the market square at Tuam said to date from his time. A silver or silver-gilt shrine of St Jarlath was known to be kept in a chapel known as Teampul na Scrine until the 1830s, but has since disappeared.

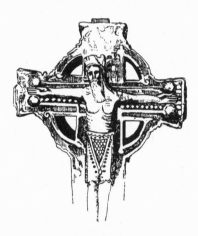

The Taum Cross

Liadain (Lelia) (fifth to sixth centuries) feast day unknown, was the mother of *Ciaran of Saighir. In the seventh century, it was thought that she had experienced a virgin birth. *Oengus describes the miraculous occurrence:

> Liadain was asleep
> in her bed, a saying which is not untrue.
> When she turned her face to heaven,
> a star fell in her mouth.
> Thence was born the wondrous child
> Ciaran of Saighir.

This unusual departure from orthodoxy can only be explained by the great respect in which she and Ciaran were held, and the great stress placed by the *Céili Dé* on virginity.

After Ciaran founded Clonmacnoise, Liadain, who was probably a widow, went to the monastery with a group of virgins 'to serve God and Ciaran' and founded a religious house for women.

Monnena (Monnine, Darerca, Modwenna, Bline) (*c.* 517), 6 July, is considered to be an early and important pioneer of religious life for women in Ireland. Her Life was written by a monk named Conchubranus (probably Conchobar, a common Irish name of the period), between 1000 and 1050, and there are indications that his account was based on an earlier Life. Conchubranus frequently travelled between *Brigid's foundation at Kildare and Monnena's foundation at Killeevy (both in County Armagh), and says that the two abbesses were contemporaries and friends.

Monnena's original name was Darerca. A priest living near her home at Killeevy instructed her, and she founded a nunnery with eight virgins and one widow with a baby. She cared for the widow's child, Lugar or Luger, who subsequently became a bishop. She and her nuns are said to have visited *Bishop Ibar for counsel, 'remaining long in his company'.

Monnena's charity to her poor neighbours was so great that her companions feared she would give all their food away, and they would be left to starve. They had to move from the place of their original foundation in order to be secure from interruptions, but finally settled in a remote spot at Slieve Gullian, in the shadow of a mountain. They do not seem to have had any help from local monasteries. There are hints in the story told by Conchubranus of considerable difficulties in founding and maintaining a religious community for women without positive support from monks. Monnena sent at least one of her companions, Brignat, across the sea to *St Ninian's *Candida Casa* at Whithorn in Galloway, to learn good monastic practice, and there is a tradition that she went to Whithorn herself. Her adopted name, Monnena, could be a feminine version of 'my Ninian'.

Oengus refers to Monnena as

> Moninde of the mountains,
> Cuillin, a beautiful pillar.
> She gained a triumph, a hostage of purity,
> A kinswoman of great Mary.

The *Annals of Ulster* record her death as occurring in 517 or 519.

Senan of Scattery Island (*c.* 544), 8 March. Scattery Island is off Kilrush, in the mouth of the Shannon. Senan was born near Kilrush, Co. Clare, where his father was a landowner. He was forced into military service by a chieftain, but was apparently not cut out to be a warrior: he went to sleep in a barn, and got left behind. Subsequently, he had a conversion experience while driving his father's cattle across the north shore of the Shannon at dusk: the tide came in and filled the inlets, and he had a narrow escape from drowning. He said, 'Sufficient for me is the length of time I have been at this layman's work,' and he broke his spear into a cross.

Senan wanted to avoid the company of women, and was disconcerted when a woman named Canair the Pious came to his island, and asked his permission to live there as a recluse. He refused to allow her to land, and told her to go and live on a neighbouring island with her sister, but Canair replied: 'Christ is no worse than you. Christ came to save women no less than men. Women have given service and ministry to Christ and his apostles. Women enter the heavenly kingdom no less than men.' Senan gave way, and allowed her to stay. The island was evidently quite large enough for both of them, for he built several churches there. The ruins of some of them can still be seen. He also made several foundations on the mainland. The shrine of his bell is in the Royal Irish Academy.

3

Ireland: the Consolidators

In the seventh century, the Irish Church faced two pressures – from some of its leaders to tighten penitential discipline, which had grown comparatively lax with the passing of the years; and from others to join the Continental Church by accepting the Roman system of papal and episcopal jurisdiction.

The internal reform movement was associated with the name of the *Céili Dé*, the Elect of God. The original asceticism of the Irish monasteries had declined, and *Céili Dé* was an attempt to return to the virtues of austerity. There were stringent rules to ensure poverty and chastity, and severe penalties for infraction. The most celebrated of the reformers was *Maelruain of the monastery of Tallaght, and *Moling was its 'familiar pet saint', according to *The Irish Saints*. *Céili Dé* was later to be corrupted into 'Culdee' and used in Scotland to denote the unorthodox and shaggy hermits whom Queen Margaret (1046–93) brought into conformity with Benedictine practice; but in its original form, it was a major reform movement in the Irish Church, promoted by men of piety and learning.

The movement towards Rome focused on what became known in Ireland as 'The Great Paschal Controversy'. It was primarily about power and authority in the Church, not about arcane calculations connected with the phases of the moon. The overt demand from distant Rome, was that the Celtic Church should accept 'the correct date of Easter', but much more was involved: submission to the decrees issued in the name of the pope, and, more immediately, the control of Irish monasteries by papally appointed bishops with authority over abbots and territorial jurisdiction over dioceses. It meant abandoning the monasteries' independence, their newly restored frugality and their asceticism for a system which many of them regarded as increasingly distanced from the simple values of the Primitive Church.

Bede records that between 605 and 610, Laurence, Augustine's successor as archbishop of Canterbury, 'sought to extend his pastoral care to . . . the Irish of Ireland adjacent to this island of Britain'. Augustine had failed to convince the Welsh Church leaders of the need to accept Roman jurisdiction, but the clerics of Canterbury 'imagined that the Irish must be better' – that is, more amenable than the Welsh; but when an Irish bishop named Dagan visited them, they complained that he refused to eat with them, or 'even to take his meal in the same house'. There may have been a misunderstanding: perhaps Dagan was fasting, perhaps his Celtic stomach could not cope with an Italian diet; but misunderstandings multiplied, and attitudes hardened on both sides.

Eventually some of the Irish leaders went to Rome to explore the situation. Cumian Fota, abbot of Durrow, took a party of Irish monks in 621, and came back to report to Segene, abbot of Iona, that he had been converted to the Roman cause. He and his party had been in the same lodging house as a Greek, a Hebrew, a Scythian and an Egyptian, all of whom acknowledged papal supremacy. On Easter Day, they had all attended the great basilica of St Peter. Everyone had told him that the same date of Easter was observed through the rest of the world. His letter earned him a stiff rebuke from Segene and other senior abbots. Segene wrote two letters to successive popes defending the Celtic system and asking for tolerance. He pointed out that the followers of the Roman Rite and the followers of the Celtic Rite were all followers of Christ, and expressed the hope that they might respect each other's positions without bitterness.

Through several brief pontificates, the response from Rome was a brusque demand for compliance expressed in terms of frank contempt. Pope Honorius I (625–38) exhorted the Irish clergy

> . . . not to consider their small number, situated at the ends of the earth, wiser than all the churches of Christ, ancient and modern, throughout the world, and not to celebrate a different Easter

contrary to paschal calculations and the synodical decrees of all
the bishops in the world.

The Irish abbots wrote in reply in the same year; but their letters
remained unanswered when Honorius died. His successor, Pope
Severinus, died after being in office only for a few months. An
answer finally came from Pope John IV (640–2), when still pope-
elect, acknowledging that the letters had not been dealt with:

> In order that a matter of such importance should not be left
> longer in obscurity, we opened them, and found that some of
> your province, in opposition to the orthodox faith, are striving to
> revive a new heresy out of an old. In the darkness of ignorance,
> they reject our Easter, on which Christ was sacrificed, and
> contend that it should be celebrated on the fourteenth day of the
> moon with the Jews.

To two errors – for the Celtic calculation of Easter was no new
invention, and it was not identical with the Jewish calculation for
the Passover – the letter added a third, accusing the Celtic clergy of
Pelagianism. It was admittedly a difficult time for the papacy, and
the papal advisers had many other issues to deal with – not least,
the problems of the Eastern Churches which were also deaf to
papal demands for uniformity; but it was precisely this kind of
ignorance about the Irish Church which most roused the appre-
hension of its leaders.

At least four synods were held, at which the matter was urgently
and anxiously debated. The Irish clergy realized only too clearly
that they would lose their own traditions if they gave way, and it
was in this period that they were most assiduous in recording their
own heritage through the Lives of their saints.

The seventh and eighth centuries were the great age of the
Irish monastic chroniclers. Lives of earlier saints were compiled,
and records instituted. Many of those which were compiled in
this period were lost when the monasteries were sacked by the
Norsemen, and many which survived this process were subsequently heavily revised after the Norman Conquest. The earliest

documents we have for this period, like the records of *Columbanus at Bobbio and *Fursey at Péronne, were preserved in less troubled Continental monasteries. Documents like the *Annals of Innisfallen*, the *Book of Armagh*, the *Martyrology of Tallaght*, the *Annals of Ulster*, the *Book of Mulling* (*Moling), and the *Book of Lismore*, like the *Félire* of *Oengus, are now only available in post-Conquest copies; but in spite of some obvious biases introduced by editors, they provide the basic information from which the life of the Celtic Church in Ireland has since been reconstructed.

Aedh Mac Brice (588 or 589), 10 November, was the son of Bricc or Brice of Clan Cholmain, a branch of the southern Uí Neill. Aedh worked on his father's land, but there were several sons, and according to the Irish laws of inheritance, his father's land had to be divided between them on his death. Under pressure from his brothers, Aedh had to leave his family home, and forgo his inheritance. He had no formal education: his Latin Life says that he had not been taught by a master in his youth, and knew nothing of literature or the liberal arts; but a bishop from Offaly took him away, educated him, and after his ordination, sent him to found a monastery at Cell Air (Killare) in Co. Westmeath, his home district. Aedh developed skills in herbal medicine. In his Irish Life, he is called *sui liag*, a master physician, and a hymn dating from the seventh or eighth century invokes his aid against headache. He visited *Molaise at Devenish, and *Ciaran's Clonmacnoise (possibly after Ciaran's death). He was known for his care of women's communities, and may have visited Ciaran's mother, *Liadain. He was a contemporary of *Columba, who was also of the Uí Neill. *Oengus says:

> Aed son of Brece, of the kingfolk,
> he was almost greater than death,
> he is high in the great kingdom,
> he is champion of the race of the hundred-battled Conn.

Brendan of Birr (*c.* 573–653), 29 November, is known as 'the chief of the prophets of Ireland'. He studied under *Finnian of Clonard, and was known as 'Brendan the Senior' to distinguish him from

*Brendan of Clonfert. He was the founder and abbot of Birr, and a friend and disciple of *Columba. He supported Columba at the time when he was driven into exile, and Columba asked his advice on where he and his kin should go. It was Brendan who sent him to Hy or Iona. Later, Brendan became influential in synodical affairs. When Columba was excommunicated by a synod for some trivial offence (perhaps because of persistent clan rivalry or jealousy of the success of Iona), he went to face the synod in person. Brendan saw Columba approaching the gathering, and 'went quickly to meet him, bowed his face, and kissed him with reverence'. The assembled abbots and bishops, shocked, asked why he did not shrink from rising and kissing an excommunicate, but he spoke out strongly against Columba's excommunication, saying, 'In no sense does God excommunicate him in accordance with your wrong judgement, but rather glorifies him more and more.' The charge was dropped.

In about 580, Brendan visited Cashel for the inauguration of the new king of Munster. Since the royal bard was not a Christian, Brendan sang the service. The tomb of the revered *Ailbe of Emly, who had died many years earlier, was discovered on the site during this visit, and the royal bard, greatly impressed by these experiences, became a Christian and asked for baptism. Brendan baptized him, and he also became an Irish saint as *Colman of Cloyne.

Brendan and Columba were so close that when Brendan died, Columba is said to have known intuitively of his death before the news reached Iona, and had already prepared to say a Requiem Mass for him. Brendan's monastery at Birr became a leading centre of learning, and its scribes were responsible for the compilation of the *MacRegol Gospels*, now in the Bodleian Library at Oxford.

Cainnech (Kenneth, Canice, Canicus) (c. 525–600), 11 October, was a friend and colleague of *Columba and *Comgall. The son of a celebrated bard in County Derry, he was educated by *Finnian of Clonard. For a time, he had a community at Glasnevin, but it was scattered by plague. He went to Llancarfan in Wales to study under *Cadoc, then returned to found monasteries in both northern and southern Ireland, the most important being Aghaboe in Laois.

Inchkenneth on Mull, Kilchennich in Tiree and the abbey of Cambuskenneth also bear his name, but it is not clear whether they were his personal foundations, or whether they were dedicated in his name by later disciples. He was a close friend and colleague of Columba, and they were together in Scotland on the celebrated occasion when Columba went to see King Brude at Inverness. A number of foundations in Scotland were dedicated in his name, and the first king to unite the Picts and Scots, Kenneth Mac Alpin, was probably named for him. Kenneth, who ruled Scotland in the ninth century, had Celtic clergy at his court at Dunkeld, though the Benedictines were in Edinburgh.

Cainnech visited Iona on a number of occasions. He and Columba are said to have been so close in spirit that one of them knew when the other was coming to see him, and in danger. On one occasion, Cainnech was in his own monastery of Aghaboe and about to begin a meal when he had an intuition that Columba and his small party of monks were at sea in bad weather, on their way to visit him. He left the table at once, and ran to the church to pray for the visitors with such haste that he had 'one shoe on his foot, and the other left behind in his hurry'. Columba and his monks landed safely.

Cainnech was evidently prone to absent-mindedness. *Adamnan also tells a story of how he left Iona on one occasion to return to Ireland, and forgot his pastoral staff. It appeared miraculously in Ireland, to his great thankfulness (perhaps brought by a monk who realized that he had forgotten it, and tactfully left it near at hand. Adamnan attributed a great deal to direct divine intervention).

Like most Celtic founders, Cainnech liked to escape to the quiet of the islands, and many stories are told about his relations with animals. He is said to have expelled the mice from one island for nibbling his shoes, and to have reproved the birds for singing on Sundays when, as God's creatures, he thought they should have known better. He devoted his time to copying many manuscripts in solitude. If comparatively little is known about Cainnech, this is probably because of his quiet habits and his closeness to Columba, who somewhat overshadows him; but he has long been one of the best-loved Celtic saints, a man of peace and courage.

Colman of Cloyne (Colman MacLenin) (530–606), 24 November, was the royal bard at the court of Ulster who was converted on the great occasion when *Brendan of Birr visited Cashel for the inauguration of the new king of Munster, and the tomb of *Ailbe was discovered. *Oengus describes him as 'the son of Lenin the vehement', ninth in descent from the kings of Munster, and says he was born in Cork. He was about fifty years old at the time of his conversion. Brendan taught him the elements of the faith, and sent him to *Jarlath of Tuam. He became a priest, and then a bishop, working in Limerick and Cork. He built the first church at Cloyne, and one at Kilmaclenine, of which the ruins and the holy well may still be visited.

Colman's ministry is of particular interest because he was a mature convert or 'ex-layman'. Although such mature conversions were common among the early Irish saints, many of whom had borne arms and some of whom were married and had children, by his time the usual mode of entry to the priesthood was for a boy to be educated and trained from his early youth, dedicated and celibate. 'Ex-laymen' seem to have been regarded as a special class – acknowledged as bringing special gifts to the ministry because of their experience in the world, but suspected of worldliness and possible corruption. A royal bard, with long experience at court, was thought to have had many opportunities for wrong-doing. Colman was investigated at the Synod of Cashel on a charge of simony, but cleared. He is said to have had six saintly sisters, but their names have not been recorded.

The remains of Colman's oratory, round tower and holy well can still be seen at Cloyne, and there are also ruins at Kilmaclenine.

Colman of Kilmacduagh (632), 29 October, was born about the middle of the sixth century. He became a monk at Aranmore, and later a hermit at Burren in Co. Clare. He lived alone apart from one disciple, on a diet of vegetables and water, and had the Celtic monk's affinity with animals – a cock would wake him for the night office, a mouse stopped him from going to sleep again, and a fly kept his place in his service book. Eventually, according to the post-Conquest accounts, he was 'unwillingly consecrated bishop'. This

probably means that other monks came to share his solitude, and
eventually he had to become their abbot. He founded a monastery
at what is now Kilmacduagh, i.e. the church of the son of Duagh.
Part of his pastoral staff is in the National Museum at Dublin.

Colman of Llan Elo (611), 26 September, was a nephew of
*Columba and visited him on Iona. *Adamnan says that Colman
visited both Iona and Scotland on several occasions, and was
drawn to 'exile for Christ'; but Columba thought that he should
found his own monastery in Ireland, and sent him home again. He
founded Llan Elo (Lynally) soon after, and it became a celebrated
monastic centre.

Colman is thought to have been the author of the *Alphabet
of Devotion*, a series of instructions from a monastic teacher to
his pupil. This includes the general principles on which a monk's
life should be based, and shows a gentle care for the pupil with
repeated reassurances that his master's questions are 'not hard to
answer':

> The three enemies of the soul:
> the world
> the devil
> a sinful teacher.
>
> What should a man learn?
> – not hard to answer:
> steadfastness in holiness,
> shortness of words,
> gentle brotherliness,
> smoothness in giving,
> fulfilling the rule without injury,
> rising before dawn,
> walking in obedience to God.

When *Mo-Chuta wanted to join Colman's community,
Colman judged that the younger man had the capacity to become
an abbot, so he repeated Columba's earlier advice to himself, and

told Mo-Chuta to go and found his own monastery. The two became close friends, and there were frequent visits between the two monasteries, Mo-Chuta's Rahan and Llan Elo. Colman also visited Clonard and Clonmacnoise, and preached a powerful sermon at the latter. The day was long remembered by the Clonmacnoise monks as 'the preaching of Colman Elo'.

There is a story in Colman's Life of 'British' monks trying to murder the founder – *secundum irascibilem Brittonum natura*, following their angry British nature. One text has a marginal note, '*Brittanorum colera*', the anger of the Britons. A similar story appears in Mo-Chuta's Life. The two monasteries were not far apart. If both had 'British' monks, the disaffection may have spread from one to the other – or one chronicler may have borrowed the story from another at a later date. The 'British' monks, who were angry enough to contemplate killing their abbot, were probably Welsh monks who had fled from Wales to Ireland to escape the plague or Viking raids. Perhaps there was not much sympathy for asylum seekers in these small, clan-based monasteries, and if they came in sufficient numbers to band together, they may have formed dissident groups; but if Abbot Colman was threatened, he was at least not physically attacked like Mo-Chuta.

Cumian Fota (*c.* 590–665), 12 November, was the son of King Fiarchna or Fiachne of West Munster. The *Félire* of *Oengus mentions under 12 November, 'There has been given with wisdom, science and much prudence, to me Cumian of beautiful warfare, the fair, tall (*fota*) son of Fiachna.' He became a monk, was in charge of the monastery school at Clonfert, and eventually became abbot of Durrow. He headed a delegation of Irish monks to Rome, and returned as a strong advocate of the case for accepting Roman jurisdiction. The Synod of Mag Lene was held on a plain near his monastery in 629–30 to consider 'the correct date of Easter', but although some of the monasteries in Southern Ireland gradually developed links with Rome, those in the North remained strongly opposed to change.

Cumian Fota's *Penitential* was widely used by the monasteries of the *Céili Dé* in the eighth century. It was based largely on the teachings of the Byzantine monk John Cassian, who was heavily influenced by the work of the Desert Fathers. The penalties (for much the same range of sins) were even more severe than those of *Finnian of Clonard, including perpetual pilgrimage for a man who committed murder or incest with his mother. Great reverence was shown to the Eucharist: a priest who let the consecrated host fall from the patten or the consecrated wine spill from the chalice was given fifty days' penance. In the case of the host, everything in the place was to be burned, and the ashes placed under the altar. In the case of the wine, the priest was required to lick it up from the floor with his tongue. Penance is described as 'the health-giving medicine of souls'.

Cumine (Cuimine) (688), 24 February, is listed in *Kalendars of the Scottish Saints* and described as the grandson of Fiachna, which suggests that he was the nephew of *Cumian Fota. The two are often confused. The clan was a celebrated one, and both were related to other abbots of Ireland and Scotland. Cumine was a monk on Iona, and founded a monastery at Kilcummin. He wrote a hymn, *Celebra Juda*, the last three stanzas of which are in the *Book of Mulling*, preserved in the Library of Trinity College, Dublin.

Diarmaid (Dermot) (sixth century), 10 January, was a native of Connacht, an abbot of royal blood who founded a monastery on the island of Inchcleraun (Innis Clothran) on Lough Ree, and is associated with *Senan of Scattery Island. The ruins of six churches can be found on Inchcleraun. He was buried there, and it became a place of pilgrimage.

Fechin (Mo-Fecha, Vigean, Virgin) (665), 20 January, came from Bile Fechin in Connacht, and was trained at Achonry in County Sligo by a priest named Nathy who was placed there by *Finnian of Clonard. Nathy urged Fechin to seek ordination so that he could offer 'the King of heaven and earth' to the people. Later he founded a community at Fore or Fobhar (Westmeath), and his name is also connected to foundations at Ballysadare, Cong, Imaid Island,

Omey, and Ard Oilean. He followed the penitential practice of standing in running water to recite his night prayers, and is thought to have died of the plague, which raged in Ireland in the year of his death.

Fechin is mentioned in the *Félire* of *Oengus, and there is a long metrical poem in his honour in his Life. There was a cult in his name in Scotland in the Middle Ages, but it is thought to have been taken there by his monks. There is no evidence that Fechin went to Scotland himself. Ecclefechan (*ecclesia sancti Fechani*) preserves his name, as does the parish of St Vigean near Arbroath, where there was traditionally a fair on his feast day, known as 'St Virgin's market'.

Finan Cam (sixth century), 7 April, was identified by his appearance: 'Finan' means fair-haired, and 'Cam' means that he had a squint. He came from County Kerry, and trained at Clonfert under *Brendan. He made a foundation of his own at Kinnity, in the shadow of the Slieve Bloom mountains. There was a strong local devotion to him, though he became confused in some martyrologies with *Finan Lobur.

Finan Lobur (sixth century), 10 March, was of Munster descent, born in Leinster. He suffered from a chronic disease which was later thought to be leprosy, though it is unlikely that leprosy had reached Ireland at this time. The word *lobur* means no more than 'infirm'.

Whatever the nature of his chronic ill-health, Finan Lobur became abbot of the monastery of Swords of Colmcille, possibly founded by Columba, north of Dublin, and of Clonmore, where he was buried. Little is known about him, but there was a strong devotion to him right through the Middle Ages, which suggests that he was an outstanding abbot.

Finbar (Barr, Barry, ?Vinnianus, ?Uinniau) (*c.* 560–610), 25 September, is the patron of Cork, born at Lisnacaheragh, County Cork. He is known as 'the lovable man', and his name means 'fair crest'. He was the son of a metal-worker and a bondwoman, and he probably followed his father's trade. Excavations of the site where he was born have revealed a metal-worker's equipment dating from the sixth century, including crucibles and moulds, a half-completed brooch, pottery and coins which are identified as evidence of Eastern Mediterranean trade.

He is thought to have gone to an Irish monastic school, trained for the priesthood and been ordained. He became a hermit before founding his monastery at Cork. Like *Moling, Finbar was prepared to join in the manual work of constructing the buildings for his community, which grew into a great school of learning. He made a number of foundations in the Cork area, and eventually became patron of Cork. He is also patron of the island of Barra in the Outer Hebrides, but it seems unlikely that he ever went there. Some of his monks carried out a mission to Barra after his death, and made dedications in his name.

Richard Sharpe suggests in *Medieval Irish Saints' Lives* that this Finbar (there are others of the same name) may have been *Columba's teacher. He points out that *Adamnan, in his Life of Columba, uses three different names for this one teacher: Finnbar, Uinniau and Finnio. He thinks that he may have gone to Wales from Ireland: Uinniau is a Welsh form of his name, and Finbar is known to have consulted *Gildas. He may also have been the teacher of *David, and if these identifications are correct, he must rank as one of the most influential and respected of all the Celtic saints.

Fintan Munnu (635), 21 October, abbot of Taghmon, Co. Wexford, was of the Uí Neill of Northern Ireland. He trained under *Comgall of Bangor, and in one of *Columba's monasteries at Kilmore. *Adamnan tells the story of how Fintan Munnu was about to set sail for Iona to enter Columba's community when he met two Iona monks. He asked them if Columba was well, and they told him that he was very well, since he was in heaven: Columba had died a few days earlier. Then they all sat down and wept bitterly. Columba died in 597.

Fintan went on to Iona to see the new abbot, Baithene, 'a friend-ly man, and easy to get on with', according to Adamnan. Columba had decided shortly before his death that Fintan should not enter the Iona monastery, judging that he had the capacity to form his own community. Columba said, 'He will not like this, for he is a rough man, therefore assure him that he will be an abbot and the head of his own congregation.' Baithene, somewhat nervous of this formidable postulant, had to pass on this decision, and to tell Fintan that he should go back to Ireland.

Fintan was sent back to Leinster, and founded the monastery of Taghmon (Tech Munnu, in the south of Leinster), which is mentioned in the Lives of *Cainnech, *Mochua and *Molua. Adamnan vouches for the story about Fintan's journey to Iona by saying that he heard it from an old monk of Taghmon, 'a priest and soldier of Christ', who had heard it from Fintan himself. Fintan died in 635, and Adamnan died in 704, so this is possible if the monk heard the story from Fintan when he was a young man, and passed it on to a young Adamnan in his own last years. The story illustrates both the care which Adamnan took to verify his sources and the importance of oral tradition in a society with few written records.

Fintan Munnu took part in the Synod of Mag Lene, in 629/30, at which he strenuously defended the Celtic system against *Molaise and others who wished to conform to the Roman pattern. He is said to have suffered from a skin disease, and to have accepted his infirmity as a cross to carry, praying that it might continue to afflict him. *Oengus calls him 'a steady flame, with the Father's fervour'.

Flannan of Killaloe (?642), 18 December, was the son of Turlough, king of Thomond in the west of Ireland, a devout chieftain who became a monk in his old age at Lismore. It is not clear where Flannan studied, or where he was ordained, but he was determined to make a pilgrimage to Rome, and legends say that he got there by floating on a millstone. There are many stories about Irish saints floating from country to country on millstones – an ancient recognition of the fact that they were sea-borne in their travels. The origin of this legend appears to be their practice of carrying a small pocket stone altar on which to celebrate the Eucharist.

If Flannan employed a more prosaic mode of transport for his journey, there is no doubt that he did actually reach Rome, unlike many other Celtic saints who were later said to have done so by Norman scribes. The detail about his consecration as a bishop is specific and convincing. He was consecrated by Pope John IV, who died in 642. When Flannan returned to Ireland, all the people of the district assembled to hear his message from the Holy Roman See; but when he had passed on his message, he was 'disappointed at the lukewarmness of his hearers', and he went to the Isle of Man.

There are cults of Flannan in both Ireland and Scotland with the same feast day, and there has been much scholarly discussion over the question of whether they refer to the same saint. There is no evidence that the Irish Flannan ever went to Scotland, though some of his monks may have taken his cult there after his death. *Flann* means red. It is possible that the traditions of two red-haired bishop-saints, one in Ireland and one in Scotland, have become fused. If so, the Flannan islands in the Hebrides, west of Lewis and Harris, are likely to owe their name to the Irish one. These islands are remote, and sailing conditions in the area difficult. For centuries, ships' crews invoked St Flannan's name as they sailed past. A small drystone chapel on one island is called the chapel of Flannan.

There are also traces of the ministry of a bishop named Flann or Flannan in the west of Ireland. There are churches attributed to him at Lough Corrib and on the island of Inishboffin.

Kevin (Coemgen) of Glendalough (*c.* 618), 3 June. Of Leinster nobility, Kevin's name means 'the Fair-begotten'. He is thought to have been educated in Wales by *Petroc. After his ordination, he went to live in a cave, where he remained for some years, eating nettles and berries, dressed in skins, and sleeping by the water's edge in summer. His metrical Life says of him:

> Coemgen was among stones,
> On the border of the lake on a bare bed,
> With his slender side on a stone,
> In his glen without a booth over him.

The mountain by his cave became known as *Disert Coemgen,*

Coemgen's lonely place. A farmer named Dima who was looking for a stray cow found him there, weak and emaciated, and had him taken down to the village on a litter. The fame of the lonely holy man grew, and disciples came to join him. When he was well enough, he took his small community to the upper lake, where they could live in silence with the water and the mountains. The Book of Leinster records 'Forty saints at Glen da Loch with Coemgen, noble priest'.

Many animal stories are told about Kevin: there was an otter which swam to the shore every day with a fish in its mouth for the monks, until one monk tried to trap it for its pelt, and it swam away, never to return. Another otter saved a book which Kevin had dropped in the river. A bird laid an egg in his hand, and he held it carefully until it hatched. Such stories may be legendary, but they speak of a close union with nature.

Glendalough, a place of scenic beauty, became one of the four pilgrimage sites of Ireland, and a place where many kings of Erin chose to be buried 'for love of God and Coemgen'. One of the Irish Lives says that he went to 'Rome', and came back with many treasures – 'No single saint ever obtained more from God than Coemgen, save Patrick only.' He went to visit *Ciaran of Clonmacnoise when the latter was dying, and received from him the present of a bell. He lived to a great age. His cave at Glendalough is now called St Kevin's Bed, and there is a rock church nearby with a Bronze Age tomb which he may have used as an altar.

Maedoc of Ferns (?628), 31 January, was baptized Aed: his fosterers called him 'Mo Aed og' or 'Little Aed', and he is also found as Moedhog, Mogue, Aedan, Aidan and Edan. There are other Maedocs, and the Lives have some suspect material which confuses them. He was born on an island in Templeport Lough, Co. Cavan, the son of a warrior who traced his lineage back to Conn of the Hundred Battles. When he was very young, he is said to have been given as a hostage from his clan to a high king. The king found him an attractive child, and offered to let him go, but Maedoc refused to leave until the king agreed to free the other hostages as well. He is thought to have been educated in Wales, and founded monasteries at Drumlane and Rossinver in addition to Ferns, which became one of the great monastic houses of Ireland. *Oengus writes

> The mighty sanctuary of Ferns
> is a flaming, radiant lantern.

Maedoc's Irish Life contains an interesting description of the construction and ordering of the monastery at Drumlane:

> Maedoc blessed and permanently established the place, arranged its ramparts and fair cemeteries, measured and marked out its temples and fair churches . . . ordered its seniors and congregations, ordained and set in honour its clergy and mass priests, its workpeople and servitors, its students and men of learning, to sow belief and devotion, to chant psalms and psalters, to celebrate the divine canonical hours, to give refection to guests and destitute and strangers. According to the proverb, 'The welcome of Erin is in Drumlane'.

By Maedoc's time, monasteries were evidently becoming large and quite highly organized.

Maedoc's bell and its shrine are in the possession of the library of Armagh.

Maelruain of Tallaght (792), 7 July. As abbot of Tallaght, Maelruain was influential in the *Céili Dé* (Culdee) reform. Though he lived after the formal submission of the Irish clergy to Rome in 715, it is evident that the spirit of *Céili Dé* continued to inspire the Irish monasteries. Maelruain is esteemed as its most influential exponent. He founded the monastery 'in the foothills of the Wicklow Mountains, south of Dublin' on a site given to him by the king of Leinster, and is thought to have been a bishop as well as abbot.

The Rule at Tallaght is thought to have been written down by Maelruain's disciple, Mael Dilgubb. The monk is enjoined, 'Do not eat until you are hungry; do not sleep till you are ready for it; speak to nobody without cause.' No meat was taken, apart from occasional wild pig or deer, and water was the only drink. There was strong spiritual direction, with frequent confession, and sternly imposed penances, involving long fasts and standing in cold water to subdue the rebellious flesh. Mass was celebrated on Sundays, Thursdays and great feasts, and the monks received the consecrated bread only, not the consecrated wine. There was a liturgical cycle of prayer, with devotion to Our Lady, angels, and the archangel Michael, and the sign of the Cross was made at the four points of the compass. The feast days were kept, and a long litany of the names of the saints (the *Martyrology of Tallaght*) was read at every Mass. *Moling and *Oengus, author of the *Félire*, were among Maelruain's students. Oengus wrote, 'May my tutor bring me to Christ, dear beyond affection, by his pure blessing, with his heart's desire!' In the *Félire*, which was written at Maelruain's direction, he describes Maelruain as 'a great sun upon the southern plains of Meath'.

At Tallaght, there was no missionary spirit: the monastery was seen as a spiritual enclave, to keep the monks from the sins of an otherwise wicked world. A number of other monasteries, including Finglas, Clonenagh, Terryglass and Dairinis near Lismore, joined the *Céili Dé* movement, which was cut short by intensified Viking attacks.

A church was built on the site of Maelruain's monastery at Tallaght in 1829, and the saint's cult was revived; but the celebrations for his feast day seem to have got rather out of hand, as there was much dancing and drinking of which Maelruain would certainly have disapproved. The Dominicans took over the church in 1836, and suppressed the cult.

Mochua of Timahoe (657), 24 December, came from Achonry. In his case, there is no indication that 'Mo' is a prefix. He was a late entrant to monasticism, having been a famous warrior for some years. His principal foundation was Timahoe, Tech Mochua, or Mochua's house. Some monasteries in Scotland claimed him as their founder, but since there are said to be fifty-nine Mochuas among the saints of Ireland, references may be to some of the other fifty-eight. Mochua of Timahoe was distinguished as a healer, and is credited with having healed two other abbots: *Colman Elo of a sudden loss of memory, and *Fintan Munnu of 'leprosy'.

Mo-Chuta (Mochuda, Mochuta, Mochta, Carthach, Carthage) (*c.* 636), 14 May. Carthach was this saint's baptismal name. His father was a rich and powerful chieftain in Lismore, who set the boy to working in the fields. He was herding pigs one day when he saw a bishop and his clergy in procession, chanting psalms, and ran to tell his father that he had never seen or heard anything more beautiful. 'The clerics sang as they went along the whole way before me, they sang until they arrived at their house, and thenceforth they sang till they went to sleep . . . I wish, O King, that I might learn [their psalms and ritual].' The bishop (or more probably the abbot) was very willing to accept this graceful youth, but the king refused to let him go: he intended his son to be a warrior, not a monk. The boy insisted, and eventually he was allowed to enter the monastery. The bishop's name was also Carthach, and 'Mo-Chuta' is an affectionate diminutive, my little Chuta. The Roman Catholic Church calls him Carthago or Carthage the Younger, approximating to his original name, but he is generally known in Ireland by the name the bishop chose for him.

After his ordination, he founded a small monastery in Kerry. He was very handsome, and found his looks a handicap, for 'maidens to the number of thirty were so enamoured of him that they could not conceal their feelings'. He built them cells and monasteries, and persuaded them to remain under his protection as holy virgins. The fact that he was driven out by opposition from other monasteries is recorded in the *Annals of Ulster* and the *Annals of Innisfallen*, under the dates 638 and 636 respectively. This seems to have related to clan rivalries, and possibly his sheer enthusiasm for missionary enterprise. An abbot, perhaps thinking that he needed more experience before taking on the responsibilities of ruling a monastery, advised him to travel and study. He spent about a year under *Comgall at Bangor, and then went to *Colman Elo, abbot of the monastery later known as Llan Elo in Offaly, who helped him to make a foundation at Rahan, only two miles from his own, thus giving him some support.

Mo-Chuta's monastery became large and celebrated. It is said that there were 887 monks under his rule, and that the régime was so severe that he would not provide them with a plough and oxen, but made them dig the soil themselves. Nor would he allow them milk or butter. He was quite old when another abbot finally persuaded him to accept the gift of thirty cows, a bull, two cattle men and two dairy maids.

There were 'British' (that is, Welsh) monks in Mo-Chuta's community, and they became restive under his régime, saying that the abbot was wrong to refuse gifts from local chieftains, and that they had to do all the heavy work. This story is also told of Colman Elo, and since the two monasteries were near to each other, and the founders worked closely together, the unrest among the asylum seekers may have spread from one to the other. When Mo-Chuta grew frail with age, the 'British monks' became impatient, and plotted among themselves, saying, 'There is no doubt that his equal in virtue or good works will never be found, therefore if he were out of the way, one of us might succeed him. Let us, then, kill him, as there is no likelihood of his natural death within a reasonable time.'

His Life records that on the basis of this specious mixture of piety and ruthlessness, they seized Mo-Chuta, trussed him up with ropes, concealed him in a bundle, and headed for the river with the intention of drowning him. However, another monk saw them, and 'at the insistence of the Holy Spirit', made them put down their bundle and open it, to discover the abbot inside.

Mo-Chuta's troubles were not over. Forty years after he had founded his monastery at Rahan, the whole community was expelled by orders of Blathmac, the High King of Tara. When he and his monks refused to move, they were forcibly driven out by soldiers. Mo-Chuta sent for his bell, and solemnly cursed Blathmac and his succession. Then the abbot and his community had to take to the road, a long and sad trail of monks and the 'lepers' from a colony which Mo-Chuta had founded.

This trail of dispossessed monks and the sick and infirm people in their care made its way south to Waterford, finally settling near Lismore, where the king of Munster gave them land. All but broken by this terrible experience, Mo-Chuta organized the building of a new monastery, and then sought a quiet retreat in a valley nearby with a few monks, where he could escape the noise and bustle of the building work. Perhaps it was at this time that he wrote his Rule, now known as the *Rule of St Carthage*. This work, of which six manuscript copies in Irish exist, is important as an early statement of the principles of *Céili Dé*. The text has been much debated by Irish scholars. It consists of a paraphrase of the Ten Commandments, followed by a detailed list of the duties and responsibilities of a bishop, an abbot, a priest, a confessor, a monk, a 'Culdee or cleric of the enclosure', and finally of a king, together with the régime for Mo-Chuta's own monastery. This last contains a great deal about fasting, though the text is rather fragmentary, but there are some relaxations. The workmen were to have 'substantial repast', and there was 'pity for the old people, who come not to their meal'. They were not to be neglected. Though the monks were to fast in Lent, except on Sundays, there was to be 'joy, festivity, reverence in the great glorious Easter' and from Easter to Pentecost, the monks were to be 'without fast, without heavy labour, without great laborious vigils, as a sign of the eternal life that will be given to us over' – presumably, in the next life.

When he knew he was dying, Mo-Chuta asked to be carried back up to the monastery, so that the other members of his community would not have to descend to the valley to see him, and then toil back to their mountainous retreat; but he died on the way, 'on the day before the Ides of May'.

Modomnoc (Midunnac) (sixth century), 13 February, came from Ulster, and was said to be, like *Columba, of the Uí Neill clan: his name is a contraction of 'my Dominic'. He went to study in Wales, and was at *David's monastery at Menevia, where he cultivated flowers in the garden, and kept the bees. According to Rhygyfarch's Life of David, the bees were so attached to him that when it was time for him to return home, a swarm settled on his ship. He returned to the monastery three times, accompanied by the bees, in an attempt to induce them to settle there again, but each time they went back with him to the ship. Eventually he received David's permission to take the bees with him, and:

> The holy father blessed the bees with these words: 'May the land to which you are journeying abound with your offspring. May your progeny never be lacking in it, and may our city for ever be abandoned by you; never may your descendants increase within it.'

In this way, bees and their honey were introduced into Ireland for the first time, and there were no more bees in Menevia.

*Oengus writes, 'In a little boat from the east over the pure-coloured sea my Domnoc brought . . . the gifted race of Ireland's bees.' The archaeological evidence is that *Gobnet and her nuns kept bees at Ballyvourney in southern Ireland rather earlier, but they may have been new to Armagh in Modomnoc's time.

Some texts of Rhygyfarch's Life of David tell another story of Modomnoc's time at Menevia. The Irishman was one of a party of monks set to dig a road up to the monastery. He reproached the monk next to him for being lazy and slow, and the monk turned to strike him with his spade or mattock; but David saw the move-ment, and made the sign of the Cross. The blow was arrested in mid-air. We do not necessarily have to accept the withering of the monk's arm. It is quite possible that a glance and a gesture from this formidable and watchful abbot was enough.

Some writers claim that Modomnoc became bishop (or abbot) of Ossory after *Moling.

Molaise (Laserian, Laisren) (639), 18 April, was abbot of Old Leighlin, and a strong supporter of the Roman date of Easter. It has been claimed that he went to Rome and was consecrated there, being created papal legate, but the *Kalendars of Scottish Saints* points out inconsistencies in the account, which is now generally thought to be untrue. *Oengus writes of 'Molaise, a name of fire', and he was clearly a very influential figure in the Irish monasteries of his day, although little is now known about him. There is a legend that he voluntarily accepted illness caused by thirty diseases at once to expiate his sins. The *Kalendars of Scottish Saints* notes that he was of royal Ulster stock, and says that he was 'taught by his uncle *Blane on Bute', but there is no confirmation of this link. He is to be distinguished from Molaise of Inismurray, another founder.

Moling (Mullins) (696), 17 June: conflicting accounts are told of Moling's origins. He came from Leinster, but some accounts say that he was the son of a wright named Faelan, while others insist that he was a descendant of the kings of Ulster. If the latter was true, there was a scandal involved. The fourteenth century *Liber Flavus* says that Moling was the son of a wealthy landowner named Faelan the Fair and his wife's sister. The girl, ashamed of her pregnancy and her betrayal of Faelan's wife, left their house, and gave birth in the snow – 'prodigious snow, so that it reached men's shoulders'. There must have been many such tragic cases. She and her child were rescued by a monk named Collanach, who kept a school for the sons of rich men and nobles. It is recorded that there were thirty sons of princes with Collanach, and that when he had completed his own studies, Moling taught them. Collanach trained him for the priesthood, and then gave him a tonsure, recited a Paternoster, and sent him to *Maedoc of Ferns.

Moling revived an earlier monastic foundation on the river Barrow in County Carlow, which became known as Tech Moling, and later as St Mullins. He is said to have lived in a hollow tree before he founded his monastery, with a pet fox, or a family of foxes, as company. A man of great physical strength and considerable energy, he is renowned for cutting a mill-stream a mile long for his community single-handed, refusing to wash or to drink from it until it was completed. He was one of the leaders of *Céili Dé*, and a figure of note in the Ferns area. He is reputed to have started the ferry service across the river Barrow which still operates today, and exercised considerable authority among the people of Leinster, settling cattle disputes and other causes of dissension. He is said to have represented the people in border disputes with the Uí Neill, and established a boundary between the two clans.

Moling had a great devotion to the Trinity, and on one occasion, seeing an inscription which invoked the name of the Father and the Son without mentioning the Holy Spirit, he not only insisted that the Third Person of the Trinity should be added to it, but ruled that all future inscriptions should do so.

*Oengus writes in the *Félire:*

> The golden bush over borders
> the splendid sun over tribes
> a high champion of the (heavenly) king
> a strong kinsman, a fair soldier.

Giraldus Cambrensis mentions Moling as one of the prophets of Ireland, ranking him with *Patrick and *Columba. The *Book of Mulling*, a ninth century Gospel book, probably based on Moling's own manuscript, contains a ground plan of his monastery. It is kept in a jewelled shrine in Trinity College Library, Dublin.

Molua of Clonfertmulloe (Lua, Lugaidh) (c. 554–606 or 609), 4 August, came from Munster, where his father was a chieftain. He was set to work in the fields, and herded the cattle; but he went often to the cell of the seven sons of Coelboth, who were all priests. His father was not willing to let him enter a monastery, and the seven priests sent for *Comgall, who came down from Bennchorr to visit them, and to convince his father that he should do. In time (probably after Comgall's death) he went to Bennchorr to study. Later, he went on to Clonard. When he had been ordained, he was sent out to make a foundation of his own. He and his small party are said to have travelled with five cows before reaching Killaloe (Munster), in the Slieve Bloom foothills, where he was founder and abbot. His principal disciple was *Flannan, who succeeded him.

Munchin (Muncius, Manchen) (seventh century), 2 January, is the principal patron of Limerick. His name means 'Little Monk'. He came of a clan on the coast of County Clare, and is mentioned in three martyrologies – those of *Oengus, Tallaght and Gorman. He was abbot of a monastery on an island in the Shannon estuary, and known as 'the Wise', but nothing more is known of his life. There is no separate Life. He may be the Manchianus (or Manichaeus) who was referred to as *doctor noster* in the Lives of some other saints, and who died in about 652, but this is not certain.

Mura (early seventh century), 12 March, was the founder of the monastery of Fahan in Donegal. Nothing else is known of his life, but three testimonies to his ministry have survived: his pastoral staff, which is now in the Royal Irish Academy, his bell in the Wallace Collection, and a stone cross preserved at Fahan as a national monument.

Murtagh (Muredoch) (fifth or sixth centuries), 12 August. Little is known about this saint, who has been variously claimed as a convert of *Patrick, or a contemporary of *Columba. He may have been the founder and abbot of a monastery on the isle of Inismurray, off the Sligo coast, where the architectural remains include a wall, an oratory, beehive cells, altar stones, and crosses. This is the most complete example of an early Irish monastery.

Oengus (Angus) (824), 11 March. Oengus studied at Clonenagh in Ulster, became a hermit, and settled in the neighbourhood of the monastery of Tallaght, near Dublin. He is said to have been received there as a servant, and to have worked at humble tasks for seven years before *Maelruain, the abbot, discovered that he was a scholar. They collaborated in writing the *Martyrology of Tallaght*, and Oengus later wrote his own long calendar of the saints, known as the *Félire* in Ireland and *Festilogium* in Latin. This is one of the chief sources of information for the early Irish saints. It was written in metrical form, and the last word of each stanza alliterates with the first word of the next, as an aid to memorization. Even in the time of Oengus, manuscripts were scarce in the Irish monasteries, and the monks must have developed prodigious memories. After Maelruain's death, Oengus returned to Clonenagh, becoming both abbot and bishop, and was one of the chief supporters of *Céili Dé*.

Ruadhan (584), 15 April, was the founder of the monastery of Lorrha or Lothra in north Tipperary, immediately to the east of the head of Lough Derg on the Shannon. There is said to have been some friction between Lorrha and the other neighbouring monasteries. *Brendan of Clonfert attempted to make a foundation in the area, but he and his monks had to move elsewhere after protests from the monks of Lorrha. The Lorrha monks thought that it was too close to their own foundation, and accused Brendan's monks of idleness and theft. Lorrha had a 'magic tree' with a sap which had the taste of delicious wine (an interesting survival of Druidic belief), and the monks of Ruadhan were accused of drinking from it.

Ruadhan came of the royal Munster line, and is said to have cursed the kings of Tara so comprehensively that their influence declined and their high places were left deserted.

Despite these evidences of conflict, Ruadhan was highly thought of in his own day. His monastery was said to have consisted of 150 monks who lived by prayer and manual labour. He is said to have been a friend of *Aed Mac Brice, and much later, *Maelruain had connections with Lorrha. Oengus praised Ruadhan generously:

> An excellent flame that does not wane
> that vanquishes urgent desires.
> Fair was the gem Ruadhan,
> lamp of Lorrha.

Ruadhan's hand, cased in silver, was kept at Lorrha until the Reformation. His bell is in the British Museum.

Samthann (739), 18 or 19 December, was traditionally regarded as one of the great women saints of Ireland. She was highly regarded in Salzburg, where her cult seems to have been introduced by *Ferghil. She refused a marriage arranged by her family, and settled at Clonbroney (Cluain Bronaig, Co. Longford, just south of Granard). There she released slaves and other captives, loved poverty, and was renowned for her wise advice. Many monks and teachers seem to have consulted her. One told her that he had decided to give up study so as to have more time for prayer; but she told him that his prayers would suffer if he did not fix his mind on spiritual things. When he said he wanted to go on pilgrimage, she told him that God was near to all who called on him, it was not necessary to cross the sea to find the kingdom of heaven.

Samthann was abbess of a community which refused to own more than six cows, and she would not accept other gifts for the community. She seems to have been a redoubtable and sensible abbess. On one occasion, she led a deputation to persuade a king to release a particular hostage – which he did. The owner of woodland near her community dreamed after she died that she had come back, belabouring him with her pastoral staff in order to get him to provide timber for her oratory. Her name, *Sam-theine*, means 'spiritual fire'.

Tigernach of Clones (549 or 550), feast day unknown, was a Leinsterman, said to have been baptized by *Conleth. He became bishop, and probably abbot, of Clones (Cluan-Enis) and the *Annals of Tigernach* bear his name. *Oengus writes:

> Sing pious Tigernach,
> For Christ's sake, he vanquished every lust.
> Out of whom comes a stream of knowledge
> Of beautiful Cluan Enis.

Ultan of Arbraccan (657), 4 September, was a scholar. He was reputed to have been the disciple of *Declan of Ardmore, and to have worked with Declan in Waterford, though the date assigned to his death does not make this credible. He certainly worked among the Deisi, Declan's people, and may have had a devotion to his illustrious predecessor. He founded a school where he is said to have illuminated manuscripts and educated and fed poor students. *Oengus describes him feeding his 'fosterlings' with porridge. Ultan collected the writings of *Brigid and wrote her Life, and he is said to have become a missionary bishop in Meath.

4

The Western Isles and Scotland

To modern readers, Scotland and Ireland are different countries with distinctive histories; but in the time of the Celtic saints, northern Ireland and western Scotland, separated only by clusters of islands easily reached by their small boats, formed a single entity. The *Scotii* of northern Ireland were of the same race as the people of the Western Isles, and the Clyde estuary; but the earliest saint of Scotland, *Ninian, derived his model of Christian mission not from Ireland, but from Gaul.

Ninian's monastery at Whithorn, *Candida Casa*, or the White House, is the earliest Christian monastery in the Celtic lands of which we have any knowledge. It was directly based on the practice of the monastery founded at Tours by St Martin. Whithorn is on the extreme tip of Galloway, and excavations in the 1980s and 1990s have revealed the existence of a trading settlement nearby. Christianity was probably brought to Galloway by traders from Gaul and Spain. Bede and Aelred of Rievaulx both record that Ninian visited Tours and that Martin personally encouraged him to make his foundation.

Candida Casa, like Martin's monastery of Marmoutier, owed much to the example of the Desert Fathers, and had a concern for mission uncharacteristic of Continental monasteries of the time. It seems to have been a prototype for monastic development in Celtic lands. For something like a hundred years, it flourished, and influenced the development of Celtic Christianity. It was known as the Great Monastery (*Magnum Monasterium*). A number of early Irish saints visited *Candida Casa* to study the monastic system and apply it to their own communities. In Ireland, Ninian was known as 'Monnen' (My Nin), which suggests both knowledge of his min-

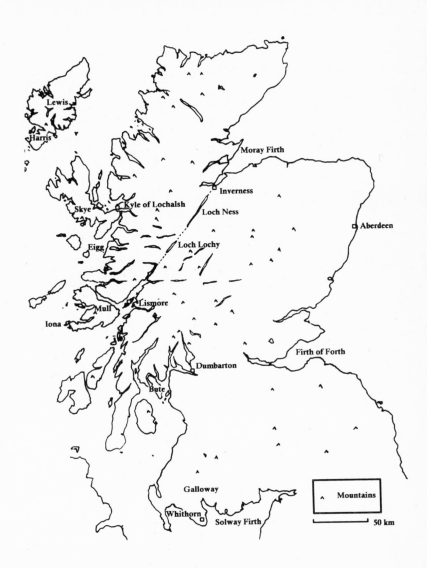

Scotland and the Western Isles

istry and affection for him; and the Irish abbess *Monnena of Killeevy, whose original name was Darerca, may have taken the feminine form of his name. She sent at least one nun to *Candida Casa*, and some accounts suggest that she went herself. She died about 519, when Ninian would still have been at Whithorn. Probably some of the Welsh saints also travelled there to learn about the monastic system – Bangor Iscoed was also known as 'the White House' for a time. Ninian and his monks may have kept to the Roman Rite, but if so, the differences from Celtic practice were not of major importance. The lines of conflict between the Roman Church and the Celtic Church had not yet been drawn. *Patrick in Ireland and *Dubricius in Wales had also carried out their ministries in the Roman tradition, and at this time, nobody was particularly concerned about 'the correct date of Easter'.

It seems that the missionary activities of Ninian and his monks at *Candida Casa* did not produce lasting results. In his *Letter to the Soldiers of Coroticus*, Patrick refers to the Picts of the area as having lapsed from the faith they had been taught, and *Kentigern found Galloway largely pagan; but if Whithorn's wider mission was not a success, the monastery set a pattern for monastic life which was adapted in other Celtic lands, and long remembered.

Probably the most widely travelled of the monks of the Western Isles (if we can believe even a fraction of what was written about him) was the remarkable *Brendan the Navigator. At the end of the fifteenth century, in the time of Christopher Columbus, cartographers were still drawing imaginative maps based on his epic voyage, in the belief that he reached the Canary Islands, off the coast of Africa; but the descriptions of marvels unknown in Ireland or the Canaries – whales, geysers and icebergs – suggest that he went north, not south, through the Western Isles and as far as Iceland. Though the account is heavily laced with Irish folklore about the Isles of the Blest and improbable meetings with earlier Irish saints such as Patrick and *Enda, the monks' sheer wonder at the beauties of the northern world is vividly conveyed.

The best known of the missionaries who left Ireland for Scotland and the more southern area of the Western Isles is *Columba, founder of the monasteries of Daire, Durrow and possibly Kells, who was driven into exile by clan warfare, and founded a new monastery on Iona, later evangelizing northern Scotland. Bede is careful to distinguish his area of mission from Ninian's. He makes it clear that Ninian's ministry was to 'the southern Picts, who live on this side of the mountain' – that is, in the southern Lowlands; while Columba went to 'the provinces of the northern Picts, which are separated from those of the southern Picts by a range of steep and desolate mountains' (the Grampians), then uncharted territory. He and his party went to Inverness, initially to secure King Brude's approval for his foundation on Iona. The 'northern Picts' had a Druidic form of worship, similar to that in Ireland in earlier times. Columba was accompanied by *Comgall and *Cainnech, which suggests that he was heading a major and important mission. They obtained the king's approval to their settlement on Iona, converted him and his court, and carried out several missions across Aberdeenshire and other parts of Pictland. A number of monks from Iona followed. How far the many place-names in Scotland associated with Columba, Comgall and Cainnech represent their own missions, and how far they represent the devotion of followers who made church dedications in their memory, is a matter for conjecture.

Columba's outstanding reputation among the travelling *Scotii* is largely due to the enduring tradition which became established on Iona. Other factors have helped to preserve it: the literary and historical quality of *Adamnan's Life of Columba, modelled on the Lives of St Antony and St Evagrius of Egypt, with which the Celtic monks were familiar; the links which Iona developed with Scotland; and circumstances which later sent *Aidan and his party of Iona monks to Northumbria.

Columba left his kin and his Irish monasteries unwillingly, and is said to have chosen a site for his cell on Iona where he could no longer see his beloved Irish coast. There were other saints who left Ireland for similar reasons: the fact that many of them were of royal or noble blood, and the strength of ties of kinship, meant that they were often drawn into conflicts which they had entered the Church to avoid; and 'exile for Christ', taking the gospel, was a recognized vocation in this small island at the edge of civilization:

a form of self-sacrifice which broke their ties with their homeland.

Bennchorr or Bangor, situated on Belfast Lough, became what would now be called a mission college. Comgall's monks went out to make many settlements in the Isles and the Hebrides. Before the dreaded Norse raiders began to attack and burn monasteries, they settled in the Orkneys and even further afield.

The Irish monk Dicuil, writing about 825, says that the monks had long known of Iceland and the Faroes. Hermits lived there for 'roughly a hundred years' before the Norsemen came. When the Norse invasions began, those who could escape went hurriedly, leaving their Gospel books, their crucifixes and even their pastoral staffs behind. Dicuil laments the loss of these quiet lands, so appropriate for Celtic hermits: 'Now, because of Norse pirates, they are empty of anchorites, but full of innumerable sheep and a great many different kinds of sea fowl.'

The monks sailed about the islands in coracles which had a wicker framework covered with many layers of hide. Some of these structures were quite large, taking twenty men or more. Though they were frail craft, they could ride the waves, while wooden ships had to plough through heavy seas. They could accommodate a number of rowers, and might have a sail for when the wind was favourable – provided that they knew where they were going. This was not always the case: a number of monastic groups sailed off with no definite objective, simply trusting in Providence to take them where they were meant to go. The islands cluster thickly around the Irish coast, and land is rarely out of sight. They had no maps or charts to tell about the vast oceans beyond. They would have expected to strike land quite soon after setting out – either meeting other monks who had settled earlier, or finding a new opportunity for mission.

Other Irish monks travelled by way of Wales to Cornwall, to the Channel Isles and to Brittany, and thence into Gaul and beyond. A few went across to the former Britannia, and so on to the Continent. The Irish Church became notable for the number and variety of its travellers; but travellers to Scotland and the Western Isles were a special breed: they developed a culture of their own, and remarkable skills in seamanship. They would have had a good knowledge of tides and currents, and they evidently used regular runs from one settlement to the next. In the Hebrides and the islands of the Clyde estuary, they faced storms, treacherous rocks and currents, while those on shore prayed for their safe arrival, and shouted against the wind as they finally helped to drag the tiny craft to the safety of the beach.

In the seventh century, what is now Lowland Scotland was part of the territory of the kings of Northumbria. Though the northern area was not fully Christianized, Celtic monasticism from Iona spread across from the Clyde to Inverness, and both north and south of this line, later meeting in the Lowlands with missions from Lindisfarne. The turbulent history of Scotland in later periods has left comparatively few traces of this activity: clan warfare, long wars with England and the activities of John Knox and his allies at the time of the Reformation left a country which had developed a fierce national pride, but a culture in which the tradition of the saints was all but lost. Bishop Alexander Forbes describes in his *Kalendars of Scottish Saints* (1872) how, at Botriffnie in Banffshire, the wooden statue of St Fumac was hurled into the flames by an enraged minister, who regarded it as 'a monument to superstition'; but the bishop comments, 'There is reason to believe that the old Celtic element remained obstinately alive for a long time . . . nay, in many places survived the Reformation.'

Baldred (Balred, Baltherus) (608), 6 March, was a disciple of *Kentigern (Mungo) who, according to the *Kalendar of Scottish Saints*, 'betook himself to the eremitic life in wild desert places and islands of the sea' after his master died (reputedly, at the age of 185). Kentigern had delegated to him the care of three churches, at Aldhame, Tyninghame and Prestonne, and he had a hermitage on the Bass Rock on the Firth of Forth. He is reputed to have performed some remarkable miracles, including moving a rock which was a danger to seamen to the shore. According to the *Breviary of Aberdeen*, when he died, all three of his churches claimed his body for burial, and after much prayer, it was found to have been miraculously triplicated during the night, so that each church had a whole body for reverent burial. Stories of the multiplication of saints' bodies are found elsewhere in Celtic legend: the explanation given was that after death, the bodies of saints were not subject to the earthly laws of space and time. It seems more likely that each of the three churches obtained some relics of Baldred as a focus for devotion.

Brendan the Navigator (Brendan of Clonfert) (486–575), 16 May, was born in Kerry near Tralee, and educated by *Erc, of Slane, who is described as bishop of Kerry. Erc's sister *Ita was his foster-mother, and later his spiritual guide. He became a monk, and then the founder of Clonfert in the west of Ireland, about 559. He is subsequently credited with foundations at Annadown, Inishadroun, Ardfert, and Mount Brandon on the Dingle peninsula, the most westerly point in Europe. His cult is also found in Scotland, Wales, and Brittany – possibly taken there by other travelling monks.

Brendan is chiefly known for the record of his epic voyage, the *Navigatione Sancti Brendanis*. This is probably largely mythical, and has many borrowings from Irish folklore and Scandinavian mythology. The position of these sea-faring peoples on the edge of the known world, facing the great and mysterious Ocean, led to imaginative ideas of what might lie, in terms of good and evil, in the sea beyond.

Brendan's *Navigatione* was written in the ninth century by an unknown Irish monk in Germany, who set down an old story based on an oral tradition. It became an immensely popular medieval romance. No less than 116 medieval manuscripts of the story survive, in Latin and other languages.

After founding his Irish monasteries, it is said, Brendan chose 'exile for Christ'. He and his companions made themselves a coracle, 'using iron tools'. The ribs and frame were made of oak, hides were stretched over the frame, and the whole rubbed with fat. He is said in the *Navigatione* to have sailed with thirty-three men, though the Book of Leinster records 'Three score men who sailed with Brendan to seek the land of promise'. Clearly the numbers rose in the re-telling. Even with thirty-three, it must have been an unusually large coracle to accommodate them all, with forty days' supplies.

In the late fifteenth century, when exploration was fashionable, it was assumed that they travelled south, and that Brendan's Blessed Isle – *terra promissionis sanctorum* – was near Madeira or the Canaries, in good Catholic territory; but it seems clear from the narrative that he went north. He is said to have visited *Patrick, *Ailbe and *Enda on his journeys. All three must have died many years earlier, and the topography is highly suspect unless he and his monks sailed right round Ireland. Patrick worked mostly in Armagh. Ailbe's monastery was at Imlech in Tipperary, and despite the discovery of his relics at Cashel, there was a legend that he did not die, but was waiting for the faithful on the Islands of the Blest, like King Arthur at Avalon. Enda's Arran island was off the south-west coast of Ireland, remote from the shipping routes. By the time the story was written down, Patrick, Ailbe and Enda had become famous and almost mythical figures of the Irish Church tradition. Claiming to have met them was almost like claiming to have met Abraham, Jacob and Moses.

The story of how the little group of monks saw an iceberg is more convincing. They had never seen such a thing before, and their marvelling comes through in the manuscript. It was a 'column rising out of the sea . . . higher than the sky . . . the colour of silver' and it 'seemed harder than marble'. It took them four days to row round it, and they thanked God for the gift of this wonderful sight. Their journey was full of terrors: there was a time when the wind failed to fill their sail, and they 'rowed and rowed until their strength failed'. They often went hungry, and had to fast for days as they drifted. They had no maps, and trusted in God to take them where they should go; but they were not shipwrecked, and there is no record of any storms. They drifted on a clear, glassy sea, wondering at the shoals of fish they could see in clear water, 'like a city on the march'. They visited an island where they saw their first volcano – 'a high mountain' which seemed to be covered with cloud, but had 'smoke belching from its peak'. 'The whole mass of rock, right down to sea-level, glowed like a pyre' and there were 'glowing masses of slag' which the savage inhabitants flung into the sea, making it hiss and boil.

On several occasions during their travels, they were miraculously greeted by shadowy personages who provided them with banquets, luscious fruits, springs or jugs of pure water, fish or even whole sheep. They saw sea-monsters – and cooked and ate slices from a dead one when there was no other food. A good deal of their concern is over provisions and they are profoundly thankful for offerings of 'extraordinary' white bread and 'incredibly tasty roots' from the shadowy personages. On one occasion, they lit a fire on an 'island' which turned out to be the back of a great whale. They went to the Island of the Birds, where the winged creatures had the gift of human speech, and sang psalms with them. They met Judas Iscariot, who was being eternally punished for his betrayal of Christ. He was sitting on a rock, lashed by gales, and tormented by demons who were trying to snatch him from it and gobble him up.

In these largely fanciful tales, what comes through is the steadiness of the monks' faith: they keep to their daily liturgical framework, celebrate the Eucharist with great joy and reverence, and keep the great feasts – Christmas, Easter, Pentecost. They are very dependent on their abbot, rushing to him at every alarm. He reassures them, and tells them what to do. Eventually, they return to their own monastery, where the welcoming monks are 'rapturous with joy' and glorify God 'for his kindness in letting them once more enjoy the sight of their father from whom they had been separated so long'. In accordance with a prophecy, Brendan died soon after, 'giving up his illustrious spirit to the Lord'.

Chattan and Blane of Kingarth (sixth century), 11 August. Chattan was an Irish monk, probably from Bennchorr, who undertook missions in the Clyde area, founding churches, and established the monastery of Kingarth on the isle of Bute, where he became abbot. Blane was his nephew, the daughter of his sister Ertha. Blane was born on Bute, which suggests that Chattan, like many of the Irish founders, took his sister and her children, and probably other members of his family, with him, as well as his disciples. Chattan sent Blane to *Comgall at Bennchorr to be trained for his ministry, and Blane succeeded him as abbot. Dunblane cathedral was later built on the site of the monastery, and a bell, reputed to be Blane's abbatial bell, is preserved there.

Columba (Colmcille) (*c.* 521–97), 9 June. The founder of the monastic community at Iona was of the royal line of Ulster, a member of the southern Uí Neill, claiming descent from Niall of the Nine Hostages. He was born in County Donegal. He received a bardic training in Irish poetry and literature, and was then allowed to study for the priesthood. This was unusual, for the southern Uí Neill were a warlike race, constantly involved in battles with other clans, and with the northern Uí Neill. According to the Life by *Adamnan, his teacher was 'the holy bishop Uinniau', who has been identified with *Finbar, and also with Uinniau or Uinnianus who taught *David. When Columba became a priest, his family gave him a hill covered with oak trees in a place which became known as Daire Choluim Cille (Colmcille's oak wood chapel) on the site of the modern city of Derry, which the English much later renamed Londonderry. There he founded his first monastery. With the support of his clan, he was able to found other monasteries, reputedly including Durrow and Kells. Columba spent fifteen years preaching and founding monasteries in Ireland before his exile. During this time, according to an old Irish Life, he went to Tours, and 'brought away the Gospel (book) that had been on Martin's bosom, one hundred years in the earth; and he left it in Daire'. Columba's love of ancient manuscripts is well attested (he was a skilled copyist), and this must have been a precious possession.

His quarrel with King Diarmaid of the northern Uí Neill gives us some interesting insights into his character, and the world in which he lived. Columba was of the southern Uí Neill, and trouble arose when the two branches of the clan came into conflict at the ceremonial games at Tara. Columba's kinsman, young Prince Cernau, caused the death of another young man. Whether this was an accident, horseplay or a deliberate act is not known, but Diarmaid had Cernau killed.

A second cause of ill-feeling arose after Columba made a visit to *Finnian's monastery of Clonard, and secretly made a copy of a beautiful book of Psalms which Finnian kept in his church. Finnian heard of this, and demanded the copy. Columba refused to give it up. Both appealed to King Diarmaid, who said 'To every cow belongeth her calf' and awarded Columba's copy to Finnian. It is claimed that this is the copy now known as the *Cathal* or Battle, now kept in the Royal Irish Academy.

Columba said that he would be avenged for the loss of his manuscript. Diarmaid imprisoned him at Tara, and he escaped. His kinsmen took up arms, and Columba prayed publicly for the victory of his own people. There was a great battle at Cuil Drebne, in which some three thousand men are said to have been slaughtered, and the southern Uí Neill were defeated. Columba was exiled by King Diarmaid, now undisputed High King. He realized that he would have to leave Ireland, and consulted *Brendan of Birr on where he should go. Brendan counselled him to settle on the island of Hy, now known as Iona, and in 561, Columba and twelve kinsmen, including a cousin and an uncle, set sail in a wicker coracle covered with hide.

Iona, about one mile wide by three miles long, lies off the coast of Mull. They landed there at Pentecost in the year 561. Columba is said to have grieved deeply over this separation from his homeland – so much so that he chose a stretch of land on the eastern side of the island for his monastery, where he could no longer see Ireland.

It seems likely that the southern Uí Neill helped in the construction of buildings and providing supplies for the monks, but once the monastery was established, the members of the community laboured on the land themselves, growing their own crops and becoming nearly self-sufficient. The new monastery developed a character of its own, closer to that of Marmoutier than to the more open Irish monasteries. At some stage, Columba is thought to have gone to Tours, and visited Martin's Marmoutier. There is a Celtic cross within the monastic enclosure at Iona with a dedication to Martin.

Though subsequent Benedictine occupation and some clumsy nineteenth century excavations have destroyed much archaeological evidence, more recent excavation has revealed a highly organized community. There was a church and a 'Great House', where meetings were held and much of the business of the monastery was carried on. The monks probably slept in recesses around the walls. There was a large guest-house (for hospitality was a sacred duty), and a complex of outbuildings: barns, stables, kitchens, workshops, a bakehouse. There was a mill for grinding corn on the stream which runs through the old monastic enclosure. There was arable farming, and the monks kept sheep and cattle. There are no lakes or rivers on Iona, but there would have been sea-fishing in the waters round the island.

The monks of Iona were never entirely cut off from Ireland. Columba was often able to return in later years, and there was a constant coming and going of monks, penitents and exiles. It was a busy life, not an isolated one. The community was disciplined, but did not go to the extremes of asceticism. Those monks who wished to live a stricter life of penance and denial went to live, temporarily or permanently, on one of the many uninhabited islands nearby.

From their base at Iona, Columba and his monks sailed among the islands and across to western Scotland. Other missionaries followed him to Iona. Both *Comgall and *Brendan of Birr are known to have established groups of monks there for a time; but Columba developed a distinctive monastic tradition which endured. Adamnan, who became the fifth abbot of Iona and collected all the traditions of his great predecessor, describes his fasting and vigils, his labours for the monasteries, and his learning, saying that he had 'joy in the Holy Spirit in his inmost heart'. Bede says that Columba's monks were distinguished for their purity of life, their love of God, and their loyalty to the monastic Rule.

For two years, Columba taught the island people and the people of Galloway, before going on to Pictland. Accompanied by a group of monks including Comgall and *Cainnech, he went to the castle of King Brude at Inverness, two miles above the head of the loch, to ask permission for this new missionary enterprise. The party probably travelled by boat, sailing up the Clyde estuary, and then through the lochs to Loch Ness. They would have needed porterage for two short land stretches between Loch Lochy and Loch Oig, and between Loch Oig and Loch Ness, but there was a good deal of traffic through the lochs, and their boats were light.

Columba was a giant of a man, with 'a voice so loud that it could be heard half a mile or even a mile off' according to Adamnan. A commanding voice was greatly respected among the monks, because it could be heard above the winds and the crash of the waves. On their way to Inverness, the Pictish wizards tried to stop them, but Columba chanted the 44th Psalm, and 'his voice was miraculously lifted up in the air like some terrible thunder, so that the king and his people were filled with unbearable fear'. When they reached the castle, facing the loch at the top of a steep incline, they found that the king had given orders that they were not to be admitted. According to Adamnan, when Columba raised a great arm and made the sign of the Cross, bolts were hastily withdrawn, and gates opened. A Life of Comgall tries to distribute the honours, saying that Comgall caused the gates of the fort to open, Columba ordered the opening of the doors of the king's house, and Cainnech subsequently prevented the king from killing them by paralysing his arm.

Adamnan says that King Brude, though greatly alarmed, welcomed the party with words of peace, confirmed Columba's possession of Iona, and gave him leave to carry out his missions. Columba himself undertook missions to Ardnamurchan, Skye, Tiree, Kintyre, Loch Ness, Lochaber and many other places. He was later credited with having evangelized Aberdeenshire and the whole of Pictland, but much of this missionary activity may have been carried out by other monks of Iona or monks from Bennchorr.

Columba kept his headquarters at Iona, where many people came to him for spiritual counsel or healing, and a great tradition of hospitality developed. He demanded extreme austerity of his followers, and practised it himself, but Adamnan describes him as mellowing in his later years, living in love and peace with his monks and with the natural world. There is a revealing story about Columba and nettle soup. On one occasion, while going about Iona, he saw a peasant woman boiling nettles for her meal. When he asked why, she said that they were all she had to eat. She had only one cow, and it had not yet borne a calf, so she had no milk. Columba decided that if nettle soup was a suitable diet for the poor, it was good enough for him, and in future, he would eat only nettle soup; but the cook, who loved his abbot, feared for his health, and devised a hollow stick with which he used to stir the soup. Through this, he poured in milk. Columba flourished on this diet, and some of the other monks asked to try it; but the demands on the milk supply became too great, and the cook had to confess his trick. After a moment of formidable anger, Columba roared with laughter, and decreed that everyone must eat sensibly in future.

Columba had an abiding love of learning, and when his great physical strength left him, he spent much time in transcribing manuscripts and writing poetry. It is said that he transcribed three hundred copies of the Gospels. In one long narrative poem, he deals with the whole epic of the Scriptures – the nature of God, the Creation, the Fall, the Last Judgement, hell and paradise. He was on Iona for thirty-six years, becoming 'an old man, worn out with age'. He was copying Psalm 44 when he died. When the monks finally left Iona in the early ninth century, his body was taken back to Kells. The *Book of Kells*, which rivals the *Lindisfarne Gospels* in its brilliant colour, the intricacy and beauty of its birds and beasts and its interlaced Celtic ornamentation, is now kept at Trinity College, Dublin. It is popularly attributed to Columba, but probably formed a memorial to him. A Victorian professor, J. O. Westwood, author of the *Paleographia Sancta Pictoria* (1843) was critical of 'the crudity of the portraits of human beings' in the paintings, but they are not crude: they display the immobility characteristic of ikons. As in the case of the ikons of the Eastern Orthodox Churches, the artist's intention was to provide a memorial of a saint or saints, but not to make his picture so lifelike that it became an object of worship in place of God himself.

Adamnan, born some thirty years after Columba's death, was his kinsman. He writes of Columba that 'he was of an excellent nature, polished in speech, holy in deed, great in counsel . . . loving unto all, serene and holy'. The monastic Rule drawn up by Columba was taken to western Europe by *Columbanus, and used by many monasteries until it was superseded by the Benedictine Rule. Iona has been so greatly esteemed in succeeding centuries that it became a burial place for the rulers of Scotland.

Comgan (eighth century), 13 October, is said to have been the son of Kelly, Prince of Leinster. He succeeded his father, but was attacked by neighbouring clans. After being wounded in battle, he escaped to Scotland with seven warriors, his sister and her children. He settled on the shores of the Kyle of Lochalsh, opposite the Isle of Skye, where he founded a small monastery, and the seven warriors became his first monks. When he died, his sister's son *Fillan took his body to Iona for burial, and built a church there dedicated in his name.

Conan (648), 26 January, was a bishop who worked in the Hebrides and the Isle of Man, where various place-names commemorate his work. He is often referred to as 'bishop of Sodor', but this is a misunderstanding: 'Sodor' is a corruption of *Suthreyar*, a Norse term meaning 'the Western Isles'. This suggests that the name came into use after the Viking raids, not in Conan's time. Conan is said to have educated *Fiacre of Breuil.

Donald (Domhnall) (early eighth century), 15 July, was a layman who lived at Ogilvy (Forfarshire). He married and had nine daughters. His wife died, and he and the daughters led a strict religious life in their own home. The daughters are known as the Nine Maidens, and the term is applied to hills and wells in the district, including a well at Glamis. When Donald died, the daughters all entered a monastery at Abernethy. The popularity of 'Donald' as a Christian name probably comes from the clan MacDonald, and not from this Donald.

Donan and his Companions (618), 17 April: Donan or Donnan was an Irish abbot, a monk of Iona who founded a monastery on Eigg, near Skye. The community was attacked by Viking raiders or pirates during Mass on 'Easter night'. This probably means the first Mass of Easter, which would be celebrated from midnight on Holy Saturday. Donan was the celebrant. Some accounts say that the invaders allowed him to complete the Mass before he and his community were forced into the refectory, which was set on fire. Those who tried to escape were put to the sword, and the entire community perished. The raid seems to have been planned in advance, and with some knowledge of monastic practice, since the raiders knew when they would find the whole community together. It is reputed to have been instigated by a woman who had lost her rights of pasture to the monastery, and devised this way of recovering them. The *Martyrology of Tallaght*, the *Martyrology of Donegal*, the *Martyrology of Gorman* and the *Félire* of *Oengus all record the massacre. At least eleven churches were dedicated in Donan's name – on Eigg, South Uist, Arran and other islands.

Drostan (*c.* 610), 11 July, was a hermit who attracted disciples, and became founder and abbot of the monastery of Deer, near Peterhead in Aberdeenshire, which became a centre for mission and learning in the area of the Moray Firth. There are dedications to him in north-east Scotland. It has been claimed that the monastery was founded by *Columba, but it was in Pictish territory, which is known to have been hostile to the Columban missions.

Fergus (early eighth century), 27 November. Fergus is a very common name in the history of the Irish saints. This Fergus is listed in the *Aberdeen Breviary* as an Irish missionary bishop. He was known as 'the Pict'. He built churches at Strogeth, Blackford and Dolpatrick, carried out a ministry in Caithness, and is believed to have died at Glamis. He may have been returning from Ireland or from Rome. There was a '*Fergustus episcopus Scotiae Pictus*' who attended the Council of Rome in 721 and has been identified with him. If this identification holds, he must have been one of the leaders in the movement to accept papal jurisdiction. According to the *Kalendars of the Scottish Saints*, 'full of years, he presignified the day of his death, and slightly bowing his head, slept in the Lord'. His shrine at Glamis was a pilgrimage site in the Middle Ages. He is listed in the *Martyrology of Tallaght*. A reliquary said to contain some of his relics is in the British Museum.

Fillan of Glendochart (Foilan, Phelan) (eighth century), 9 January, was the son of *Kentigerna, and nephew of *Comgan. He seems to have grown up in Leinster, and may already have been a monk when the family left Ireland. He lived as a hermit near what is now the modern town of St Andrews. He was asked to become abbot of a neighbouring monastery, and administered it for some years before joining Comgan at Stracht, in what is now Fifeshire. When Comgan died, Fillan took his body to Iona for burial, and built a church there in his honour. Fillan died at Strathfillan. Robert the Bruce prayed before a relic on the night before Bannockburn, attributing his subsequent success to the intercession of the saint. According to the Scots poet Hector Boece:

> As gude king Robert in that samin nicht
> Befoir the feild, at his devotioun
> Walkit that nicht into his orisoun
> To Sanct Phelan most speciall of the laif
> His richt arm bane into ane siluer cace . . .

Butler 2000 points out that Robert would not have taken the right arm in the silver case, a precious relic, into battle with him, for fear that it would be damaged or lost. Fillan's pastoral staff and bell are in the museum of the Society of Antiquaries of Scotland. His pool was one of many in which, until the early nineteenth century, 'lunatics' were taken to be dipped, and left bound and wet all night in a ruined chapel. The treatment was thought to reduce frenzy. It was probably quite efficacious – if the patient survived.

Kentigern (Mungo) (*c.* 518–612), 13 January, came of a ruling family of Picts from the Clyde valley. His mother Thedaw was the daughter of Loth, chief of the Lothians. Her legend – that of a princess who was to bear a child, refused to reveal the name of her lover, and was thrown into the river in a barrel – is one frequently encountered in the Lives of the saints, and in this case is said to have a classical Greek origin. What is unusual about the case of Kentigern's mother is that her father, Loth, is described as ' a demi-pagan', which means that he was in touch with Christian practices; and Thedaw was also called Monnena, and thought to have been taught by the monks of *Ninian's Casa Candida*. One version even says that she was a consecrated virgin. This proved so puzzling to later chroniclers that some of them conjectured that she must have experienced a virgin birth. The twelfth century monk-chronicler

Goscelin or Jocelyn of Furness had two early Lives of Kentigern before him when he wrote his version, one in Latin, and one in the vernacular. He rejected this hypothesis as 'contrary to sound doctrine', and omitted it from his own account. He evidently felt for 'the poor little pregnant woman', and suggests that she may have been given a sleeping potion or have 'suffered the sleight of hand of soothsayers' so that she was raped, but had no under-standing of what had happened to her. The use of drugs or hypno-sis is certainly possible; but the law of her people was primitive and strict. A pregnant girl who would not or could not give the name of her lover was executed. Thedaw was thrown from the top of a cliff on the southern side of the Firth of Forth in a barrel according to one account, or, more mercifully, set adrift in a coracle according to another. She gave birth to her child on the northern shore, and a nearby hermit, Serf or Servanus, heard a heavenly host singing for joy, and discovered them both. He baptized mother and child, and brought up the boy, calling him Mungo or 'darling'.

Accounts of Kentigern's later ministry have a stronger historical basis than these early stories. He was taught by Serf, and became a hermit who undertook missions in Galloway, where the people had fallen into idolatry after the death of Ninian. He also founded churches in the Aberdeen area. At one point he was driven out by infuriated pagans. There are persistent, but probably untrue, stories that he went to Wales. He is said to have been at Menevia in *David's lifetime. Later, legend says, he became an abbot at Llanelwy, where *Asaph was one of his monks, and eventually his successor. When it was safe to go back to Pictland, he was present at Asaph's installation. Then he went out of the northern door of the church and back to Scotland 'to combat the northern enemy'. Professor E. G. Bowen's conclusion, after detailed mapping of church dedications to Kentigern, is that the whole story of his visit to Wales 'smells strongly of the twelfth century'. He dismisses it as 'bogus from start to finish'.

Wherever Kentigern went, he eventually returned to Strathclyde, where his ministry was so much honoured that he became either abbot or bishop – it is not clear which, or whether he combined the two offices. He and *Columba are said to have met together with processions of their respective monks, the two processions singing psalms until they were within earshot of each other, when they sang alternate verses of the same psalms. Kentigern and Columba exchanged pastoral staffs. Kentigern is said to have lived to a great age, though the date of his death is not certain. The ring and the fish on the coat of arms of the City of Glasgow relate to a legend that he performed a miracle by finding a ring which the queen had given to a lover, and which had been lost, inside a salmon caught by one of his monks. The cathedral in Glasgow, popularly called St Mungo's, commemorates him as the first bishop of the city.

Kentigerna (733), 7 January (no relation to Kentigern), was the sister of *Comgan and mother of *Fillan. Her husband was Feredach, prince of Munster. After his death, she and her children left Leinster to live near Fillan's monastery in the Lochalsh district. When the children were older, she became an anchoress, and settled on an island in Loch Lomond, where the ancient church of Inch Calleach bore her dedication.

Kessog (Mackessog) (sixth century), 10 March, could be either Mackessog (son of Kessog) in the Scottish style, or Mo Kessog in the Irish manner. He was born in Cashel of the royal family of Munster, went to Scotland as a missionary monk, and is traditionally associated with Monks' Island in Loch Lomond. He is said to have been murdered by assassins at Bandry, and was commemorated by a pile of stones known as St Kessog's Cairn. When part of this was removed in the nineteenth century, a statue of Kessog was found inside, but nothing is known of its age or provenance.

Machan (sixth century), 28 September, was a Scottish disciple of *Cadoc at Llancarfan in Wales. He went back to his own country to carry out a ministry around Campsie, and Glasgow cathedral had an altar in his honour before the Reformation.

Machar (Mochumna, Mauritius) (sixth century), 16 November. 'Mauritius' is an unsuccessful attempt to Latinize this saint's name, and he is usually known in his native Ireland as Mochumna. He studied under *Columba at Bennchorr, and went to Iona with him, remaining there for several years. He evangelized Mull, and then moved on to the mission to the Picts, working as head of mission in the Aberdeen area. He is sometimes credited with being the first bishop of Aberdeen, but this appears to be incorrect, as is the later tradition that Pope Gregory the Great appointed him archbishop of Tours. Water from his well was long used for baptism in Aberdeen cathedral.

Maelrubba (Maelrubha, Malrubius) (642–722), 21 April, is known as the apostle of the Picts. He was a descendant of Niall of the Nine Hostages, and trained at Bennchorr under *Comgall, who is said to have been a relative on his mother's side. He left Ireland in 670 or 671, and he may have spent some time at Iona before following in *Columba's footsteps to Scotland. Both the *Annals of Ulster* and the *Annals of Tigernach* record his journey. He settled at Apurcrosan (Applecross) in Wester Ross, facing Skye, and held office there for fifty-one years. There has been some discussion over the question of whether he was abbot or prior of Applecross. His name is not in the list of abbots recited in *The Antiphony of Bangor*, though Scottish accounts refer to him as abbot. There is also debate over whether he was martyred by Vikings: Irish accounts say that he died peacefully at Applecross. *The Celtic Church in Scotland* has a map of his churches. He worked up the west coast of Scotland, and in the Isles. The short route to Scotland from Bangor was across the North Channel to Kintyre, and there are place-names connected with his name on Mull, Skye and Harris. It is said that the Gaelic exclamation '*Ma Ruibbe!*' is still to be heard on Harris. He also went across to the east coast of Scotland, which is only some forty miles wide at this point. Pilgrimages in Maelrubba's honour were stopped by the Presbyterians in the seventeenth century. A report of the Inverness and Dingwall Presbytery 1633–88 on a meeting at Applecross deprecated the survival of 'superstitious practices', including 'frequent approaches to some ruinous chappells and circulateing of them'.

Maughold (MacCuill, Maguil, Maccul, Machallus) (498), 27 April or 28 December, bishop of the Isle of Man, but not the first bishop (see *Germanus). According to legend, Maughold was a ferocious pirate who was converted by *St Patrick. As a penance for his sins, Patrick is said to have told him to put to sea (on the eastern side of Ulster, where the islands cluster thickly) in a coracle without oars. He landed at the Isle of Man, where he was received by two earlier disciples sent by Patrick, named Romulus and Conindrus. He eventually became a missionary bishop. Maughold is the Manx form of his name, and Machallus the Latin form, the other forms being Irish variants.

Modan (*c.* 550) 4 February, sought solitude in the mountains of Dunblane, where he is reputed to have carried out a ministry in Stirling and Falkirk, and to have been elected abbot of a monastery against his will. There is no trace of a monastery in the area before the twelfth century. The Revised Roman Martyrology places him in the seventh or eighth centuries, and says that he died at the monastery of Rosneath in Dumbartonshire. The high church at Stirling bears his dedication. There is another Scottish saint named Modan (eighth century, 14 November) at Fraserburgh, with whom he is sometimes confused.

Moluag of Lismore (Lua, Lugaidh, Luanus, Moloc) (*c.* 530–92), 25 June. It is not certain whether Moluag was born in the south of Ireland, Scotland or the Isles. *Oengus calls him 'Moloc pure – fair son (or sun) of Lismore and of Alba'. He is said to have been trained at Bennchorr, and to have headed a mission into Pictland. He went to Argyllshire and to monastic communities on the isle of Lismore, Skye and the outer Hebrides, and carried out missionary work in Ross and the province of Marr.

He is best known on Lismore. His blackthorn pastoral staff, known as the *Bachuill Mor*, and once encased in gilded metal and studded with jewels, is now in what was probably its original state, and a treasured possession of the Livingstone family of Lismore. A Latin charter of 1554 confirms their possession 'since time immemorial' of the *Magnum Baculum* or pastoral staff of St Moluag. It

The bachuill of St Moluag of Lismore

came into the hands of the dukes of Argyll for safe-keeping, but in 1973, the then duke of Argyll determined to return it to its rightful owners. On a notable occasion, he and the duchess, with their eldest son, the bishop of Argyll and the Isles and a small party of clergy, embarked in a coracle to return it to its hereditary keeper, Alastair Livingstone of Lismore, who bears the title of Baron of Bachuill. Almost the whole population of Lismore turned out for the ensuing ceremony. On 25 June 1992, the fourteen hundredth anniversary of the death of St Moluag was celebrated on Lismore, and his staff is still carried in procession on ceremonial occasions.

Ninian (*c.* 362–432), 6 August: Aldhelm, bishop of Sherborne (639–709) visited Ninian's church of *Candida Casa* at Whithorn, and wrote to the Benedictine monks who then kept the shrine. By that time, southern Scotland had submitted to Roman jurisdiction, and the bishopric was revived – or instituted, since no-one was quite sure whether Ninian had been a properly consecrated bishop in the first place. Bede, writing rather later (he completed his *Historia Ecclesiastica* in 731) describes Ninian as 'a most reverend and holy man of British race', who was 'regularly instructed in the mysteries of the Christian faith in Rome'. He says that he had an episcopal see 'named after St Martin, and famous for its stately church'. There is no indication that Ninian ever went to Rome, or that he administered anything resembling a Roman episcopal see. Bede is merely repeating the Roman claim to the foundation of *Candida Casa*; but he does add two other comments which are of some historical importance. The church was known as *Candida Casa* (the White House) because it was built of stone, which was 'unusual among the Britons'; and Ninian's body and the bodies of many saints lay at rest there.

Bede's single paragraph on Ninian, before he turns to the work of *Columba, reads as though he knew people who had been to Whithorn and seen the shrines of Ninian and his followers. Ninian built a stone church at a time when churches in the Celtic lands were usually build of timber and thatch. Stone churches were common in Gaul, so he probably learned of this from Martin in Tours. When his monastery was complete, he heard of Martin's death, and dedicated his church in Martin's name. Martin died in or about 397, which fixes the date of the monastery's foundation within a year or two.

Aelred, who was abbot of Rievaulx from 1143 to 1166, went to Galloway to visit *Candida Casa* in 1164. There he was shown a book written in 'a barbarous language' which had been composed at the request of Christianus, then bishop of Galloway. Presumably this was translated for him, and he reproduces some of the information, 'bringing it forth into the clear light of Latin diction'. By Aelred's time, it was of fairly dubious authenticity, for over five hundred years had passed since Ninian's death, but at least it contained the local traditions. He says that Ninian was born near the shores of the Solway Firth, that his father was a Christian, and that he was given the name of Ninian in baptism. He was educated in the Christian faith, and soon surpassed his teachers with his knowledge and his questions. He went on a journey to Rome over the Alps, studied in Rome for several years, and came back via Tours. There he met St Martin, who was then bishop of that city, and had long discussions with him. They parted with 'embraces, kisses and tears'. Martin gave him two stone-masons to help him build his own church. When he heard of Martin's death, Ninian dedicated the new stone church in his name. He had a ministry among the southern Picts in Galloway, but there is no mention of an episcopal see.

Aelred is much more interested in miracles attributed to Ninian after his death than in the facts of his life; but recent research into fifth century patterns of Celtic travel does help us to place his statements in context. There is no reason to doubt that Ninian was born in Galloway, at or near Whithorn, or that he came of a Christian family. The Solway Firth would have been on the trade routes which ran from the Mediterranean to the west coast of Scotland, and there may well have been a large trading post in that area where traders from France and Spain had settled. An ancient Irish Life says that Ninian's father was a king, and his mother a Spanish princess. Once we allow for the fact that many of the kings were local chieftains, there is no difficulty in accepting the proposition that he was probably a chieftain's son, and his mother may well have been a chieftain's daughter of Spanish descent, a Christian from the Roman province of Spain. The Christian travellers from the Continent would have brought their clergy with them, so there would be scholarly men to teach him, and to encourage him in his desire to travel and learn further.

He probably went to the Continent with a party of other young men. The fifth century was not a time for solitary pilgrims or backpackers. Where did he travel to, and what route did he take? Bede and Aelred assume that he went overland to Rome, and this became the established view. The editor of *Pinkerton's Lives of the Scottish Saints* (1889) was so convinced of this that he appended a long footnote describing Ninian's probable tribulations as he struggled over the Alps in winter; but more recent writers think that his travels may not have taken him so far. Given Whithorn's geographical position and the sea-routes, it is far more likely that Ninian travelled by sea rather than risking the long and dangerous journey overland. And he may have gone no farther than Tours.

Tours was already renowned as Martin's bishopric, and Martin was still bishop when Ninian travelled. Alcuin's account of Martin's encouragement of Ninian's project has been supported by archaeological findings. At that time, there were no stone-masons in Pictland, where churches were constructed of wood with thatched roofs; but Continental churches were commonly built of stone. Excavations at Whithorn have uncovered the remains of three walls of a fifth century stone church, the fourth wall being replaced with that of the east wall of a medieval priory. The walls are constructed of local rock, shale and slate, and traces of the original white finish (a coarse cream mortar) are still visible. Further excavations have revealed a large trading settlement close to the site.

Haddan and Stubbs note that *Candida Casa* was 'frequented by the Irish' in Ninian's time. *Enda, *Monnena, *Moluag of Lismore, *Finnian of Moville, *Tigernach and *Donan are all said to have studied there, learning from the monastic system which Ninian had brought back from Tours.

Ronan of Kilmaronen (seventh century), 7 February, was a Scottish missionary, described by Bede as a bishop, who defended the Roman date of Easter. Bede calls him 'a most zealous champion of the true Easter', who had been 'instructed in Gaul and Italy in the authentic practice of the Church'. He is reported to have disputed against *Finan, *Aidan's successor as abbot of Lindisfarne, in the controversies leading up to the Synod of Whitby.

He is evidently not the same person as the Scottish hermit Ronan, who lived on the island of Rona north-east of Lewis, in the same century. The legend of the hermit is that he went to Rona to avoid the evil tongues of the women of Euroby on Lewis. He had a sister named Brenthilda who was exiled to a nearby island, but he refused to see her, and she died pining for her brother. This has all the making of a really interesting story, but there is no information about what the women said or why Brenthilda was exiled, so this is one of the many loose ends which students of the Celtic saints have had to accept.

Rule (Regulus) (?4th century), 17 October, is known to us through the legend of St Andrew, patron saint of Scotland. The story, which occurs in many versions, and in at least three ancient manuscripts, is that Rule was the custodian of the tomb of Andrew the Apostle, who was reputedly crucified at Patras, in Greece, and buried there.

Rule was inspired by a vision to take the saint's relics 'towards the ends of the earth' and finally took them to the city on the east coast of Fife which now bears the Apostle's name. This is why the saltire or diagonal cross of St Andrew is the national flag of Scotland, and appears on the Union Jack.

The Victorian historian of Scotland, W. F. Skene, attempted to sort out the tangled and often contradictory strands of legend. He found evidence to suggest that about the year 345, the Emperor Constantine ordered St Andrew's shrine to be taken to Constantinople; but that, as often happened in such cases, some of the relics were kept back, and remained at Patras. Much later, a priest-custodian of the shrine took them to Scotland, landing at Muckross. At Matha, he met Ungus or Hungus, king of the Picts (identified with Angus McFergus, king from 731 to 761) at the head of his troops. Ungus was about to lead an expedition against Eadbert of Northumberland. He pitched his tent on the spot where the royal hall now stands in St Andrews, received a blessing from the priest, and gave the place and the city to God. He declared that the church to be founded there was to be 'the head and mother of all the churches in the kingdom of the Picts'.

Dr Skene came to the somewhat eccentric conclusion that the legend was so inherently unlikely that there might well be some truth in it. He visited Patras, and could find no church there dedicated to St Andrew; but in a 'small and very old-looking' Greek monastery, he was shown what the then custodian claimed to be the saint's sarcophagus, which was empty.

We do not know who St Rule (sometimes called 'Bishop Regulus') was, or his nationality. Unsuccessful attempts have been made to identify him with a French St Rieul and an Irish St Righail. If he was from anywhere in western Europe, it seems very unlikely that he would have been in a position of trust in a Greek monastery in the ninth century, when the Eastern Church had all but severed its links with Rome. The transportation of Christian relics from the Middle East to Europe did not begin until the late eleventh century, at the time of the First Crusade, so it is more likely that relics or reputed relics of St Andrew were brought to Scotland at that time.

The movement of relics from the Middle East occurred on a large scale during the Crusades, for a variety of reasons. There was the urgent need to save shrines which had attracted great devotion in the first Christian millennium from desecration by the advancing Islamic armies. There was an acute sense that, though Christianity had started in the Middle East, it had developed in the West, and Western churches needed their own devotional links with the earthly life of Christ and his Apostles; and there was the undeniable fact that the possession of relics enabled a diocese or monastery to claim precedence over others, and to attract pilgrims. In Scotland, the legend of St Andrew enabled the church in the city which came to bear his name to claim greater antiquity than the work of the Irish *Columba and the monks of Iona – or even that of *Ninian.

Scotland has at least the distinction of being the only constituent part of the United Kingdom which has one of the Twelve Apostles as its patron.

5

Wales: the Founders

To the Romans, 'Britannia' was the name of their most westerly province, and only barbarians lived beyond it; but by the sixth and seventh centuries, the Britons or Brythons were the people of Wales. When Bede wrote of 'British bishops' meeting Augustine, he was in fact referring to Welsh monks, led by their abbots. They are thought to have met on two occasions, the first at St Augustine's Oak somewhere in the West Country, and the second time near Bangor-on-Dee. The Celtic clergy consulted *Dinwydd, abbot of Bangor Iscoed, as to how they should proceed, which suggests that he was a very senior and respected figure. He told the Celtic party that if Augustine proved to be meek and lowly in heart, they should take it as a sign that he bore the yoke of Christ, and enter into discussions with him; but if he was haughty and unbending, they should not listen to him. This was shrewd thinking: it would test whether the Romans still regarded themselves as *superiori*, or whether they were ready to co-operate on equal terms with the Celtic clergy. The Celtic group were not used to Roman manners, and were not aware that Roman bishops were accustomed to receive their guests sitting down. When they arrived, Augustine remained seated. The Celts became angry when he compounded this apparent discourtesy by lecturing them on the subject of the 'correct' date of Easter, and the importance of conforming to Roman practices. Interpreting his attitude as one of arrogance, they reasoned among themselves that 'if he would not rise to greet them in the first instance, he would have even less regard for them once they submitted to his authority', so they withdrew. Quite basic misconceptions complicated the strained relations between the Celtic and Roman clergy for another two and a half centuries.

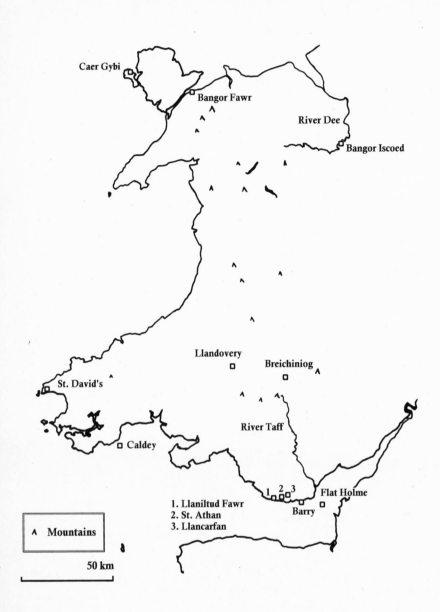

Wales

Bede, who tells the story of the meetings with Augustine entirely from the Roman point of view, noting that the Celts 'stubbornly preferred their own customs to those in universal use among Christian churches', records almost with satisfaction that 'divine judgement' followed. In 603, there was a battle between the Britons and the Anglo-Saxons at Chester, near Bangor Iscoed. The monks of Bangor Iscoed gathered to pray for their countrymen, and stood between the warring parties in an attempt to secure peace; but the Anglo-Saxon king Ethelfrid ordered his troops to attack the praying monks first, though they were unarmed. About twelve hundred of what Bede calls 'the faithless Britons who had rejected eternal salvation' were massacred, and their monastery was razed to the ground.

North Wales and South Wales do not relate easily to one another. The massive structure of the mountains across the centre of Wales hampers communication. In the days when transport was slow and difficult, North Wales tended to relate to northern Britain and Armagh, while South Wales related to Cornwall, southern Britain and Cork. There were ethnic differences, too, for the brawny, red-haired people observed by Tacitus tended to predominate in the north, while the smaller, dark, 'Iberian' people were more common in the south.

Romano-British influence was stronger in Wales than in Ireland or Scotland. The Romans had penetrated the Welsh valleys, building forts at Caerleon-on-Usk, Carmarthen and Caernavon; but the Welsh Church also had contacts with Ireland, and in the south, contacts with Gaul and the Mediterranean. Of the five great early monasteries, *Illtud's monastery, later called Llaniltud Fawr (now Llantwit Major), was on the south Glamorgan coast, and *Cadoc's Llancarfan was also in Glamorgan. Bangor Fawr on the Menai Straits and Bangor Iscoed in Clwyd, both founded by *Deiniol, have a clear link with the Irish Bangor or Bennchorr on Belfast Lough, and acquired names which made that connection clear. Sometimes Welsh monasteries were referred to as 'bangors' in the chronicles.

Some were apparently very large monasteries. Bede, who is more careful with numbers than most of the Irish chroniclers, records that in the time when St Augustine was at Canterbury (597–604) Bangor Iscoed had over two thousand monks – 'so many monks that although it was divided into seven sections, each under its own head, none of these sections contained less than three hundred monks'. The arithmetical precision of his statement carries some weight. The massacre of twelve hundred monks from Bangor Iscoed which he records must have been a terrible blow to the Church in North Wales.

Though the Church in eastern and southern Britain was all but wiped out in the fifth century, it is likely that some Christian communities, like the one which *Patrick came from, survived intact if they were close to areas fortified by the Romans. The earliest of the Welsh saints of whom we have definite knowledge is *Dubricius, whose Welsh name is Dyfrig. He is better known by the Latin version of his name which is used even in the earliest chronicles. He was a bishop, working principally on the borders of Hereford and Gwent, along a Roman road, and exercising episcopal functions in Illtud's monastery, in Glamorgan. We know that he ordained *David and *Samson, and he is thought to have died about 550. The next in seniority of whom we have knowledge are Deiniol, founder and abbot of the great monasteries of Bangor Fawr and Bangor Iscoed in North Wales, and Illtud himself. *Paulinus, David, Cadoc, *Teilo, *Gildas, and Samson of Dol were all among Illtud's disciples. The Irish *Finnian, already abbot of Clonard, also went to study under him to enrich the life of his own foundation, and went on to other Welsh monasteries on what seems to have been a sort of protracted study tour. The links between the Irish and Welsh Churches became so strong that *Columbanus, writing from Italy, referred to them jointly as 'the Western Churches'.

There were Welsh colonies in Brittany, often centred on coastal trading-posts. Illtud, who was born in one of them, kept his links with Brittany, and a number of his disciples went there, often via Cornwall and the Channel Isles. The Lives of the Welsh saints indicate that Wales suffered very badly from a series of disasters in the fifth decade of the sixth century. Large groups of monks fled the country in the face of internal warfare, such as those who went to

Bardsey after the destruction of Deiniol's Bangor Fawr, and the 'British monks' who caused so much dissension in Ireland at the monasteries of *Mo-Chuta and *Colman Elo. Parties of Norse pirates attacked the cost, burning and killing; and Wales was racked by a plague of cataclysmic proportions which came from the East, probably along the sea-routes. John Davies, author of *A History of Wales* (1995), writes:

> The plague originated in Egypt in 541: it had reached Britain by 549, when it carried off Maelgwn Fawr. It would appear that it did not attack the English because they, unlike the Britons, lacked contacts with the shores of the Mediterranean.

He continues, 'The plague of 549 is believed to have been as devastating as the more famous plague of 1349.' If this was the case, it could have killed a third of the population. The death of Maelgwn Fawr is recorded in the *Welsh Annals* in the year 547, with the words: 'A great death in which Maelgwn king of Gwynedd died. Then was the yellow plague'.

The fourteenth century Black Death was due to bubonic plague, and produced characteristic swellings in the groin and armpit. The Yellow Plague had different symptoms: its chief characteristics were that it turned people yellow and then killed them. It is described in an older account incorporated in the *Book of Llan Dav*, which is specific about the symptoms:

> It was called the yellow pestilence because it made everyone it attacked yellow and bloodless. It appeared to men in the form of a column, consisting of a watery cloud passing over the whole region. Everything living that it touched with its pestilential breath either died straightway or became sick unto death.

The record says that 'vast numbers of all conditions and ages died, and the very beasts and reptiles also perished'. The symptoms resemble those of yellow fever, which is still a major threat today in Africa and Central America. The infection causes jaundice, hepatitis, vomiting and internal bleeding, and can result in coma and death in three days.

This was a major disaster; but there were other plagues, a whole series of them, in Wales in the sixth century, and there must have been other migrations. Very large numbers of people left Wales – not only monks and whole monastic communities, but families and extended kinship groups, the inhabitants of whole localities, men, women and children.

Among the groups of kin who moved to escape the effects of the Yellow Pestilence or one of the other calamities were the family of *Germoc, and some of the mysterious and numerous 'children of *Brychan'. If they and others fled in terror, they travelled in faith, spreading the gospel as they went. Many of them went to Cornwall and on to the Welsh settlements in Brittany, where there are accounts of how the ships bringing immigrants were not always welcome, because it was feared that they brought the plague with them.

David's monastery of Menevia (Mynyw) was on a remote promontory jutting out from South Wales towards Ireland in the place now known as St David's. It seems to have been clear of the disaster areas, and to have continued its work and its links with the Irish monasteries when other Welsh monasteries were razed to the ground or left deserted. Thanks to the eleventh century Welsh monk Rhygyfarch, we know much more about David than about Dubricius, Deiniol, Illtud or Paulinus, all of whom were senior to him, and greatly revered in the Celtic Church in Wales.

Only fragments of the Lives of the Welsh saints, written soon after their deaths, have survived. New Lives were compiled by Norman ecclesiastics after the Conquest, and though they often used material which is now lost, they tended to shape it to their own purposes. These Norman accounts were often circulated with charters attached to them, claiming that land had been granted to their monasteries in the past, and asking for it to be returned under the new dispensation. Ironically, the most trustworthy Lives of the Welsh saints tend to come from Welsh monasteries in Brittany rather than from those in Wales.

A key feature of the Lives of the Welsh saints is that many of them are said to be connected, either by kinship or by monastic master–student relationships. The kinship relationships may not always have been as close as they appear in the ancient Lives, since it was the custom to refer to other members of the *gwely* or extended family in their own generation as cousins, or even brothers and sisters, and to those in the preceding generation as uncles or aunts. This still happens in Wales: the terms do not have the precision they have in England. Monastic relationships often developed from family relationships, and these also were described in family terms, the most confusing to later generations being *Papa*; but if the references are not as precise as they seem, they do indicate that the people concerned belonged to the same extended family, and lived at roughly the same time. They are repeated in different Lives from different sources often enough to date nearly all the major Welsh saints to the first half of the sixth century. One major event involving a number of the leading Welsh saints was the Synod of Brefi, which took place at a date between 546 and 548. Dubricius, Deiniol, Paulinus and David were all present, and David astounded the assembled abbots and bishops with the excellence of his discourse.

Wales had experienced a golden age of learning which was coming to an abrupt end. Whether the synod was held just before the first waves of the Yellow Pestilence struck the country, or whether it was called in a desperate attempt to seek divine aid in the face of disaster, is unclear; but the lack of information about the Celtic Church in Wales and its leaders after this time is striking. Gildas's account of 'The Ruin of Britain' and Nennius's account of 'The Loss of Britain' give ample evidence of the chaos which ensued as a result of all the cumulative disasters: famine, despair, and the 'thickets of tyrants' who preyed on the survivors when the fragile law and order established by the chieftains broke down. The strength of the Cambrian monastic system moved to new witness and new foundations in Brittany.

Asaph (sixth to seventh centuries), 2 May, was a cousin of *Deiniol, a nephew of *Dinwydd, and related to *Tysilio. He is said to have become a disciple of *Kentigern (Mungo) during the period when Kentigern was an abbot in Wales, but this link with the patron saint of Glasgow, told by his Norman chronicler Goscelin or Jocelyn, is suspect.

The story of how the young Asaph brought live coals to make a fire to warm his master does seem to be Welsh in origin, and may relate to a master other than Kentigern. His master was reciting the Psalter, all 150 psalms, while standing in the coldest water he could find. Asaph carried the coals in his apron, and it was accounted a miracle that the apron was not burned. Similar stories are told of *Cadoc and *Cybi, and there may be a simple and practical explanation. The holy penitents must have been at risk of hypothermia, and their young assistants would have been anxious to warm them when their penance was completed (compare the otters or beavers who warmed *Columba's feet when he came out of the sea). To kindle a fire on the banks of the river, they probably used the same method which was used by most housewives right up to the invention of matches: taking a shovel of coals from an existing fire to start a new one elsewhere. The handle of the shovel would become hot, and a sensible boy would wrap it in his leather apron to avoid burning his fingers.

In the monastery, Asaph was esteemed 'a venerable boy . . . the dearest and best loved of all', and he was raised to the priesthood as soon as possible. He eventually became abbot. His influence on the monastery and the locality was so strong that after his death, the monastery was renamed in his memory. In the twelfth century St Asaph became the centre of a Norman diocese covering the whole of the principality of Powys, and the episcopal authorities would have used any legends, such as the one involving Kentigern, to reinforce their position.

Barry (Barnic, Barruc) (sixth century), 27 September, came from the Glamorgan region. He was a disciple of *Cadoc, and probably contemporary with *Gildas and *Deiniol. According to Baring Gould and Fisher, he was the founder of Llancarfan, though other sources attribute this to Cadoc himself. He is said to have been one of the teachers of *Finnian of Clonard, through whom he was known in Ireland; but very little seems to be known about him. He became a hermit, settling on what is now Barry Island, and is thought to have died there.

Beuno (seventh century), 21 April, was a holy man, the brother of *St Winifred's mother. Like her, she probably came from Clwyd, and was a member of a noble family. Stanton describes him as 'the grandson of Gundleus' (*Gwynllyw) and says that he was related to both *Cadoc and *Kentigern. The relationship to Cadoc is likely enough, but it is difficult to see how he could be related to the Pictish Kentigern, the story of whose ministry in North Wales is now generally discounted.

Beuno had an oratory at Clynnog Fawr in Clwyd, and it was there that Winifred was reputedly martyred and then raised from the dead in answer to his prayers. His well, the *Ffynnon Beuno*, still exists, close to his church at Clynnog. It was the centre for processions and ceremonies on his feast day as late as the sixteenth century. There are many dedications to him in Clwyd, and there is a Jesuit retreat house named St Beuno's at St Asaph.

Brychan (Brechanus) (?fifth or early sixth century), 6 April, is said to have been king of Breichinniog (Brecon) in South Wales. A stained glass window at St Neot, Cornwall, shows a figure, said to be his, crowned and with his arms around ten children, but this has also been interpreted as 'God the Father with souls in his lap'. There are many stories of 'the children of Brychan', who are said to number anywhere between twelve to sixty-three in different genealogies.

Canon G. H. Doble notes that 'the area around Llandovery is full of Brychan associations'. It is close to Llandeusant, the monastery founded by the Welsh *Paulinus. Some commentators have explained the very large numbers of children by citing a tradition that Brychan married three times. Others hold that they represent all his descendants in several generations; or that he was a monastic teacher, and the 'children' were his disciples; but a number of the 'children' were women, which makes this last explanation unlikely. The probability is that they were an extended family with broader kinship ties.

The genealogies of the 'children of Brychan' include a number of saints: *Gwladys, mother of *Cadoc, *Non, mother of *David, *Nectan, *Clether, *Endellion, Morwenna, *Dwyn, *Keyne and

St Brychan: stained glass window at St Neot's

*Tydfil, some remembered in Wales, some in Cornwall, and some in Brittany.

Cadfan (fifth to sixth centuries), 1 November, is said to have been born in Brittany. He was a half-brother of *Winwaloe, whose mother *Gwen Teirbron was twice married, and the cousin of *Padarn (or one of the Padarns). He may have been a soldier at one time, like *Illtud: a thirteenth century Welsh poem by Llywelyn Fardd describes him as 'the guardian of battle' and 'a hero', and there is a statue of a man in military dress at Quimper, which is said to be his.

In Wales, he founded a church at Towyn (now in Gwynnedd), and later became abbot of a monastery on the island of Bardsey, off the Lleyn peninsula in North Wales. Bardsey became a refugee centre for monks after the massacre at Chester and the consequent destruction of Bangor-on-Dee in 603 (see *Dinwydd). There was predictable chaos: 'there were no cells, but everyone did as he chose'. Later the monastery settled down, with about 500 monks, to a regular way of life. Its importance in the life of the medieval Church was such that three pilgrimages to Bardsey are said to have counted as the equivalent of one to Rome, and in Wales it ranked as second only to St David's. It became so celebrated that even in the eighteenth century, centuries after its destruction, fishermen would remove their hats and say a prayer when they sailed past.

Cadoc (Cadog, Cadfael, Catwg) (?570), 21 September, was the son of *Gwynllyw, a South Wales chieftain, and his wife *Gwladys, one of the 'children of *Brychan'. One of Gwynllyw's bands of soldiers stole a cow from an Irish hermit named Meuthi, who promptly went to ask for it back. We do not know the fate of the cow, but Meuthi stayed to baptize the royal couple's first child. The child was named Cadfael, but known as Cadoc, which was probably a diminutive. Later, he was sent to a school which Meuthi taught in Caerwent. When he grew up, he refused to succeed his father, having decided that he wanted to be a priest. He went to his uncle, Paul Penychen (*Paulinus), who had been the ruler of a district south of Brecon, and was a disciple of *Illtud. Paul, who taught both *David and *Teilo, also taught Cadoc, later offering him land for a monastery. Cadoc made a valley settlement at Llancarfan, and built a hill fort at Llanfeithin nearby, as a refuge in case of attack. As a chieftain's son and a descendant of Brychan, he probably had quite a large force of followers and labourers. There is no indication that he lived for long periods as a hermit, and the suggestion that he did so may arise from confusion with another Cadoc who earlier advised Illtud; but it is probable that, like many Celtic monks, he sought solitude for Lent or Advent retreats.

At some point, Cadoc went to Ireland, and studied for three years, traditionally with *Ciaran of Saighir. He came back with a large party of Irish and British monks, including *Finnian of Clonard, who was older, and already an abbot. The monastery at Llancarfan grew. Cadoc's biographer Lifris says that he 'daily fed a hundred clergy with a hundred soldiers and a hundred workmen and a hundred poor men, with the same number of widows', so even allowing for some exaggeration, it sounds like a large household. The monastery became of great influence and importance. Cadoc and *Gildas were close colleagues, going on retreat together to Steep Holme and Flat Holme (Echni), islands in the Bristol Channel, for prayer and meditation. Gildas is known to have visited Llancarfan, which became 'one of the three great bangors of Llandaff'.

At some point – probably at the time of the Yellow Pestilence – Cadoc and his monks had to emigrate to Brittany, but they returned when the plague had run its course. His chronicler Lifris, writing in the late eleventh or early twelfth century, tells the story of how, when Cadoc died, his body was miraculously spirited away to Benevento in Italy in a white cloud. This was probably an inspired invention by the monks of Llancarfan to conceal Cadoc's shrine. The church of St Peter's, Gloucester, was given jurisdiction over Llancarfan after the Norman Conquest, and would have been very anxious to acquire the relics of such an illustrious Welsh saint if they could have found them. As far as we know, Cadoc died at Llancarfan.

At the time when Lifris wrote his Life, Anselm, archbishop of Canterbury, was asserting jurisdiction over the Celtic bishops of Llandaff and St David's, thus threatening the independence of the Welsh Church. Lifris was archdeacon of Glamorgan, and the son of Bishop Herwald of Llandaff. The Life of David by Rhygyfarch, son of the bishop of St David's, was written soon after. Lifris is evidently trying to provide Roman credentials for Cadoc to please Anselm's commissioners. He says that there was a disagreement between Gildas and David over which of them should have jurisdiction over all the churches in the province (which was the sort of matter which concerned Norman bishops, but not Celtic abbots); and that Gildas had a bell which Cadoc wanted to own, but Gildas said he was going to Rome to give it to the pope. The pope is said to have refused it, after which it was handed over to Cadoc. In Rhygyfarch's Life of David, there is a different version of this story: Gildas proposed to give the bell to David; but it emitted a 'melodic sound' for Cadoc, and refused to ring for David, so it was agreed that Cadoc should keep it.

Lifris also asserts in his long, wandering and indigestible account that Cadoc went three times to Jerusalem, and seven times to

Rome, and performed many miracles, including turning wolves to stone, and that King Arthur had been in love with his mother, Gwladys, in her youth; but such stories appear to be no more than literary flourishes.

Unfortunately, no contemporary Life of Cadoc has survived – if there ever was one. Apart from casual references in the Lives of other saints he knew, subsequent scholars have been entirely dependent on Lifris and a less extensive and equally unreliable Life written by Caradoc, for what is known of his work.

Even the little which is known about Cadoc has been complicated over the centuries by confusion with two other saints: a Scots Cadoc (24 January) for whom there is no information apart from the fact that he made a foundation at Cambuslang; and a Breton Cadoc, about whom there is only a garbled story that he was in military service with Illtud in Brittany.

Collen (Colan) (date unknown), 21 May, was the founder of the church at Llangollen, Clwyd, and possibly of the church of Langollen at Finistère in Brittany. He may have studied in Gaul, was said to have a hot temper, and eventually left his monastery to become a hermit. The only Lives available are late compilations which tell an entirely mythical story of how he fought a duel with a Saracen in the presence of the pope, and slew a giantess who was terrorizing the Vale of Llangollen. Like the stories about saints who slew or tamed dragons, this account represents the triumph of good over evil in a satisfyingly dramatic form.

Congar of Wales (date unknown), 7 November, is known only by dedications and calendar listings. The dedications are in North Wales, at Llangefni on Anglesey, Ynys Gongar near Criccieth, and Llangyngar (now Hope), in Clwyd. Medieval Welsh calendars indicate that there were fairs in his honour at Llangefni and Llangyngar. This Congar has to be distinguished from a sixth century Congar (27 November) who seems to have founded a Celtic monastery at Congresbury in Somerset, and also a saint of the same name (13 February and 12 May) whose name occurs in place-names in Brittany (Saint-Congard, Rosconger, Lesconger). It is possible that the Welsh Congar and the Breton Congar are the same person, but difficult to accept Canon Doble's assertion that he was a brother of both *Petroc and *Cadoc.

Cybi (Kebi, Gybi) (sixth century), 8 November, is considered the most important saint in Anglesey. He was the founder of the monastery at Holyhead, which was called in Welsh *Caer Gybi*. Other place-names associated with him are Llangybi near Pwllheli, Ynys Gybi off the coast of Dyfed, and Llangybbi-on-Usk. Cybi is also known for his missionary work in Cornwall, where he worked between the rivers Tamar and Limar. Later, he went on to Poitiers, and is said to have worked with the bishop, St Hilary, for nearly fifty years. This is unlikely, since Hilary died in about 368, but he may well have studied for a time at the monastic school which Hilary had founded. He went back to Cornwall, and then to Wales, where he made foundations known as Llangybi and Llandyfredwys. He spent three days at Menevia, before going at the age of seventy-seven to the 'island of Aruin', *Enda's island to the west of southern Ireland, where he and his monks 'bravely dug the soil' to establish a new monastery.

They were persecuted by a local chief or the abbot of another monastery (accounts vary) named Crubtha Finta or Fintan Munir, because they were encroaching on his land. The story that he was an abbot is supported by Cybi's whole-hearted curse: 'May all thy churches be deserted, and may never three churches be found singing thy praises in all Ireland.'

Eventually Crubtha Finta or Fintan Munir drove Cybi and his monks away. They went back to Anglesey, where they were at first threatened with eviction by the king of Gwynnedd; but the king finally allowed them to stay, and ended his days as a convert, giving his fortress to 'Almighty God and Cybi as a perpetual offering of alms'.

Cybi frequently met the hermit *Seiriol for 'holy converse'. The two had a custom of meeting at midday at the wells of Clorach, near Llanerchymedd, about half-way between Cybi's monastery at Holyhead and Seiriol's hermitage at Penmon. Cybi journeyed from west to east in the morning, getting the full force of the rising sun,

1. *The Romans defeating 'barbarians', the Antonine Wall, Bridgeness*

2. *A Celtic beehive hut*

3. The Shrine of St
Patrick's Bell

4. The Temptation of St
Antony, detail of cross at
Moone, County Kildare

5. St Martin's Cross, Iona

6. *The Eagle, symbol of St John the Evangelist, from the Book of Kells*

7. *St Columba at Loch Ness. Painting by Gareth Lucas*

8. *The flag of St Perran at the Last Night of the Proms 2001*

9. St Gwen Teirbron, Chapel of St Vence

10. A page from the Lindisfarne Gospels

11. Stonework, St Saviour's Church, Glendalough

and back from west to east in the afternoon, facing the setting sun. As a consequence, he was tanned by the sun's rays. Seiriol, travelling in the opposite directions, had his back to the sun, and so was not exposed to its rays. They were popularly called *Cybui Felyn* (the Tawny) and *Seiriol Wyn* (the Fair). Their meetings are commemorated in Matthew Arnold's poem 'East and West', and the poet seems to have had more in mind than a simple case of sun-tan:

> In the bare midst of Anglesey they show
> Two springs which close to one another play
> And 'thirteen hundred years agone', they say,
> Two saints met often where their waters flow . . .
> 'Seiriol the Bright, Kybi the Dark', men said,
> The seer from the east was then in light,
> The seer from the west was then in shade.
> Ah! Now 'tis changed. In conquering sunshine bright
> The man of the bold West now comes arrayed,
> He of the mystic East is touched with night.

Arnold (1822–88) may be referring to the origins of Christianity in the Middle East, its near-eclipse as a result of Islamic conquests, and the rise of a westernized form of Christianity.

Cybi died in Snowdonia, where, according to his ancient Latin Life, he 'slept in Christ with great honour'. The Welsh name of Holyhead is still Caer Gybi.

David (Dewi) (*c.* 520–89 or 601), 1 March. There are no contemporary biographies for David, and none of his writings have survived. Accounts of his life and work rest on centuries of oral tradition and a single late eleventh century Life written by Rhygyfarch or Rhigyfarch, the eldest son of Bishop Sulien of St David's, about 1095. This was probably based on older documents which have since disappeared, and possibly written to match the Life of *Cadoc by Lifris, which had recently been completed. These two sons of bishops were evidently in some haste to set down the stories of the great Welsh saints before the Normans took over the Church in Wales: it was already clear by the closing years of the eleventh century that dioceses with territorial boundaries would be formed, Norman prelates would be appointed to rule them, and Welsh traditions would be lost. It had already happened in England, where archbishop Lanfranc's commission of Norman clerics had toured the country, changing church dedications, and substituting the names of Roman saints for Anglo-Saxon ones. Rhygyfarch and Lifris may have been to some extent in competition with one another, but they had a common cause.

Rhygyfarch makes it clear that he is basing his account on older manuscripts. Many of them were 'eaten away along the backs and edges by the continuous gnawing of worms and the ravages of passing years' and he found them very old-fashioned. He was writing a good five hundred years after the events he described – about as long as the time from Columbus's discovery of the Americas to the present day – so it is hardly surprising that he thought them somewhat dated. His chief purpose was to make a record of 'the Father's signs and miracles', so the biographical details are often somewhat imprecise, and other leading figures in the Welsh Church of David's day, such as *Dubricius and *Illtud, are virtually edited out.

Many manuscript copies exist of Rhygyfarch's Life of David. There are some variations between them due to editing, and some fairly obvious interpolations by later hands, but the basic story is that David's mother was *Non or Nonna, said to be a granddaughter of *Brychan, and his father a prince named Sant. David is still called 'Dewi Sant' in Wales, and this means both 'St David' and 'David, son of Sant'. Rhygyfarch, writing in Latin, called Sant 'Sanctus by name and by merit', glossing over his alleged violation of the virgin Non. Their child was born in a meadow near Vetus Rubus, which has been tentatively identified with Henfynyw, on the coast near St Bride's Bay in Dyfed. The Latin name suggests that it was an outlying Roman settlement beyond the Roman road which stretched from Gloucester to Carmarthen. David was baptized by *Ailbe, 'a bishop of the Munstermen', who is known to have been in South Wales about this time.

There was a monastic school at Vetus Rubus. David studied there with other students, and on one occasion, the other pupils saw a dove sitting on his shoulder, 'teaching him and singing hymns with him'. There are other stories about doves hovering near future saints – *Samson had one at his ordination. One suggestion is that the 'doves' were pigeons, and the future saints were the boys whose task it was to feed them – in which case, the pigeons might well have perched on their shoulders at every opportunity. There seems to be no information on how the Celtic monasteries communicated with one another. Can they have used pigeon post? This would explain the hovering 'doves', and also some of the many stories of one saint having a premonition when another was coming to see him.

David was ordained priest, and went on to study under *Paulinus of Wales. He remained with Paulinus 'for many years, reading and fully assimilating what he had read', and he cured Paulinus of blindness so that 'darkness was driven from his eyes'. Then Paulinus sent him out to make monastic foundations of his own. He is said to have founded twelve monasteries, including those at Glastonbury, Bath and Leominster, but this may well be Rhygyfarch's attempt to assert claims which would impress the Normans, or the work of a later hand. It seems unlikely to be fact, because the one monastery founded by David of which we have positive knowledge is as far away from this area as possible, on a promontory in the extreme west of South Wales, facing Ireland, and now called St David's.

He founded, or became abbot of, the monastic community of Mynyw (Menevia) near his childhood home. The life of his monastery was evidently modelled on that of the more austere Irish monasteries of the time. There was no concession to what Rhygyfarch calls 'the slippery slope of earthly delights'. The régime involved hard manual labour. They had no oxen, but bore the yoke of the plough on their own shoulders. They dug with spades and mattocks, including the Irish visitor *Modomnoc, and did all the labour of daily existence themselves, unlike the monasteries which employed serfs or artisans. Having worked hard, they studied and prayed hard – chanting all the psalms before supper, and spending three hours in 'watchings, prayers and genuflexions' after their meagre meal. They were up again for prayer at cockcrow before going back to the fields. When the labours of the week were over, they kept vigil from Friday evening to dawn on Sunday with continuous prayer, except for an hour's sleep after Matins, said at midnight. The Rule was strict: when the bell rang for chapel, they had to leave what they were doing immediately. If a monk was copying a manuscript, he had to stop – 'when only the tip of a letter or even half the form of the same letter was written'. In chapel, they were forbidden to yawn or to sneeze. Their diet consisted of bread, bitter herbs and salt, with water or a little milk. David was called '*Aquaticus*', because he drank only water, and his monks became known as the *Aquatici* or Watermen.

Any man wishing to join the community was made to stand at the outer door for ten days, 'as one rejected and also silenced by words of abuse'. Only if he bore this with patience was he admitted, and put to serve the elder who had charge of the gate. He was not welcomed into the full community until 'many oppositions within his soul had been broken down'. Rhygyfarch says that David 'imitated the monks of Egypt, and lived a life like theirs'. His Rule is very similar to that instituted in the Upper Thebaïd by Pachomius (292–346) who had seen service in the Roman army, and brought a military discipline to the life of monks living in community. Knowledge of the Rule of Pachomius reached the Celtic world through the writings of St John Cassian, which were well known in Ireland.

David seems to have kept aloof from Church concerns outside his own remote monastery, but when the Synod of Brefi took place, there were evidently some sharp differences of opinion among the abbots and bishops who attended. It was Paulinus of Wales, his former tutor, who urged the gathering to send for David. There has been some debate about the subject of deliberation at this synod, which was held in an old Roman fort at Loventum. Rhygyfarch and later Giraldus Cambrensis both assumed that the synod must have been concerned with Pelagianism; but Pelagianism was never a problem in the Celtic Church. The canons adopted at the synod are all concerned with penitential discipline, principally for the clergy, and that is why David was needed. The assembled clergy had reached an impasse, and some of them were preparing to go home when Paulinus made an impassioned speech, saying:

There is one who . . . has not attended our synod; a man of eloquence, full of grace, experienced in religion, an associate of angels, a man to be loved, attractive in countenance, magnificent in appearance, six feet in stature. Him I advise you to summon here.

Three times messengers were sent to Menevia, but David refused to attend, even for his old tutor. Eventually, according to other accounts, Dubricius and *Deiniol, the most prestigious members of the synod, went themselves. David, who did not bind his visitors to his own sparse diet, offered them fish, but they refused to eat with him until he agreed to accompany them. He did so reluctantly, saying that he would not speak, but would go with them and offer his prayers. However, when he reached the synod and had been welcomed, he was persuaded to ascend a hill or mound where they had left their outer garments (they were in the open air, and perhaps it was a hot day). Then 'his voice rang out like a trumpet' to the waiting assembly.

This last passage sounds like the recollection of an eye-witness. We may disclaim the inevitable dove which came to perch on his shoulder, and the assertion that he was immediately proclaimed archbishop of all Wales (was Rhygyfarch scoring off Lifris?), but the story of David's desire to keep aloof from controversy, his agreement in answer to the pleas of the two senior and holy men, and his final understanding of the situation and what he had to contribute, rings true. The personal details – the meal of fish, the clothes on the mound, the sound of his voice – reach us through the centuries.

Rhygyfarch tells his readers that David went to the Holy Land with *Teilo and *Padarn, and was consecrated archbishop by the patriarch of Jerusalem; the Lives of Teilo and Padarn have the same story, but with notable variations, each of the three chroniclers claiming that his saint received special commendation. In Teilo's Life, Teilo is recognized as the most holy of the three, and in Padarn's, it is Padarn's singing voice which impresses the patriarch and his companions. Rhygyfarch claims that David was consecrated as archbishop of Wales in Jerusalem; but there was no archbishop of Wales before the Norman Church assumed control. The story of the visit to the Holy Land, in whatever version, may safely be dismissed as a piece of embroidery intended by the chroniclers to impress the Normans and safeguard their privileges.

David is mentioned in the eighth century *Catalogue of the Saints of Ireland*, which dates from about 720. The *Martyrology of Tallaght* records the date of his death, 1 March. Perhaps the story that he had been consecrated archbishop of Wales by the patriarch served its purpose. His reputation, unlike those of his great contemporaries Dubricius, Deiniol, Illtud, Cadoc and Paulinus, became so celebrated that his cult was approved by Pope Callistus II in 1150, and two pilgrimages to St David's were declared to be equal in merit to one pilgrimage to Rome. Both William the Conqueror and his grandson Henry II are known to have visited David's shrine.

In Wales, his name is sometimes spelled Dafydd, which may be the origin of 'Taffy' as a generic term for Welshmen. The tradition of his fellow countrymen wearing leeks or daffodils on his feast day is an ancient one, but the explanation for it remains obscure.

Deiniol (Daniel) (?584), 11 September, was the founder and abbot of two monasteries in North Wales, Bangor Fawr on the Menai Straits, and Bangor Iscoed or Bangor-on-Dee, near the former Roman military base of Deva (Chester). Both were large and celebrated monasteries: Bede tells us that in 603, there were over two thousand monks in Bangor Fawr, and Bangor Iscoed became a notable school of monastic learning and piety. We know surprisingly little about Deiniol, though Bishop Forbes in the *Kalendars of Scottish Saints* refers to him as *Deiniol Fawr*, Great Deiniol.

His son, Deiniol the Younger, succeeded him as abbot of Bangor Fawr, having been brought up by his grandfather near the monastery. This suggests that, like several of the well-known Welsh saints, Deiniol Fawr was a late entrant to monastic life, possibly following the death of his wife, or her retreat to a nunnery. He may, like *Illtud, have fought in Brittany as a young man: he is thought to be commemorated by the names of Saint-Denoval at Matignon and Plangenoual in the Côtes du Nord. He is said to have been a disciple of *Cadoc, and to have been sent by him to establish Bangor Iscoed. He was a leader in the Welsh Church when he and *Dubricius jointly persuaded *David to attend the Synod of Brefi, and he lived for about another forty years after that. The *Welsh Annals* note under 584 'the burial of Daniel of the Bangors'.

In Norman times, Deiniol was regarded as 'the first bishop of Bangor', on the assumption that he ruled a diocese on the Menai Straits; but Lives and chronicles telling of his ministry as a famous abbot, which must have been compiled in his monasteries, have completely disappeared. The most well-known dedication to him is that of St Deiniol's, Hawarden, where W. E. Gladstone's great library is still available to readers.

Derfel (Gdaen, Cadarn) (sixth century), 5 April, was a warrior who won distinction at the battle of Camlan in 537, and was celebrated by Welsh bards as 'Cadarn the Mighty'. A Breton tradition says that he was the brother of *Tudwal. He became a monk, and Llanderfel is named as his church. Later writers say that he became abbot of Bardsey.

In Henry VIII's time, Thomas Cromwell, as Commissary-General for the St Asaph diocese, wrote a letter asking what should be done about a statue of 'Darvel Gadarn', 'in whom the people have so greate confidence, hope and truste, that they cumme dayly a pilgrimage unto hym, some with kyne, others with oxen or horsis, and the reste with money'. It was a wooden statue showing the saint on horseback, holding a pastoral staff, and the people were so attached to it that they offered the large sum of £40 to be allowed to keep it; but it was deemed to be an object of superstition, and taken to London, where it was cast into the flames. This took place immediately before the burning at the stake of Catherine of Aragon's confessor, Dr John Forest, and the occasion has been quoted as fulfilling a Welsh prophecy that the statue would 'set a whole forest on fire'.

Dinwydd (sixth to seventh centuries), no known feast day, was the abbot of Bangor-on-Dee in 603, when the group of 'British bishops' were to meet St Augustine and his clergy to discuss the differences between the Latin and Celtic churches. Bede calls him 'Dinoot'. It was on Dinwydd's advice that the Welsh clergy looked for humility in the behaviour of Augustine – and failed to find it. We do not know whether he was leading his monks, whom Bede calls 'faithless Britons', when twelve hundred from his great monastery were massacred at the Battle of Chester. The Anglo-Saxon forces went on to sack and loot the monastery. Some monks escaped and took refuge at Bardsey (see *Cadfan).

It is perhaps understandable that Roman Catholic Calendars of saints have never included Dinwydd among their number, with the result that he has no feast day, though he is much respected in Celtic tradition.

Dubricius (Dyfrig) (*c.* 550), 14 November, was one of the earliest known and most respected saints of South Wales. He was probably a bishop in the Roman tradition, and he carried out ordinations at Llaniltud Fawr in *Illtud's time as abbot. In the seventh century Life of *Samson, he is called *Papa*, and *Sanctus Papa*, titles which indicate a wide affection for him, but which were later misunderstood by post-Conquest chroniclers. His name occurs in many other saints' Lives. He confirmed *Gwynllyw; he installed *Deiniol as an abbot; he ordained Samson, who had been prepared for the ministry under Illtud, and later consecrated him; he went with *Teilo to induce *David to attend the Synod of Brefi. Dubricius was buried at Llantiltud Fawr, and when Samson was dying, he asked to be buried at the same spot 'on account of the extraordinary love which he had for his dearest teacher'.

Rhygyfarch, in his Life of David, says that Dubricius was *magister* of a monastic school near Hennlann (Hentland), then close to the Roman city of Arconium (near Ross-on-Wye). He seems from place-names to have carried out his ministry along a Roman road in the Wye valley, and may have had more contacts with the old Roman centres than most of the Celtic saints. He made many foundations, and placed his disciples in charge of them.

No Welsh Life of Dubricius has survived, though the Life of Samson makes a number of references to the 'holy father Dubricius' who supervised Samson's spiritual development. His importance in Welsh ecclesiastical tradition was such that after the

Norman Conquest, Norman chroniclers made strenuous efforts to link him to the Latin Church. He was given a Latin name. The *Book of Llan Dav*, claiming for the Llandaff diocese all the property which had once been in his care, described him as 'archbishop of the whole of southern Britain' (i.e. South Wales), and '*summus doctor*'. A Latin Life by Benedict of Gloucester says that he died in November 652 (which is demonstrably incorrect), and that he was a contemporary of Germanus of Auxerre, who died in 446. The fourteenth century chronicler Geoffrey of Monmouth, who was never averse to flights of fancy, named him as archbishop of Caerleon, primate of Britain, and 'legate of the Apostolic See', and adds for good measure that he crowned King Arthur.

In his later years, Dubricius retired to the island monastery of Caldey. He died at Bardsey, and his relics were taken to Llandaff cathedral in 1120. His shrine in the cathedral was destroyed at the time of the Reformation. Canon Doble calls him '[o]ne of the chief figures in the creation of Christian Wales'.

Dwyn (Donwen) (?547), 25 January, was a virgin, reputedly one of the 'children of *Brychan'. 'Donwen' or 'Dwynwen' means 'Blessed Dwyn'. Sir Dafydd Trevor wrote in the late fifteenth century in praise of 'the holy maid of Breichinniog'. Unusually for one of the 'children of Brychan', she is best known in Anglesey; but she is also known in Glamorgan, where the cave of Dwynwen lies between Llantwit Major and St Donat's. Some commentators have also associated her with St Douine or Twine of Brittany, where some of the 'children of Brychan' went to live.

The cult of Dwyn in Anglesey was very strong. She is traditionally known as a consecrated virgin, and Llandwyn and Porthdwyn preserve her name. In this remote place, she is said to have healed the sick, both humans and animals, and her name was invoked at her holy well for healing until long after the Reformation. In the Middle Ages, her church was one of the richest in Wales, as a result of thank-offerings at her shrine. She is also the patron saint of Welsh lovers: a story about a rejected suitor who was turned to ice and unfrozen in answer to her prayers is told to account for this attribution, but she may have been a counsellor as well as a healer.

It is possible that there are two saints of the same name. It is certainly out of character for one of the 'children of Brychan', particularly a woman, to break away from her family, who were moving south from Brecon to Cornwall and Brittany, and to travel the length of Wales to settle alone in Anglesey.

Germanus of Man (?410–75), 3 July: accounts of the life of Germanus are sparse and dubious. There are some puzzling references in Nennius, the early ninth century chronicler, to a St Germanus who 'execrated and condemned' the fifth century tribal

The Calf of Man Cross on the Isle of Man

chief Vortigern for marrying his own daughter, but he seems to be referring to Germanus of Auxerre. Baring Gould and Fisher insist that Germanus of Man was a Celt, born in Brittany, who went to Ireland to stay with *Patrick about 440, then went to Wales to the monasteries of *Brieuc and *Illtud, and became bishop of Man about 466. *The Oxford Book of Saints* repeats this account, but notes that the dates are 'highly conjectural'. They certainly do not fit with the dates now assigned to Patrick, Brieuc and Illtud, and though he may have been a missionary bishop, Germanus would not have been 'bishop of Man', a Roman styling. It is not clear whether he is thought to have preceded other missionary saints on the island, such as *Maughold.

Baring Gould and Fisher, who were Anglicans, argue that Germanus of Man was responsible for evangelizing a large part of North Wales, and that references in the Welsh literature to 'Germanus' as a senior and respected bishop all apply to him rather than to Germanus of Auxerre. This seems to be an attempt at a counter-attack to the often-repeated view of Roman Catholic scholars that early Welsh and Irish saints were often linked to the monastery at Auxerre, and ordained or consecrated there. The 'Germanus' references may be, like the frequent references to Rome, no more than an attempt by twelfth century Norman scholars to provide a respectable Latin background for some unconventional saints who in their view required validation. There are also dedications in Cornwall (see *German) which confuse Germanus of Auxerre and Germain of Paris with a Germanus who could be the saint of the Isle of Man.

All that can reasonably be concluded is that Germanus of Man lived in the fifth or sixth century, studied in Ireland or Wales or both, and carried out a ministry in the Isle of Man and along the adjacent North Wales coast.

Gildas (?500–570), 29 January. Gildas tells his readers that he was born in the year of the battle of Mons Badonius (Mount Badon) and that he is writing his *De excidio Britanniae*, *The Ruin of Britain*, in his forty-fourth year. This would be very helpful if we knew in what year the battle of Mount Badon took place. It is usually dated to somewhere between 500 and 506. Older accounts say that Gildas came from the Clyde valley and conclude that he was a Pict, but this seems highly improbable. He denounces 'foul hordes of Scots and Picts like dark throngs of worms who wriggle out of fissures in the rock when the sun is high and the weather is warm'. He says that they make 'dreadful and devastating on-slaughts' on what he knows as civilization, so he was evidently neither a 'Scot' nor a Pict. He probably came, like *Ninian and possibly *Patrick, from one of the Clydeside trading settlements.

Gildas is said to have studied for seven years in Gaul, after which he entered the monastery at Llaniltud Fawr. Later, he went to Ireland, and then to Brittany before settling on an island in the Bristol Channel to write his *De excidio Britanniae*. He was well acquainted with events in Dumnonia (Devon and Cornwall). He was evidently working the western sea-ways. A puzzling factor is that he is fervently pro-Roman. In *De excidio*, he looks back with longing to the age when the Roman legions kept order, describing them as 'a splendid army' and 'our worthy allies' and referring to their 'superior prestige'. This only becomes comprehensible in the light of three factors: he was writing, without records, about a near-mythical golden age nearly a hundred and fifty years before his own time; he probably came from a Romanized settlement in the Clyde valley; and his time in Gaul may well have been spent, like Ninian's, in Tours, where some semblance of Roman order survived in his lifetime. He seems to have had a good Roman-style education: his Latin is elegant, though sometimes tortuous. At Llaniltud Fawr, where he was a disciple of *Paulinus, he was known as 'Gildas the Wise', and he is said to have had Irish saints among his own disciples, including *Finnian of Clonard.

The Life of *Cadoc describes Gildas as 'an eminent Briton, a scholar and a very excellent writer, a skilful artist', though Lifris gives no indications of what form his artistic abilities took. However, the Life of *Kea rather surprisingly calls him 'a skilful bell-founder', and it may be that the bell which *David coveted, and which figures in the eleventh century Lives of both David and Cadoc, was of Gildas's own making. Bells played a large part in the organization of the monasteries, and an abbot's bell was a prized possession, so a skilled metal-worker who could make bells was highly esteemed.

At some point in his life, perhaps during the Yellow Pestilence, Gildas went to Brittany. He settled as a hermit on an island in Quiberon Bay, gathered some disciples there, and eventually founded a monastery. The island is still known as the Île des Moines. A Life written by a ninth century Breton monk says that he had four brothers, a sister, five sons and two grandsons: this need not be taken literally, but he may have been part of a large extended family which emigrated together. St Géran in Brittany is said to have been named after his grandfather, Geraint.

Later, he returned to Britain, and was a hermit for a time on Echni (the island of Flat Holme in the Bristol Channel). He is thought to have written *De excidio* there, in response, as he says, to 'the pious entreaties of the brethren'. It is a very puzzling work. It begins with a lyrical description of Britain, 'decorated with wide plains and agreeably set hills', its mountain pastures, its 'clear fountains and brilliant rivers'; but it goes on to say that all this natural beauty has been spoiled. There is a fiercely denunciatory attack in the tradition of the Old Testament prophets, insisting that the devastation caused by Anglo-Saxon raids and the consequent collapse of society represent divine judgement on the sins of the rulers and the clergy. Though Gildas is often taken to be referring to the whole of Britannia, it is clear in the context that he is referring only to what he knows – the coastal areas of the Clyde, South Wales and Devon and Cornwall. He has been blamed by generations of English historians for greatly exaggerating the effect of Anglo-Saxon raids on Britain. They regard his history as lamentable and his political judgements as unreliable because they take 'Britain' to include the Roman Britannia; but he was writing about the lands of the Brythons, which suffered very badly from the raiders. He may have witnessed the sack of Pevensey. His account may represent a fair picture of the ruinous state of Wales and the south-west after the Yellow Pestilence. He may not have understood the major causes of the disaster he witnessed, but he is reliable enough about what he saw for himself.

Gildas also wrote a Penitential from which we can infer that the monasteries of his day had their problems: sexual sins, drunkenness, stealing, disrespect of the consecrated bread and wine, laziness and disobedience of the abbot's orders are all listed, though the penalties are notably milder than those in some of the Irish Penitentials.

Gwladys and Gwynllyw (Gundleus) (sixth century), 29 March, were the parents of *Cadoc, and Gwladys is listed in some of the genealogies as the eldest of the 'children of *Brychan'. Gwynllyw was the son of Glwys, king of the 'southern Britons', i.e. of Glamorgan. When he inherited his father's kingdom, he divided the seven *cantrefs* of Glamorgan, keeping one himself, and allotting the others to his six brothers (of whom *Paulinus was one), while retaining overlordship.

There is a story that he kidnapped Gwladys – which must have been a standard way of acquiring a bride in those turbulent times; and in view of his later behaviour, this sounds quite possible; but later accounts represent him as a responsible king who lived in some state, and carried out the negotiations for the marriage with dignity. He was 'a most favoured conqueror in warfare, pacific after conquest . . . a victor never vanquished', according to one ancient Life. He lived in a 'lofty palace' in a forest in the foothills of the mountains. He sent messages to the king of the Breichinniog folk, saying that he had heard of the gentleness and beauty of his daughter, and asking for her hand, 'that he might delight in lawful marriage'. The transaction was achieved with treaties of friendship and the exchange of property between the two kings.

The Life of Cadoc by Lifris says that Gwladys was 'of very high reputation, elegant in appearance, beautiful in form, and adorned with silk vestments', but he gives a very different account of Gwynllyw's character. He says that Gwynllyw 'disgraced his life with crimes', and Gwladys pleaded with him repeatedly to lead a Christian life. It was she who persuaded him to let their child be baptized and educated by *Tathai (Athan). When Cadoc had grown up and become a priest, he added his injunctions to his mother's. He urged his father to repent, and Gwladys said, 'Let us trust our son, and he will be a father to us in heaven.' Gwynllyw finally reformed. He 'gave up his malice and wickedness', and they

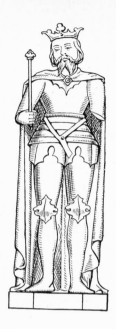

St Gwynllyw: statue at St Woolno's

apparently 'left the world', and lived in ascetic retreat in a place near Newport, Monmouthshire. St Woolno's church at Stowe Hill commemorates this period in their life – 'Woolno' is a corruption of Gwynllyw; but eventually Cadoc advised that they should not continue their married life together, and so they separated in response to their son's direction. We have no way of knowing whether this was simply monkish disapproval of the married state on Cadoc's part, or whether Gwynllyw, even after repenting of his sins, was very difficult to live with. Cadoc could have been protecting his mother. Gwynllyw and Gwladys each lived in solitude thereafter. There is a church dedicated to Gwladys at Pencarnon.

Hwyn (Henwyn, Hewin) (dates unknown), 1 or 6 January, was a monk trained at Llantwit, who became abbot of Bardsey. He was the patron of Aberdaron on the Lleyn peninsula, where pilgrims used to take a boat for Bardsey. His feast was celebrated there in the Middle Ages, but his name does not occur in ancient calendars.

Illtud (Illtyd, Aeltut, Hildutus) (early sixth century), 6 November, was brought up in a Welsh colony in Brittany. He was the son of princely Christian parents, and his father was a famous warrior. His name is said to have come from the Latin *ille* and *tutus,* meaning 'he who is safe'. He was 'instructed in literature', which meant religious literature, from an early age, but he rejected the scholarly life, became a soldier, and married.

He was on a hunting expedition when he met a local holy man named Cadoc. (This is unlikely to be the *Cadoc, who was one of his pupils at a later date). The holy man told him:

> Thou wast formerly a very celebrated soldier, rewarded by many kings. But now I bid thee to serve the King of kings. Remember how thy parents dedicated thee to a clerical pursuit; thou didst study, devoted to a divine comradeship. Then thou didst despise what was not despicable, giving thyself to spear and sword. Seek again what thou hast left.

Illtud was also told to leave his wife, Trynihid. 'What, pray, is carnal love but a horror and a source of sin?' enquired the hermit. 'He who shall abstain and forbear from sexual union shall be exalted and set on an everlasting seat.' Trynihid was very distressed when Illtud insisted on their separation, but armed with the hermit's advice, he 'drove her off', saying, 'Thou shalt not cling to me further.' His rejection of married life left her 'cold and trembling'.

Still wearing his military dress, Illtud went to see *Dubricius in the Wye valley. With the bishop's approval, 'he shaved his head, he cut his hair, he blessed his crown' (this last phrase suggests a Roman-type tonsure), and became a hermit. He lived very simply, growing his own food. Later, Trynihid went to see her former husband in his hermitage, and found him digging the soil, with his face covered with mud. She pleaded with him to return to his family, but he refused. We may discount a rather spiteful later story that she was stricken with temporary blindness for her presumption in approaching her husband, but the chroniclers make short work of her distress. We are told that she went away and devoted herself to prayer, living devoutly, comforting 'innumerable widows and poor nuns', and developing a liking for mountain solitude.

It is not clear where Illtud received his monastic training – he was later said to be 'learned in Scripture and philosophy' but suggestions that he was taught by Germanus of Auxerre are pure fantasy. Germanus died in 446, and there is no evidence that Illtud went anywhere in Gaul outside Brittany. Dubricius eventually found land where he could start a community, and archaeologists suggest that this may have included an old Roman villa. He founded the great monastery later known as Llaniltud Fawr, setting to work with great energy and administrative capacity:

> He appoints labourers, cultivators of husbandry throughout his fields. They increase seeds, they duly perform labours with great profit. He feeds the poor, he covers the naked, he visits the sick and those cast into prison. He had a hundred in his household, as many workmen, clerics, and a hundred poor persons daily.

Many scholars came to be taught by him. The Lives say that as abbot, he still looked like a soldier, but he was a man of peace – evidently of high intelligence, great knowledge and deep piety.

Llaniltud Fawr (Llantwit Major) became one of the most influential monasteries in South Wales, with hundreds of monks. Illtud worked closely with Dubricius, the roving bishop, and *David, *Gildas, Cadoc, *Samson and *Teilo are said to have been among his monks. He was present as abbot at the ordination of Samson by Dubricius, but not at his consecration – he may have been in Brittany at the time. He seems to have returned to Brittany at least once, because he had an inheritance there. There is a story that he organized corn ships from Wales to relieve a famine in Brittany, and some Breton churches have a dedication to him. He is known at St Pol-de-Léon, Tréguier and Vannes.

Norman chroniclers made much of Illtud's life – unfortunately providing very little information, and many fanciful inventions. Like Dubricius, he is said to have been at the coronation of King Arthur, and he is credited with many unlikely miracles. After the Norman Conquest, the monastery at Llaniltud Fawr, by then much reduced in size, was appropriated by the abbot of Tewkesbury, and became a collegiate church with canons. Illtud asked to be buried in his Welsh monastery, but by the time of William of Malmesbury, his shrine had been moved to Glastonbury. Breton accounts insist that he died in Brittany, and was buried at Dol.

Non (Nonna, Nonnita) (fifth century), 3 March, is the traditional name of the mother of *David. According to Rhygyfarch, she was a virgin, and a prince named Sant (*rex concupiscens*) saw her walking in a meadow and took her by force (the Latin word is *oppressit*). Rhygyfarch dwells more on David's princely ancestry than his mother's misfortune, saying that Sant later gave up his rule and entered a monastery. *Non* in Welsh means a nun, and the story developed in the Middle Ages that Sant had violated a nun. Since the story was a very old one by the time that Rhygyfarch heard it, he may have been simply trying to endow his saint with a holy father as well as a holy mother. According to other (later) sources, Non was the daughter of a Pembrokeshire chieftain, and was married to Sant. The author of *The Oxford Book of Saints* suggests that she may have become a nun when she was a widow.

There is also a tradition that Non was one of the 'daughters of *Brychan', which would make her sister to *Gwladys and aunt to *Cadoc. In this case, David and Cadoc would be first cousins; but the Brychan traditions, though pervasive, are extremely vague.

Non was commemorated as a holy woman in Cornwall and Brittany in the Middle Ages. The church and well of St Non are at Altarnon in Cornwall, and there is a shrine in Brittany at Dirinon, Finistère; but Canon Doble thinks these relate to a male saint called Non, and not to David's mother. William Worcestre reports that he saw an entry in the Tavistock Calendar for 15 June, which read 'Sanctus Nin, Martyr'. Either this contains four errors – the date of the feast day, 'sanctus' for 'sancta', 'Nin', for 'Non', and a non-existent martyrdom – or it refers to a totally different saint.

Roscarrock says that Non was also known as Melaria, that she was the sister of *Gwen Teirbron (another 'child of Brychan'), and the aunt of *Cybi, as well as being the mother of 'a most vertuous, learned and religious bishopp named St David'.

Oudoceus (Eudoggwy) (born *c.*546), 2 July, is said to have been a nephew and disciple of *Teilo. The Life of Teilo is the only source of information about him, but it may be based on earlier manuscripts. He was the son of a princely Breton family which migrated to Wales about 625, and was born there shortly before the outbreak of the Yellow Pestilence. He was a monk at Llandogo, became a bishop, and persuaded the abbots of Llancarfan, Llantwit Fawr and Llandough to act together against a corrupt chieftain. For this reason, he is sometimes regarded as the original founder of the see of Llandaff. His name occurs in many medieval Calendars, and he is named as one of the four saints of Llandaff cathedral.

The account is inherently unlikely, for three main reasons: there is nothing distinctive in the Life, the story consisting of weak parallels with the Lives of *Dubricius and Teilo; the contention that Oudoceus acted to create a diocese with territorial boundaries is quite foreign to the thinking of the Celtic Church; and the Life is accompanied in the *Book of Llan Dav* by fourteen land charters representing gifts of land alleged to have been made to the 'diocese' by eleven different kings. Canon Doble comes to the conclusion that the Life of Oudoceus is a 'not very skilful' creation of the twelfth century Norman monks of Llandaff to validate their own territorial claims.

If Oudoceus existed at all, he was probably a monk at Llandogo, the only place where there is a dedication to him. The later claim that he went to Canterbury and was consecrated by Augustine is certainly Norman wishful thinking, since his birth date is long after Augustine's death. He is sometimes confused with *Judoc (Iudocus) of Brittany.

Padarn of Wales (Paternus) (fifth to sixth centuries), 15 April. In addition to the Welsh Padarn, there are two other Celtic saints also Latinized as Paternus: one is *Padarn of Vannes, and the other, who may have been a cousin of *Cadfan, is commemorated as Paternus of Avranches. According to his ancient Life, Padarn of Wales was born in Brittany of noble Welsh stock. He was an only child. Soon after his birth, his father went to Ireland to lead the religious life, while his mother lived piously and brought up their child. When he grew up, Padarn decided that he should follow his father in becoming a monk. He and some cousins joined a group who were setting out for Wales. Later, he founded monasteries at Llanbaddan Fach and Llanbaddan Fawr, and was both abbot and bishop for some twenty years. He evangelized the area close to a Roman road, and may have had more contacts with the Romano-British Church than most of the Welsh founders. He is thought to have been a contemporary of *David and *Teilo, and is said in the *Book of Llan Dav* to have gone with them to Jerusalem. The only personal detail which emerges in this apocryphal story is that Padarn was an excellent singer, which was why the patriarch of Jerusalem allegedly made him a gift of a silk choral cope.

Paulinus of Wales (sixth century), 10 October, is usually given his Latin name, but is also referred to as Poul, Paul, and Paul Penychen. Ancient Lives say that he was the son of the king of Breichinniog, with jurisdiction over a large area of land south of Brecon, and thus, the brother of *Gwynllyw, king of Glamorgan. Gwynllyw had six brothers: when he inherited the kingdom from their father, he divided it into seven *cantrefs*, ruling one himself and allotting the other six to his brothers. Paul presumably had charge of the *cantref* of Penychen.

    Like all secular princes of the time, Paul must have borne arms, and he may have fought in Brittany – perhaps supporting Gwynllyw and his family, who emigrated from Wales before *Cadoc was born. Baring Gould and Fisher state from Breton records that *Illtud fought in Paul's service. At some point, Paul left the world to study under Illtud at Llaniltud Fawr, which suggests a friendship between them, and a very interesting reversal of roles. Evidently Illtud was respected for his scholarship even during his military career. Paul was *David's teacher. In the Lives of both Illtud and Cadoc, Paul is bracketed with David, *Samson and *Gildas as being one of Llaniltud Fawr's most distinguished students. He taught Cadoc, David, and *Teilo, so he was probably some years senior to them. Eventually he went with Illtud's blessing to found his own monastery at Llancarfan, some distance from Llaniltud up the Taff valley. He had a reputation as a wise man, and Illtud seems to have sent his best students to study with him. He was a senior figure at the Synod of Brefi, when he urged the clergy to send for

David to resolve their differences. Rhygyfarch's Life of David makes the standard pro-Norman claim that Paulinus was a disciple of Germanus of Auxerre, but Germanus died in about 475, and there is no evidence that Paul went to Gaul to study.

Little attention has been paid to Paulinus, who must have been a very influential figure in the early Welsh Church. The reason for this is that Norman chroniclers assumed that he was identical with the better-documented and more highly-regarded Paulinus of York (d. 544, 10 October), whom Augustine of Canterbury sent to the court of King Edwin of Northumbria. The two still share the same feast day because of this misunderstanding; but Paulinus of York was a Roman bishop who escaped back to Canterbury when Edwin was killed, and later became bishop of Rochester. It would have been completely out of character for him to make a dramatic dash to Wales to evangelize Celts of whom he would have known little or nothing.

Paulinus of Wales is described in early Welsh Lives as a teacher of great distinction. In addition to helping Cadoc with the foundation of the monastery at Llancarfan, he is said to have founded another at Llandeusant (which means the church of the two saints) with his brothers Notolius and Potolius. There was an annual fair to celebrate the two saints of Llandeusant right through the Middle Ages, though at some stage a revisionist bishop changed the dedication and decreed that it should be held in honour of St Simon and St Jude.

From these rather confused stories, we can discern the outlines of the career of a teacher in Glamorgan who was of royal blood, trained under Illtud, tutored some of Illtud's best students, and founded one or possibly two monasteries. It is more difficult to judge whether he is also the *Paul Aurelian who founded the great monastery of St Pol-de-Léon in Brittany. Paul Aurelian's Breton chronicler, Wrmonoc, treats them as the same person, devoting roughly half his narrative to Paul's career in Wales and half to his career in Brittany. Later commentators have questioned the identification on the grounds that it simply contains too much to be incorporated in a single individual's lifetime. (The two are listed separately here: see Chapter 7 for Paul Aurelian.)

Welsh sources have claimed that Paulinus remained in Wales, and died there. The claim rests on the evidence of an inscribed tombstone found in a field north-west of Llandovery, with an inscription (in Latin): 'Preserver of the faith, constant lover of his country, here lies Paulinus, the devoted champion of righteousness'; but this sounds more like the epitaph of a secular leader than that of a saint and respected teacher.

Pyr (late fifth to early sixth century), does not appear to have a feast day. He was abbot of the community on Caldey island, off the coast of Dyfed, where *Dubricius had been the visiting bishop and spent his last years. The early seventh century Life of *Samson describes Pyr as 'an eminent man and a holy priest', but the community developed many problems, and Pyr is said to have been a heavy drinker. In the less strict monasteries, the monks drank both beer and wine, the wine coming from Continental traders. Whether Pyr's drinking habits were the cause of the lamentable state of the community, or a result of his inability to cope with his fractious and quarrelsome monks, is not clear. A Breton Life suggests a deeper cause, saying that he was a very sick man, and if this was the case, perhaps both his contemporaries and subsequent chroniclers might have dealt with him more charitably.

One dark night, while Samson was staying at Caldey, Pyr 'took a solitary stroll into the grounds of the monastery, and . . . fell into a deep pit. Uttering one piercing cry for help, he was dragged out of the hole by the brothers in a dying condition, and died during the night'. His death was attributed to intoxication. The bishop, when he heard of the occurrence, instructed the monks to remain where they were and to spend the night together. In the morning, there was a council, and Samson of Dol was elected to succeed him. Monastic discipline was so lax by this time that the young monks were ungovernable, and Samson resigned after a year and a half.

Seiriol (sixth century), 1 February, was the founder of Penmon church on Anglesey and Ynys Seiriol, now known as Puffin Island. He was known as '*Seiriol Wyn*', Seiriol the Fair, because of his frequent meetings with *Cybi, when he travelled with his back to the sun, thus preserving his pale skin while Cybi, travelling towards the sun, became tanned. The two, celebrated in Matthew Arnold's poem 'East and West', are the principal saints of Anglesey. Seiriol's well, the *Ffynon Seiriol*, and the remains of his cell can still be seen at Penmon, and there are traces of a settlement on Puffin Island. It seems that some Norsemen at least came to Anglesey in peace, and they are said to have flocked to listen to Seiriol, 'to acquire useful and religious knowledge'.

Tathai (Tathan, Tatheus, Athan, Atheus) (fifth to sixth centuries), 26 December, was the son of an Irish chieftain. In his youth, it is said, he studied incessantly 'without aversion'. Evidently his chronicler found the educational process harder, and regarded an inclination to study as little short of miraculous. He says, 'Well-ordered knowledge shone from him as fruit developing from the best of flowers.'

Tathai and eight disciples found a boat on the seashore without sails or oars, and set out on an adventurous mission 'wherever the blowing of the wind directed them'. They sailed up the Severn estuary and landed in Gwent. Caradog, king of Gwent, heard of their arrival, and sent a messenger to invite the party to his court; but Tathai refused, saying that it was not fitting for monks to stay in a secular household. Caradog was impressed rather than offended, and went to visit Tathai in the company of twenty-four knights. He gave Tathai land for a monastery at the place which became known as Llantathan (St Athan's). Tathai became known as 'the Father of all Gwent', 'the defender of the woodland country', a man of gentleness, charity and hospitality.

Teilo (Elidius, Eltud, Delo) (sixth century), 9 February, was born in Dyfed, probably near Tenby, and was one of the group of outstanding monastic students taught by *Illtud and *Paulinus of Wales. Eventually he founded his own monastery in Carmarthen, which the monks called *familia Teliavi*, and which became celebrated as Llandeilo Fawr. He was one of the few Welsh Church leaders who combined the role of bishop and abbot. He had a number of other missionary bishops, and they made foundations over a wide area. Baring Gould and Fisher list a page and a half of place-names in South Wales which involved a dedication to him, including the small town of Llandeilo Fawr, now in Powys.

Teilo's monasteries were badly affected by the Yellow Pestilence in 547: some of his communities went to Ireland, but Teilo himself led a large party, with some bishops and many monks, which went first to Cornwall, where the parish of St Dillo may owe its name to him, and then to north Brittany, where they sailed up the river Rance and landed at Dol. Teilo stayed at Dol with *Samson. There is a story about the two of them laying out an orchard together which suggests that they were old friends, and that Samson was still in the process of establishing his own monastery. According to one account, Teilo became a missionary bishop at Dol, and many place-names – Llandélion, St Thélo, Lande-de-Saint-Eliau and others – testify to his work in the region. He was given land for his foundations by his brother-in-law, King Budic. Apparently he travelled about on horseback, though a fifteenth century stained glass window at Plogonnec, Finistère, shows him riding on a large and spirited goat, wearing his mitre.

Eventually he went back to Wales (after seven years and seven months, according to the Breton chroniclers, who recorded every-thing in sevens), in the hope that 'the British nation may be renewed in holiness after the pestilence'. He took the three sons of his sister and King Budic with him, and *Oudoceus was one of these nephews.

Teilo died at Llandeilo Fawr, and was greatly reverenced in Wales. The story in the *Book of Llan Dav* about his visit to the patriarch of Jerusalem with *David and *Padarn is designed to exalt his reputation at the expense of the other two saints: it is recorded that three thrones were set out for the visitors, two magnificently enriched with gold and carvings, and one of plain cedar wood. Teilo chose the plain one, saying that it was of the same substance as Christ's cross. All three were raised to the episcopate, but Teilo was regarded as 'the successor of Peter' because of his greater holiness. Further to emphasize Teilo's superior status, the chronicler of the *Book of Llan Dav* includes the story of a miracle: Teilo went to Rome, and the bells of the city rang out unaided to welcome him.

Theodoric (Tewdrig) (fifth to sixth centuries), 1 April or 3 January, was a king of Morganwg, Glamorgan, known only from the *Book of Llan Dav*, and very different from the tyrant Tewdric who figures so largely in the accounts of the saints of Cornwall and Brittany. Theodoric founded many churches, including those at Bedwas, Llandow and Merthyr Tydfil, and gave property to monasteries. In his old age, he resigned his kingdom to his son, and became a hermit at Tintern; but when there was a Saxon invasion, he returned to help his people. He stood at the head of his troops to defend a bridge over the river Wye, but though the Saxons were put to flight, a blow from a lance felled the old king. He was carried to Mathern, near Chepstow (formerly known as Merthyr Tewdrig), on the banks of the Severn, where he died, and was buried. He is listed in old Welsh Calendars as 'King and Martyr'.

In 1617, the bishop of Llandaff had Theodoric's coffin at Mathern opened, and the skeleton was found to have a badly fractured skull.

Trillo (Terillo) (?fifth century), 26 January, is said to be a saint of Bardsey. Llandrillo in Gwynedd has his oratory built over a spring, to an Irish pattern. Traditionally, all the water for baptisms in the parish was taken from it. The bishop of St Asaph and the vicar of the parish had a right to a tithe of fish from the nearby weir: fish caught every tenth day in the fishing season, from 13 May to 18 October. There is another Llandrillo in Denbighshire with a healing spring, famous for the treatment of rheumatism.

Tydfil (?480), 23 August, was a woman hermit in Wales, said to be one of the 'daughters of *Brychan'. She was killed by pagans while she was on her way to visit her father in his old age. If she was a 'daughter of Brychan', this could have meant a journey to Cornwall or Brittany, but she evidently did not get far. The place where she died and was buried became known as Merthyr Tydfil. 'Merthyr' is generally taken to mean that she was a martyr, though this was not always the case by the seventh century, when it sometimes denoted simply a place of death.

Tysilio (Tyssilio) (seventh century), 8 November, was the son of a reigning prince of Powys. Some accounts make him first cousin to *Deiniol and *Asaph. His father insisted that he should follow a military career, but Tysilio was determined not to bear arms. When he failed to convince his father of his repugnance, he told his brothers that he intended to enter a monastery, and took refuge at the abbey of Meifod. His father, furiously angry, sent a company of soldiers to bring him back. Their leader berated the abbot for filling the boy's head with religious ideas, and eventually the abbot produced Tysilio – in a monk's habit, and with his head shaven in the Celtic manner. Tysilio steadfastly refused to return to his father's court, and since they were unwilling to violate sanctuary, the soldiers eventually went back without him. He went to an island on the Menai Straits for seven years as a hermit before returning to Meifod, where he eventually became abbot. The town of Llandysilio bears his name, and there are scattered dedications in Powys, Clwyd and Dyfed.

There is a cult of Suliau (29 July) in Brittany, who may or may not be the same saint. The story which connects them says that after his brother died, he was pressed to become the ruler of Powys, but he refused. He and his monks were persecuted by his brother's widow, who seized the revenues of the monastery, and they had to emigrate to Brittany; but the Breton Suliau was probably a different person, though he may, like so many of the Breton saints, have been Welsh in origin.

Winifred (Winfrede, Gwenfrewi) (*c.* 680), 3 November, is the much-loved saint of Ellis Peters' *Brother Cadfael* mysteries. She was a real person, though fictional stories have surrounded her memory for centuries. There are two medieval Lives, both written some five hundred years after her death. She came of a noble and wealthy family in Clwyd, and, unusually for a girl, was educated – possibly by *Beuno, her mother's brother. Since she was an only child, her father was anxious for her to marry, so that he would have a male heir. She is said to have been beautiful, 'made up of white and red . . . fair in form and face', and Caradog, son of Alaric, 'sprung of royal stock', wanted to marry her.

The twelfth century Latin version of her Life suggests a somewhat stilted dialogue between them. Caradoc said, 'O damsel most dear, assent to my proposals by joining with me in the intimacy of wooers, for I desire thee vehemently.' Winifred tried to dissuade him, saying, 'My lord, what utterance is this of a man so noble as thou to a handmaid as ignoble as I?' At this, Caradoc forgot about diplomacy. Filled with fury, he replied, 'Cease talking these silly, frivolous, trifling things, and consent to be united with me. Marry me, and I will take thee for a wife.' Realizing that he was very angry, Winifred told him that she was betrothed to another man, and that she must go to prepare for the ceremony. She fled to the oratory of her uncle, the hermit Beuno, at the far end of the valley; but as she arrived at the door, Caradoc galloped up behind her, and cut off her head.

Beuno came out of his oratory to find 'bloody Caradoc still standing with his gory blade in hand' and cursed him; and immediately Caradoc 'melted in his presence like wax before fire'. Winifred's parents were 'drowned in piteous misery', but Beuno put her head back on her body, and prayed; and 'the body with power received back the soul' with not a scar showing except a thin one at the neck. Then Beuno gave her his oratory as a place to live in, and she was 'openly by all named White Wenifred, for she discoursed with radiance of wisdom, and lived steadfastly thereby'. Eleven other virgins came to join her, and she became their abbess.

The dramatic details of Winifred's beheading and her resuscitation after Beuno's prayers are the stuff of legends, but the account may have been based on a real incident: the details are perhaps exaggerated rather than false, and she may have been wounded by her angry suitor rather than killed outright. Great veneration was paid to her in the Middle Ages. and her miraculous spring at Holywell, *Tre Ffynnon*, was the centre of many pilgrimages and claims of miraculous cures, particularly of people with dropsy and epilepsy.

Her relics were translated to the Benedictine abbey at Shrewsbury in 1138, and from 1148, her feast was kept throughout the province of Canterbury. Henry V made a pilgrimage to Holywell after the battle of Agincourt, which suggests that she was one of the many saints he invoked before the battle took place. The wealthy and pious Lady Margaret Beaufort, mother of Henry VII, enclosed the well in its present buildings.

In 1917, when mining works threatened the supply of water to the well, there was considerable local anxiety until further excavation re-connected it to a subterranean reservoir. Winifred was included in the Roman Martyrology of 1596 by Cardinal Baronius. Working in the Vatican, Baronius can have had no knowledge of the complex racial history of the British Isles. To the disgust of her Welsh devotees, he described her as an English virgin saint rather than a Welsh one.

6

Cornwall: the Travellers

Much has been written about the 'saints of Cornwall', but nearly all of those who can be identified were Irish or Welsh in origin; and most of them went on to Brittany, where there were already Welsh colonies based on trading posts. Cornwall and the Channel Isles were primarily stopping-places on the way.

In Roman times, Isca Dumnorum (Exeter) was a fortified city, but the Romans made little attempt to penetrate the land beyond it. Cornwall was an isthmus across which sea-captains sailing from Ireland or South Wales to Gaul sent their cargoes and their passengers by land to avoid the cross-currents round Land's End. A study of the sea-routes suggests that Cornwall may well have been *Patrick's 'desert'. For those travelling south, the only two safe harbours on the north coast of Cornwall were on the rivers Camel and Hayle. The land routes ran from what is now St Ives or Hayle south to Penzance (roughly the route of the A30 and A374) or from Padstow to St Austell or Fowey (A339, A39). In both cases, there are many place-names derived from the names of saints on the way. The Celtic saints who ended their travels in Cornwall were either solitaries looking for a quiet place, or families who decided to travel no further – perhaps because some of the group were too old or too sick for further travel.

They were mostly people on the move: a number of celebrated 'Cornish saints' are more appropriately classified as saints of Brittany, because that was where their main ministry took place. *Samson of Dol left no mark on Cornwall, though there is an island named for him in the Scilly group, and his companions *Austell and *Mewan, like *Budoc and others, are remembered by Cornish place-names. They moved on to the better-populated

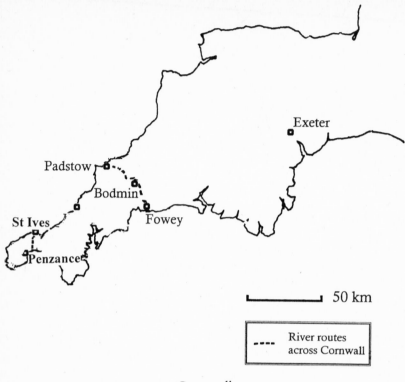

Cornwall

shores of Brittany, leaving only small churches and a scatter of hermits. The only Cornish monastery of which we have any information is *Petroc's at Padstow. There are no traces of large monasteries with libraries and scholars, of the kind which developed in Ireland or Wales, and later in Brittany. If there were chronicles and relics, they were removed and taken to Roman monasteries in the west of England after two separate invasions, the first by the Saxons, and the second by the Normans.

There was still a king of Dumnonia in the early eighth century, when Wessex was Christian and in communion with Rome. The territory of Dumnonia had shrunk to the Cornish peninsula, and the kings of Wessex had landed estates there. Aldhelm (639–709), abbot of Malmesbury and Sherborne, went to urge the Celtic clergy to submit to Roman authority. He wrote a poem describing his journey 'through dire Devon and cheerless Cornwall', which suggests that the prosperous Benedictines of Anglo-Saxon Wessex were distinctly unimpressed by the scattered groups of monks and hermits in these territories. In the ninth century, Egbert, king of Wessex, consolidated his grip on the West Country. By that time, the Cornish chiefs were making border attacks on his territory, siding with the invading Danes, and in 815, he 'harried Cornwall from east to west'. There was a renewal of Cornish insurgence in 825 and again in 828, but the defeat of the Cornishmen at Hingston Down, near the valley of the Tamar, in the latter year spelled the end of Cornish independence – though an independent Cornwall still has its advocates, and is now symbolized by the flag of *St Perran.

The takeover of what remained of the Cornish Church continued in the reign of Egbert's grandson Alfred the Great (849–99), who became king of Wessex in 871. As a boy, Alfred had been taken to Rome and confirmed by Pope Leo IV. He had also spent time in Frankish monasteries, and became a scholar of note. Alfred reigned for twenty-eight years, during which time he revived the religious scholarship of Wessex. Priories were set up at Sherborne, Bodmin, Tavistock and Exeter. Under his patronage and that of his friend and colleague Bishop Asser of Sherborne, Roman-educated clergy were encouraged to appropriate shrines and to take into their own keeping what chronicles were available in Cornwall. Under Alfred's grandson Athelstan (895–939), the process was virtually completed. What little was left was appropriated by the efficient administration of the new dioceses after the Norman Conquest, when Archbishop Lanfranc instituted the suppression of Celtic and Anglo-Saxon saints alike. While some effort was made in the twelfth century to re-write the Lives of the earlier Celtic saints, the material was often not available. We know that in the case of *Rumon, and possibly of Perran, chroniclers simply reproduced the Lives of other saints, doing no more than changing the names. The Normans reduced most of the Anglo-Saxon priories to the status of local churches. Shrines and relics were moved again, taken to the large new monasteries at Glastonbury, Bath or Winchester, and the heritage of the Celtic saints was virtually lost. Only local tradition kept it alive.

The result of these depredations is that information about the 'saints of Cornwall' is disappointingly thin, and largely based on traditions collected by amateur historians and antiquaries such as William Worcestre in the fifteenth century and John Leland in the sixteenth. In the early twentieth century, Canon G. H. Doble of Truro made a sustained effort to order this material in a series of pamphlets, but many of the saints he deals with were in transit across Cornwall, their lives better dealt with in the context of Wales or Brittany. Most of those who stayed in Cornwall are very shadowy figures.

In Cornwall as in Wales, many of the saints of whom we have some record are said to be related. Two royal families who left Wales and adopted the religious life crop up repeatedly in different Lives: the 'children of *Brychan' and the children of *Germoc. The numerous family of Brychan, king of Breichinniog, seem to have left their father's kingdom to move south. According to the Life of *Nectan, his brothers and sisters (twenty-three of them in this version) followed him, each to live as a hermit in the wooded valleys of their new land, and meeting at his cell in a sort of family reunion once a year. They include *Clether, *Endellion, Morwenna and *Keyne. The accounts of Germoc (who is also reputed to have been a king) and his family include *Breage, *Helen, *Selevan and *Crowan, some of whom may have moved on to Brittany. As in the Welsh Lives, the relationships may not always have been as close as they are claimed to be, but there is certainly evidence to suggest migration by kinship groups related to former chieftains.

These travelling nobles would not have received much help from the kings of Dumnonia. There are some fleeting references to the Christian king Mark of Cornwall, whose name appears in the Arthurian legends, and some to Arthur himself: but these are probably later elaborations at the hands of some scribe with an interest in medieval romance. The two kings of Dumnonia who make a credible appearance are both much-feared chieftains whose robber bands preyed on the travellers as they crossed the peninsula. *Constantine, branded by *Gildas as 'the tyrannous whelp of the unclean lioness of Dumnonia', was eventually converted, reputedly by Petroc. Tewdric or Theodoric appears in the Lives of *Euny,

*Gwinear, Petroc and *Kea, and also in that of *Meriadoc of Brittany. It is possible that the threat from this cruel and blood-thirsty pagan prince was the main reason why so many of the emigrants from Wales decided not to remain in Cornwall, but to move on to Brittany, where the rulers were of their own kin, and likely to be more hospitable to refugee Christians.

Breage (Breaca, Bray) (?sixth century), feast day unknown, is said to have come from Laois, and to have been a nun at *Brigid's foundation in Ireland. She travelled to Cornwall with members of her family, including *Germoc, *Helen, *Selevan and *Crowan. In the legends of all these saints, they are said to have been of royal blood, and in Breage parish church, there is a sixteenth century fresco showing Germoc as a king with a crown and sceptre. Helen, or Elin, a priest, is described as Germoc's brother, and Breage and Selevan as Germoc's children. Selevan was (or became) a monk, possibly a bishop, and Crowan is said to have been Breage's woman companion. Breage was probably a widow, since the Life of Selevan records that she visited him with her two children.

If Breage and her companions were Irish, they may have taken ship from the south of Ireland to Cornwall, or via Wales. Germoc, Selevan and Crowan (as Crozon) are all to be found in chronicles in south Brittany. There is no indication of whether Breage accompanied them. According to Leland, some of the group were killed by Tewdric, which may be why the rest of them moved on.

John Leland asserts that in 1540, he saw a Life of Breage, since lost, from which he copied seven sentences. These include, 'Breaca came to Cornwall accompanied by many saints, among whom were Sinninus the bishop, Germocus the king, Elwin, Crewenna, Helena . . .' He tentatively identifies 'Sinninus' with *Sithney, and 'Elwin' with Helen the priest or bishop; but the mention of 'Helena' suggests that the document is of a fairly late date. A mistaken belief arose that 'Helen' was a woman, and the name was identified with that of the Empress Helena, mother of Constantine the Great – who died in 330, and certainly never visited Cornwall.

Clether (Cleer, Clarus, Cleder) (?sixth century), 4 November, is said to have been one of the 'children of *Brychan'. He lived in Wales, probably as a hermit, close to the River Never, and later settled in north Cornwall at the place which now bears his name. A parish church was built there in his memory in the eleventh century, and his oratory and well were rebuilt in the fifteenth century. He may be the St Cleer who gave his name to another village in the same area.

Constantine (?596), 9 March. This 'tyrannical whelp of the unclean lioness of Dumnonia' (the description comes from *Gildas) is credited, among other misdeeds, with disguising himself as an abbot and murdering two Saxon princes before the altar at Winchester, thereby committing both violation of sanctuary and sacrilege; but this story comes from Geoffrey of Monmouth, whose imaginative powers far outstrip his skill as a chronicler. It is very unlikely that Constantine's tyrannies extended into the heart of Wessex.

According to the Life of *Petroc, Constantine was hunting a stag when he discovered that Petroc was sheltering it from him. He tried to strike Petroc, but his arm became rigid, and he was unable to do so. This incident led to his conversion, and that of twenty of his soldiers who witnessed it. Rhygyfarch's Life of *David tells how Constantine abandoned his kingdom, and 'bent his proud head, previously unbowed' in David's cell. Evidently David thought it would be inadvisable for him to stay in Wales, given his reputation and the number of his enemies. He went to 'a distant land, and built a monastery there'.

An Irish account says that Constantine went to Ireland. He entered *Mo-Chuta's monastery at Rahan, and remained there unknown for seven years as a penance, being employed in the heavy task of carrying sacks of grain. One day, he was heard to say to himself (perhaps for the benefit of anyone who was listening), 'Am I Constantine, whose head has carried so many helmets and whose body has worn so many corselets? That I am not.' A monk who overheard him duly reported this news to the abbot. Constantine was relieved of manual labour, and trained for the priesthood, eventually being ordained.

The *Aberdeen Breviary* somewhat rashly claims him as a Scottish 'king and martyr', and gives his feast day as 11 March. It claims that he did not die in Ireland, but went to Scotland, and served with both *Columba and *Kentigern. He became an abbot, and prayed that he might die a martyr's death. During a mission to Kintyre, he was murdered by 'certain wicked men' (presumably Norsemen), who according to the chronicler, 'landed to fulfil in their sin what the good man had sought in his piety'. In the Irish martyrologies, he becomes confused with another Constantine, a Pict and the son of Fergus. Baring Gould and Fisher claim to have found six Constantines – 'all the material for confusion' – but the story of the chieftain of Dumnonia, condemned by Gildas and converted by Petroc, who served seven years' penance at Rahan, seems the most probable.

Crowan (sixth century), ?1 February, was the woman companion of *Breage. She is identified and known as Crozon in Brittany, which suggests that Breage and her children may have accompanied the party which left Cornwall. She may have been a consecrated virgin or a nurse for Breage's two children. All we can say for certain is that she was not Cronan of Roscrea – a male Irish saint with whom she has sometimes been confused.

Endellion (Endellient) (sixth century), 29 April, is described in a twelfth century manuscript as the sister of *Nectan, and another of the many 'children of *Brychan'. She was a consecrated virgin. Two wells and part of her tomb survive at St Endellion in Cornwall. She also had a chapel at Tregony. Nicholas Roscarrock, who was brought up in the manor house of Roscarrock in the parish of Endellion in the seventeenth century, and knew the local traditions well, tells a curious story. The lord of Tregony killed Endellion's one cow, on which she depended for milk and butter, and her godfather, said to be King Arthur, had him killed in reprisal. Endellion revived the dead lord by her prayers. No doubt she was given another cow. It is unlikely that King Arthur (if he existed) was as ubiquitous as such stories suggest, but the story does tell us that Endellion was of noble blood, that she was living the simple life of an anchoress, and that she had powerful relatives in the area to protect her interests. The group of migrants of which she and her godfather formed part clearly ran into hostility from the local landowner.

The tomb which is thought to be Endellion's shrine is now used as an altar in the south aisle of the church at St Endellion. Her feast was formerly celebrated on Ascension Day, and St Endellion's Fair took place in the village on the second Tuesday in September.

Erc of Cornwall (Erth, Ercus, Herygh) (sixth century), 31 October, is the patron of St Erth in Cornwall. William Worcestre found a local tradition that he was an Irishman who landed at Hayle Bay in Cornwall, and was the brother of *Euny and *Ia. Canon Doble and other commentators assume that he is Erc of Slane, who is known as one of the very early Irish saints, and died, in Ireland according to the Irish Martyrologies, in 512; but this identification seems unlikely. Bishop Erc was brother to the Irish *Ita, not to the Cornish *Ia, and the two women saints are now clearly distinguished. Bishop Erc's feast day is 2 November. While the editor of *The Oxford Dictionary of Saints* suggests that the two Ercs were the same, and that the feast day was moved at some point to 2 November to avoid All Souls' Day, it seems more likely that Erc of Cornwall is a different saint whose record has been largely lost.

William Worcestre introduces another false trail when he tells his readers that Erc's tomb lay 'in a certain church beneath the holy cross of St Paul's in London'. This is a confusion with the Saxon bishop of London, Earconwald or Erkenwald (30 April) who died in 693.

Euny (Uny) (?sixth century), 1 February, is said by William Worcestre to have been the brother of *Ia and *Erc, and to have migrated with them from Ireland to Cornwall. The parish of St Uny is near St Michael's Mount. Euny is said to have travelled with 777 monks to match Ia's 777 virgins. Even if we discount the almost certainly exaggerated numbers and the recurring sevens, which are a common feature in both Cornish and Breton accounts of the saints, it remains possible that Euny, Ia and Erc all had disciples who travelled with them; but it seems more likely that they travelled as part of a larger kinship group, which would have included lay people as well as the members of religious communities. The focus on the names of individual saints commemorated by church dedications has tended to obscure the nature of what were essentially mass clan migrations.

Euny is said to have been martyred. Breton accounts place his martyrdom in Brittany, but there is a farm near St Uny in Cornwall named Maroony, which could be a contraction of Merthyr Uny. Cornish accounts suggest that, like *Gwinear and his sister, he was killed in Cornwall by the murderous and pagan Tewdric. He is the patron of Lelant and Redruth, and boys in the Redruth district were often given Euny's name at their baptism until the time of the Reformation.

German of Cornwall (dates unknown), no feast day, may be a lost Cornish saint: the town of St Germans in Cornwall has been associated at various times with Germanus of Auxerre (d. 446), who is unlikely to have ventured beyond south-east Britain on his two visits; with *Germanus of Man (c. 410–75); and with Germanus (Saint Germain), bishop of Paris (496–576). By the tenth century, the minster church of St German in Cornwall had adopted the patronage of Germanus of Auxerre, and a 'proper' or special liturgical service for German's feast day stated (quite erroneously) that the saint was sent by Pope Gregory the Great in the time of Augustine to be the 'lamp and support' of the Cornish people. In 1284, by which time it was an Augustinian priory, St German's church had also adopted the feast day of Saint Germain, bishop of Paris, presumably under the impression that they were the same person. In the fourteenth century, the church acquired relics of Germanus of Auxerre, whose feast was also observed at Bodmin priory and elsewhere.

Nicholas Orme, a recent writer on the Cornish saints, dismisses the possibility of an original dedication to a lost saint of Celtic origin, regarding tenth century evidence from Wessex church records as reliable; but what has been established about the systematic suppression of the devotion to earlier local saints in Cornwall and their replacement by saints acceptable to Rome suggests that, under the layers of false attribution, there may be the record of the original patron of the Church of St Germans.

Germoc (?sixth century), 24 June, is the patron of the parish of Germoc in Cornwall, some three miles from St Michael's Mount. According to the legend of *Breage, he was her father, an Irish king or chieftain who travelled via Wales to Cornwall with his family, and thence to Brittany. From what we know of the movements of the Irish saints, this seems more likely than the alternative suggestion that he may have been a bishop travelling with his religious community. A stained glass window of a crowned king in Breage parish church may represent him. The accepted date of his feast is 24 June, but William Worcestre states that when he visited the parish, it was observed on 'the day of John in *festo natalis*', which would give the alternatives of 19 August or 27 December.

Glywys Cernyw (Gluvias, Gluviac) (?sixth century), 3 May, was not Glywys the father of *Gwynllyw, but a Cornish saint, Glywys the Cornishman. He is said to have been the nephew of *Petroc, which would confirm the Welsh origin suggested by his name, and place him firmly in the sixth century. He may have been a grandson of the elder Glywys, or a grand-nephew.

Glywys is the patron of St Gluvias in Cornwall. A shrine at Merthir Glivis in Glamorgan is mentioned in the *Book of Llan Dav*, and some fifteenth century documents refer to him as a martyr. He may have joined Petroc for a time, and then gone back to Wales, where he met his death.

Goran (Gonnan, ?Wron) (sixth century), 7 April, is the patron of Goran, Cornwall. He apparently lived on Bodmin Moor until *Petroc arrived there with twelve disciples, when, realizing that Petroc intended to set up a monastery, he decided to move a day's journey south for solitude. Goran in the deanery of St Austell is the place to which he retired, and his well and cave survive there.

Gwinear (Guigner, Fingar) (fifth or sixth century), 23 March, is the patron of Gwinear in Cornwall, and is thought to have gone there from Wales with *Meriadoc. They both went on to Brittany, where Gwinear is commemorated by a stained glass window in the church at Pluvigner, near Vannes. This shows him hunting a stag with a cross on its antlers, like the stag in the legend of St Eustace, patron of hunters. Gwinear and his companions are said to have been martyred by 'Theodore, king of Cornwall'.

There are also Irish, Cornish and Breton accounts of two saints, Fingar and his sister Piala, otherwise known as Guigner and Ciara (14 December). They were the children of a king, and among the early settlers in Brittany, where the ruler gave them and their companions land, and they were able to follow the religious life. After some years they felt called to undertake a mission in the kingdom of Dumnonia. (The Breton chroniclers say it was to 'the Saxons of southern England', but they were notoriously weak on both history and geography across the water.) Fingar and Piala set out with a large missionary force said to number about 700, including seven bishops. When they landed in Cornwall, the entire company was massacred on the orders of a pagan ruler called Tewdrick or Theodoric in 453. Fingar said to Tewdrick, 'You son of a devil, do your work quickly,' and was beheaded. If we discount the shaky numbers and the uncertain topography, this story closely resembles the story of Gwinear.

Breton chroniclers list Gwinear and Fingar as different saints, recording that the 'Irish' Fingar and his sister were martyred in Brittany by a local ruler; but Tewdric of Dumnonia (otherwise Theodoric or Teudar) is, in Canon Doble's words, 'a well-known tyrant of Cornish folk-lore'. It was this vicious prince who persecuted *Kea, whose man-eating dragon was tamed by *Petroc, and who is the villain in the *Beunans Meriasek* (see *Meriadoc). It is possible that Tewdric also had lands in Brittany, and carried on his persecutions there as well as in his native Dumnonia; but it seems more likely that the massacre of the missionaries from Brittany occurred in Cornwall, and that the story was taken back to Brittany by subsequent migrants to the places where Fingar/Gwinear's Breton ministry was remembered.

A medieval Life of Fingar was written by a cleric named Anselm in the thirteenth century. This has frequently been cited as the work of St Anselm (1033–1109) and published among his works, but it is now regarded as the work of another scribe.

Helen of Cornwall (Elin, Elwin) (early sixth century), 6 or 7 October, was the brother of *Germoc and uncle of *Breage. He was a priest of royal blood who went on to Brittany and later into Gaul. Breton records say that he and his party were well received by the bishop of Rheims, St Remigius (d. 533), and settled at Bucciolus, near Biscuit on the Marne. Churches in Cornwall with a dedication to St Helen were probably originally dedicated to him, and not to the Empress Helena, mother of Constantine the Great. There are also two villages on the north coast of Brittany named Saint-Helen and Lanhelen.

Ia (Hya, Ives) (sixth century) 3 February and 27 October, is the woman patron of St Ives, Cornwall, and needs to be distinguished from the patron of St Ives in Huntingdonshire, Ives or Yves. The latter was male, and it has been suggested (on rather slim evidence) that he was a Persian bishop. Ia was Irish, a virgin of royal ancestry, the sister of *Euny and *Erc, and a disciple of *Finbar. She had planned to travel from Cornwall to Brittany with Fingar and Piala (see Gwinear), but they left without her, and she and her community travelled with another party. They settled at Pluvé (which means the parish of Ia) near Carhaix, and she was martyred there. We have no way of knowing whether this was a massacre of a group of new settlers, or whether she was the only one to suffer. William Worcestre notes that he saw a Life of Ia at St Ives, but this has now disappeared.

Kea (Quay or Ké) (sixth century), 5 November, knew *Gildas, who is said to have made a bell for him. He was reputedly the brother of the *Congar who went to Brittany. Either in Cornwall or Brittany, he encountered the tyrannical Tewdric, who chased a calf right up to Kea's door, and then led it away with seven oxen and two cows. Kea made no protest, because of Tewdric's violent reputation. Later he went to ask for his cows back, but Tewdric hit him, and caused him to lose a tooth. Kea went and washed his bleeding mouth with water from the holy spring by his hermitage, and was healed. Tewdric is said to have become very ill, and to have repented, giving the cows back, and asking Kea's pardon, but this reads like the happy ending demanded by the listeners to medieval stories of saints. In one version, the tyrant is said to have fallen off his horse and broken his neck.

Kea had a hermitage at Cleder in Cornwall, where Baring Gould and Fisher lamented (in the first decade of the twentieth century) that they found his statue was 'of shabby and lamentable appearance'. He went on to found a monastery on the Côte de Léon, north-west Brittany. His Breton Life says that he was a bishop in 'one of the cities of his country' before he commenced his travels, but no great credence can be placed on this statement, since the Celtic Church did not attach bishops to cities, and there were no Roman-style cities in either Wales or Cornwall.

Kea is the patron of two places in Cornwall, Kea and Landkey, and also of Saint-Quay and Portrieuc, near Brieuc in Brittany.

Kew (Cuet, Kywere, Kigwe) (?sixth century), 8 February, is reputed to have been the sister of *Congar, and therefore also of *Kea. The place known as St Kew was formerly under the patronage of Congar, but after the Norman Conquest, it became 'the king's manor at Kew', and by the fourteenth century, it had come under the patronage of Exeter cathedral.

There is a legend that Congar refused to let his sister live near him unless she tamed a wild boar, presumably thinking this beyond her capacities. Kew, a woman of spirit, tamed the boar. Thereafter Congar permitted her to have conversation with him, and came to the conclusion that his initial refusal had been wrong, since she was a person of 'rare vertue and holiness'.

The old name of the parish of St Kew in Cornwall is Lon-Docco, and there was a monastery of Docco there in *Samson's time. Docco may be another name for Congar, though attempts to identify him with the Irish St Docco mentioned in the *Annals of Ulster* as an abbot and a bishop who died in 473 are not credible.

Keyne (Cain, Ceinwen) (?sixth century), 8 October, is said to be another of the 'children of *Brychan'. When the others in the party went on to Brittany, she stayed in Cornwall to live as an anchorite, but *Cadoc met her at St Michael's Mount, and persuaded her to go back to Wales. She is the patron of St Keyne, Cornwall, where her hermitage and well were well known as a pilgrimage centre in the Middle Ages.

Nicholas Roscarrock, with his local knowledge of the traditions of the Cornish saints, thought that Keyne was a daughter of Brychan, and so Cadoc's aunt. He reports that she was beloved by the local people, who resisted her desire to go back to Wales, and that she died in Cornwall, being buried in her own oratory. He was not sure whether she was a widow: 'Capgrave maketh her a virgen, so I knowe not what to determyne.' Canon Doble mentions speculation that Keyne was in fact a man, but Cadoc's concern seems to make that unlikely – as does the legend of the Well of St Keyne, which is an early example of feminine wiles in a male-dominant age. According to the legend, the husband or wife who drank its water first after their marriage would 'gain the mastery' of the other. This is the topic of Robert Southey's well-known poem: a bridegroom heads for the well as soon as the wedding ceremony is over – only to find that his new wife had a better idea – '*she* took a bottle to church'.

Lide (Elid, Elidius) (dates uncertain), 8 August, was a Cornish saint who settled in the island of Scilly now called St Helen's, but which bore his name in medieval times. There was a small community of monks there, and he seems to have been considered of some importance before the Reformation. Pilgrims who visited the shrine were granted a seven-year indulgence, and pirates who raided the site in 1491 were excommunicated.

William Worcestre thought that Lide was a man, and was not sure whether he was a king or a bishop. John Leland mentions Lide's island disparagingly as a place of 'great superstition'. He thinks that Lide may have been a woman, though most other authorities disagree. There was certainly a hermitage and a shrine on the island: the remains were excavated in the early 1960s.

Madron (Madern) (sixth century), 17 May, was renamed 'Maternus' some time after the Norman Conquest by a bishop of Exeter, but he is the patron of the Cornish town of Madron. This town was a pilgrimage centre until long after the Reformation, the saint's feast day being marked by processions through the town. Anglicans and Methodists still hold annual services in Madron's chapel; but who he was is difficult to determine. He has been identified with *Padarn (Paternus) of Wales, which seems improbable; with Medran, a disciple of *Ciaran of Saighir, a hypothesis now abandoned, since Ciaran of Saighir was never in Cornwall; with *Perran, of whom we know very little once the Ciaran of Saighir link is discounted; and with Matronus, a disciple of *Tudwal, who worked with him in Cornwall and Brittany. The last of these seems the most likely.

Mawnan (Maunanus) (eighth century), 18 or 23 December, was a Cornish saint, possibly a roving bishop from Ireland. He is said to have been 'of a restless disposition'. He was much given to cursing his enemies and practising extreme austerities. He visited *Maelruain of Tallaght (d. 792), one of the more advanced ascetics, and asked him for advice on how to deal with a beggar who refused to work, preferring to live on alms. The two agreed that the man should be refused the services of the Church.

Mawnan is also remembered for his prophecy:

A time will come when girls shall be pert and tart of tongue; when there shall be grumbling and discontent among the lower classes and lack of reverence for elders; when churches will be slackly attended, and women shall exercise wiles.

The town of Mawnan commemorates him.

Meriadoc (Meriasek, Mériadec) (sixth century), (7 or 9 June), was the companion of *Gwinear. He is the subject of a Cornish religious play, *Beunans Meriasek*, written in Middle Cornish, apart from a few curses rendered in English, French and Latin. The play was discovered in Peniarth in 1869, and dates from 1504. It was revived in 1924 at Redruth.

Like Meriadoc's twelfth century Life, it contains much which is legendary, and very few historical facts. Meriasek is the son of a duke of Brittany, renowned for his learning and piety. The king of Brittany wants him to marry an heiress, but he refuses, becomes a priest, and sails for Cornwall. There he is in danger from an evil Cornish lord accompanied by demons. The Cornish lord is named Teudar, so he is probably the tyrant Tewdric (see *Gwinear, *Kea and *Petroc); but this form of his name suggests a sly comparison with the Tudor Henry VII, whose financial exactions were very unpopular in Cornwall at the time when the play was written.

Meriasek escapes back to Brittany, living for a time as a hermit at Pontivy. The next scene is in Rome, where Pope Sylvester converts Constantine the Great (a popular, but apocryphal story), Christianity is established in the Roman Empire, and Meriasek is ordained by the pope. He is then escorted back to Dol, where he is consecrated in *St Samson's church, clothes the naked, heals lepers, and finally dies, surrounded by sorrowing clergy and attended by the archangels Michael and Gabriel. At the end, Christ makes an appearance, saying,

> My angels, fly to the earth,
> To fetch me, very gently,
> Meriasek's soul.

It would be interesting to know more about the origins of the play; but it contains very little that is plausible about Meriadoc, except that he was a Welshman, travelled with Gwinear, and was highly regarded in Brittany.

There is a holy well at Meriadoc, a rock bearing his name, and a local tradition that he was the founder of the parish church at Camborne, where his feast was traditionally observed on the first Friday in June. He is the patron of Camborne. The parish of Gwinear is close by.

In Breton accounts, based on a manuscript at Morlaix and lessons for his feast day (7 June), he appears as 'Mériadec', a Welshman of illustrious stock who lived at the court of the king of Brittany. He became a priest, lived a life of voluntary poverty as a hermit, and became bishop of Vannes. He refused to leave his hermitage, and the people dragged him out to his consecration. (This reluctance to be promoted occurs frequently in the Lives of the Celtic saints, and was probably very much like the practice of dragging the new Speaker of the House of Commons to the chair of office. It indicated a commendable humility.) As bishop, Mériadec was noted for his charity to the sick and poor. There are chapels dedicated to him in the Pontivy area, and one at Stival, three miles from Pontivy, claims to have his bell.

Nectan (sixth century), 17 June, is said to be one of the 'children of *Brychan', though he is not mentioned in the Welsh accounts of Brychan. There was a twelfth century Life of Nectan. William Worcestre worked from it in the late fifteenth century, and Nicholas Roscarrock's friend William Camden, himself a well-known antiquary, actually found it in a book in Martine (Merton) College library in Oxford a century later. Camden wrote a brief note to Roscarrock, telling him of his find. 'I importuned to get me a coppie of the life at large, which by report was not very longe'; but when Mr Camden went back to the library, he found that it had been 'imbazzled, being cutt out of the booke and carried away'. Library thefts are evidently nothing new. In the mid-twentieth century, what is probably this Life was discovered in the Library at Gotha, and it forms the basis of Canon Doble's account of the saint.

Nectan is said to have been the eldest and the most celebrated of the 'children of Brychan'. His father is called 'Brocanus' or 'Brocatus', from 'Brekenauk' in the land of 'Kambria'. Nectan decided 'to imitate Antony, the greatest of the hermits, and the other Egyptian Fathers of godly living'. He 'entered alone into a certain boat . . . leaving behind him everything he possessed, and all that he had loved in the world'. He landed at 'a certain wooded solitude' in north Devon, at what is now Hartland, living alone in the forest. The other members of his family (there is a list of twenty-three brothers and sisters) came to live near him. Most of them settled in Cornwall, and they met once a year 'on the Vigil of the Circumcision of the Lord in the cell of the blessed Nectan' to confer together. After that, they returned to their separate hermitages 'mutually edified and rejoicing with great gladness'.

Nectan is said to have come to a tragic end: he helped a swineherd to find a missing sow and its litter, and the swineherd rewarded
him by giving him two goats. Nectan did not want to take them,
but having regard for the 'offering of brotherly love' he accepted
them with thanksgiving. Then robbers came to steal them. He
attempted to convert the robbers, and they killed him.

Nectan's relics were rediscovered in the tenth or early eleventh
century, and he was greatly revered as a martyr. His shrine at
Hartland became a pilgrimage centre. Earl Godwin and Countess
Gytha, the parents of the Saxon king Harold, visited it after the earl
had survived a storm at sea by invoking Nectan's aid. They
enriched the church with benefactions, and had his staff decorated
with silver, gold and jewels. Augustinian canons took over his
church after the Norman Conquest.

Worcestre says that the town of Hartland was named Nectan at
one time. There was a medieval fair at Launceston on his feast day,
and there are several church dedications.

Neot (*c.* 877), 31 July, was probably not a Celt but a Saxon. King
Alfred's adviser and biographer, Bishop Asser, says that he was of
royal blood, either from Wessex or East Anglia, and that he entered
the monastery at Glastonbury. He subsequently became a hermit in
Cornwall, and Alfred visited him at a church where 'Sanctus Guerir
lies in peace, and now Sanctus Niot lies there as well'. We have no
records of a saint named Guerir. *Guérir* is the French verb meaning
to heal, and Nicholas Orme suggests that he may have been a local
healer. An eleventh century Latin Life states that Neot came from
Huntingdonshire, but that he retired to Cornwall, where King
Alfred had estates, and Alfred visited him there between 871 and
878 to seek counsel from him. The place of his hermitage in
Cornwall, where he died, is called St Neot. A Saxon earl and
countess from Huntingdonshire visited the place, and took relics
back to a church in Eynsbury, which changed its name to St Neot's.

A second Latin Life, dating from the twelfth or thirteenth
centuries, draws on the first, and claims Neot as a prince of
Wessex. It makes no mention of Huntingdonshire connections. It
is a more literary effort than the earlier Life, and gives the saint a

simple companion, a sort of Sancho Panza, named Barrius. There is one vivid reference which may reveal something about the real Neot: he is said to have been 'so small in stature that he had to stand on a stool in order to say Mass'.

The Domesday Book records a church at St Neot, Cornwall, with clerics who had 'their maintenance allowed them'. Anselm, who was abbot of the Norman abbey of Bec from 1078 to 1093, visited St Neot's, Huntingdonshire, and found a strong devotion to the saint there. He had the tomb opened, and the body was found to be intact except for one arm, which was said to be in Cornwall.

Leland reports that Neot was said locally (in Cornwall) to be King Alfred's brother 'or very near kinsman', who went to Glastonbury abbey, became a Benedictine monk, and later withdrew for solitude into Cornwall, to a place 'ten miles from Bodmin which desert was after called of him Neotestowe'. By Leland's time, the story had been embroidered: it was claimed that Neot had a brilliant ecclesiastical career. He is said to have visited Pope Martin IV in Rome, acted as permanent adviser at the court of King Alfred, become director of Divinity at Oxford, and to have had a hall at the University named after him which subsequently became New College. The re-telling of the story of Neot bears all the marks of the way in which the Church in Wessex appropriated Celtic traditions. Whatever his origins, the account of the little man who sought solitude by the tomb of a Cornish saint of whom we have no record is more compelling without these accretions.

Perran (Piran) (?sixth century), 5 March, was probably a Welshman, and his name is perpetuated in Perranporth, Polperran and Perranzabuloe. There was a minster church with his dedication at the time of the Domesday Book, when the dean and canons of Exeter were reported to hold land at Perranzabuloe. A Life of Perran written for Exeter cathedral in the twelfth or thirteenth centuries was a direct copy of the Life of *Ciaran of Saighir, with only the name changed. This could have been a genuine mistake on the part of the scribe, because 'P' in Brythonic dialects becomes 'C' in Goidelic; but it was to mislead scholars for centuries.

In medieval times, Perran's shrine was a centre for pilgrimages, but in time his oratory and hermitage became covered by shifting sands. They were rediscovered in the sixteenth century and excavated in 1835, but the shrine was badly damaged by vandals, and the sands shifted again to cover the site. An ancient Celtic cross nearby marks the spot.

However, Perran has not been forgotten in Cornwall. He is the patron of Cornish tin-miners, and an accounts book in the Great Work mine in the parishes of Breage and Germoc for the period 1759–64 shows that miners kept St Perran's feast day in March each year. The men were given a shilling, and the boys sixpence, for 'Perrantide'. Many of them spent the money in the ale-house, and a man of 'unsteady step and festive appearance' was called a 'Perraner'. In recent times, with the economic revival of Cornwall, and the prospect of a University of Cornwall, there has been an initiative to make Perran the patron of the county, with a black flag bearing a white cross as his emblem.

Petroc (Pedrog) (sixth century), 4 June, was reputedly the son of a Welsh king or chieftain, and may have succeeded his father. William Worcestre, who visited his shrine in the late fifteenth century, recorded that he was 'once king of the Cumbrians'. According to the medieval Life from Saint-Méen in Brittany, which is thought to be a copy of an earlier one from Bodmin, he and a group of followers entered the religious life and studied in Ireland for some twenty years. This is confirmed from the Life of Kevin (*Coemgen). Then they took a ship to Cornwall, sailed up the estuary of the river Camel, and entered the monastery at Lan-wethinoc, named for its founder Wethinoc. Later, the place became known as Padristowe and ultimately Padstow in honour of Petroc. Little Petherick and Trebetheric also bear his name. Petroc lived an ascetic life there for thirty years (by which time, he must have been a very old man by the standards of the time).

Petroc encountered the 'cruel and fierce ruler' of Dumnonia named Teudur or Tewdric. In order 'to punish thieves and criminals', this tyrant had 'with savage cruelty caused various serpents and all kinds of noxious worms to be collected in a marshy lake' into which they were thrown. When he died, his son, who succeeded him, forbade this practice, and the ravenous beasts consumed each other 'by frequent attacks with livid tooth' until there was only one left: a 'horrible monster of enormous size'. Petroc was sent for. He bound the monster with a handkerchief and led it out to sea, where it perished. This story bears a strong resemblance to the Breton stories of *Samson, *Paul Aurelian and other saints, who similarly bind and destroy dragons. These are probably symbolic stories of Christian values overcoming the tyrannies of secular rulers.

An account of Petroc's life by John of Tynmouth, which the editors of the *Acta Sanctorum* classified as *acta suspecta*, says that he made pilgrimages to Rome and Jerusalem. When he returned to his monastery to tell the monks of the marvels he had seen, there were heavy storms battering the walls. Petroc prophesied that the bad weather would end on the following day – and when the storms got worse, he accused himself of vainglory in thinking that the Holy Spirit had inspired him. He went back to Jerusalem as a penance. On this second journey he is said to have travelled as far as the 'East Ocean', which may mean that he went south from Jerusalem to the Gulf of Aqaba; but Middle Eastern folklore is woven into these accounts, to provide some unlikely marvels: he reaches India, travels in a shining bowl to a remote island where he stays for seven years, and returns to find a wolf patiently guarding his staff and sheepskin.

Wherever he went, after his final return to Cornwall, Petroc spent his time in prayer and in deeds of charity, and he developed a great reputation as a holy man. Several legends that appear to have originated in Cornish folklore are told of him: he is said to have healed many sick people; tamed a local monster; and prescribed for a dragon which came to him with a splinter in its eye. This last is a pleasant variant on the usual dragon story, describing how the dragon meekly waited outside Petroc's cell for three days, hoping that he would help it. The story may owe something to the much older story of Androcles and the lion. He also saved the life of a stag which was being hunted by the tyrant *Constantine of Dumnonia, and converted Constantine, thus setting in train his long penance and ultimate sainthood. Details of a more practical nature come from a version of the Saint-Méen Life made by a canon of Bodmin, and included in a fourteenth century manuscript found at Gotha in 1937. This describes how Petroc built a chapel and a mill at Little Petherick, where he established a second community. Later he withdrew to a remote place on Bodmin Moor, and again some of the brothers joined him. When he knew that his life was coming to an end, he went on a last visit to Little Petherick and Lanwithenoc. He was between the two places when his strength failed, and he died in the house of a man named Rovel. The present farmhouse of Treravel may mark the spot.

In the reign of Henry II, Petroc's relics were stolen from Bodmin priory by a monk named Martin, and taken to the abbey of Saint-Méen in Brittany. Nothing is known of the circumstances of this theft. Possibly the relics were about to be moved to Winchester or Glastonbury, and Martin was trying to preserve them in one of the few remaining monasteries with a Celtic tradition. The prior of Bodmin appealed to the king, and the chronicler Roger of Howden describes how the prior went to claim the relics, bringing back 'the body of blessed Petroc in an ivory shrine'. The shrine, which may have been a gift from Count Walter of Coutances, the keeper of the Great Seal, was presented to Henry II at Winchester with great ceremony, and the king and all his court prostrated themselves in front of it.

This same reliquary, of exquisite Sicilian-Islamic workmanship, was seen in Bodmin, and greatly admired by William Worcestre. It disappeared at the time of the Reformation, but in the eighteenth century it was discovered, empty, in the room above the south porch of Bodmin church, where it had been hidden for safety. It remained in the parish church until 1970, and is now in the British Museum.

Probus (dates unknown), no feast day, is the titular saint of the town of the same name, between St Austell and Truro. St Probus is listed in a tenth century calendar, and the place is recorded under the same name in the Domesday Book. Sherborne abbey, a Saxon foundation, was known in Saxon times as *Llanprobi*, the cell or oratory of a (Welsh?) saint named Probus.

There has been considerable discussion over the question of

whether Probus is a lost Celtic saint, or whether the name is simply a Latin word meaning 'honest'. We know that the church of Santa Sophia in Constantinople carries not the name of a woman saint, but a dedication to Holy Wisdom. Probus may have originated in a dedication to Holy Honesty – or to a saint whose name meant 'honest'.

The death of an early ninth century Irish priest, Probus of Mainz, is recorded in the *Annals of Fulda* in Germany, and he may be the Probus who wrote a Life of *Patrick. For centuries his name was thought to be an adjective, and the authorship of the manuscript was assigned to Bede. A prophecy that Patrick would baptize the *Scotii*, the Welsh, the Angles and the Normans is thought to be an unskilful later interpolation.

Rumon (?sixth century), 30 August: several places in the West Country commemorate Rumon. He is the patron of Tavistock and of Ronansleigh, Devon, and of Ruan Lanthorne, Ruan Major and Ruan Minor in Cornwall. Ruan Lanthorne was a Celtic monastery, but Rumon's shrine was moved to Tavistock in 981. William of Malmesbury visited it in 1120, recording that he was a bishop, and regretting that nothing more was known about him. A local canon thereupon produced a Life by the simple expedient of taking a Life of *Ronan of Locronan, and substituting 'Rumon' for 'Ronan' throughout. This led to considerable confusion between the two saints, and Rumon was not fully recognized as a separate personality until the twentieth century. Canon Doble has found evidence to suggest that he was a monk of Glastonbury who founded a monastery at the Lizard, and subsequently went to Brittany.

Selevan (Selyv, Levan, Salomon) (sixth century), ?14 October, was a Cornish hermit of Welsh extraction, possibly the brother of *Breage and son of *Germoc. A ruined chapel and well at St Levan in Cornwall are thought to be his, and Breage and her children are said to have visited him there. Later, he went to Brittany with his father and brother. The reason that there is doubt about his feast day is that for centuries he was confused with a Breton king named Selyf in Breton calendars, and so not allotted a separate day for commemoration.

Selevan is a corruption of the Welsh or Cornish form of the Old Testament name Solomon, and there are several Cornish legends about this saint, mainly concerned with fishing. One story tells how the saint was on his way to fish for his dinner on a Sunday, when he was reproached by a local woman named Johana for breaking the Sabbath. She was picking herbs at the time, and Selevan maintained that it was no more sinful for him to take his dinner from the sea than for her to take hers from the garden. The place is still called 'Johana's garden'. The tradition is that no child named Johana or Joanna was subsequently baptized at St Levan: parents wishing to give a daughter that name had to go to the vicar of a neighbouring parish.

Sithney (Sezni) (?sixth century), 4 August, was a hermit who settled at the place now known as Sithney near Helston in Cornwall. He may be 'Sinninus the bishop' who accompanied *Breage and *Germoc and their party. Later, he went to Brittany, where there is a well thought to be his at Guissény. In the medieval period, villagers took sick and mad dogs there to drink in the hope of a cure.

There is a Breton legend that Sithney had had a vision, in which God told him that he was to be the patron saint of girls. The hermit was appalled at this prospect, protesting that they would pester him for husbands and fine clothes. God enquired whether he would prefer to be the patron of mad dogs, and Sithney thankfully accepted this alternative. He has remained the patron of mad dogs ever since.

7

Brittany: the Settlers

According to modern tourist brochures, Brittany has seven thousand, seven hundred, seven score and seven saints. Though some of the early saints commemorated on the eastern boundaries are of Frankish or Roman origin, nearly all the place-names of saints on the coast of Brittany, along the *Côte d'Émeraude*, the *Côte de Granit Rose*, the *Côte de Léon* and the *Côte de Cornouaille*, all the way round the coast from Mont-Saint-Michel to Saint-Nazaire, come from Wales, or from Ireland via Wales.

Brittany was not much settled in prehistoric times, because the coastal areas are mainly granite: sheer rock-face, with no caves to live in. In Roman times, it was sparsely populated, and of no strategic importance to the Roman Empire. The Romans took little trouble with it, apart from massacring a powerful sea-going tribe called the Veneti, establishing a few towns and constructing coastal roads. This slender infrastructure, and the proximity to the land of the Franks, who claimed suzerainty over Brittany, may explain why there were some bishops with territorial dioceses on the Continental pattern in Brittany, though there were also monasteries on the Celtic pattern.

Immigrants from Ireland and Wales seem to have begun to settle in Brittany about 450, when the Roman legions had withdrawn, and the Roman cities were falling into disrepair. The major wave of migration came after the Yellow Pestilence, but there were other plagues which swept the valleys of South Wales in the sixth and seventh centuries, and the Norse invaders were an increasing menace along the coasts, so there may have been many other group migrations from particular areas which were threatened. Procopius, a sixth century Byzantine historian, recorded that 'every year the

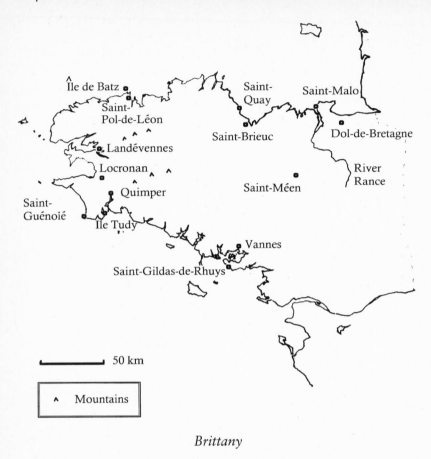

Brittany

Brittones emigrate with their women and children, and go to the land of the Franks, and the Franks allow them to settle in the parts of their land which appear to be more deserted'.

Some of the migrants were going to places where there were already established Welsh trading posts; but in the early days, they were often pioneers, clearing scrubland to grow crops, felling trees to make corner-posts for their huts, and fighting off pirates, Norsemen and the remaining Armoricans who opposed their settlement. They travelled out via Cornwall in ship-loads: monks, families, whole clan-groups. This may explain why, apart from one or two notable exceptions such as *Congar and *Sithney, their saints were kinder in their attitudes to women than the monks of

Ireland or Wales: they protected their mothers, their sisters and the groups of virgins in their company.

Many emigrated from Wales to Brittany in the sixth century to make a new life in a new land, but by the seventh century, there was a considerable two-way traffic. Young Welshmen often did military service in Brittany, supporting their Welsh overlords or members of their families. Those who wished to enter the religious life some-times went back to the Welsh monasteries, principally to Llantiltud Fawr. *Illtud's monastery was the most accessible on the sea-routes, and Illtud himself was born in Brittany of a Welsh family.

The Roman name for Brittany was Armorica. The immigrants called it *Bretagne Armorique*, Armorican Britain, to distinguish it from *Bretagne insulaire*, the British Isles. The monks who chroni-cled the Lives of the Breton saints are usually reliable enough when referring to recent events in Brittany and the northern territories of the Franks, though they are often very vague about the history and geography of *Bretagne insulaire*. Some of them are even ignorant of the distinction between Celt and Saxon; but they provide a lively picture of the religious life of a society which has been largely over-looked by historians, with some interesting insights into its customs and values.

Right down to the time of the French Revolution, northern Brittany was divided into five bishoprics: Dol, St Malo, St Brieuc, Tréguier and St Pol-de-Leon – all founded by monks from South Wales. The 'Seven Saints of Brittany' are *Samson of Dol, *Paul Aurelian, *Malo, *Padarn, *Brieuc, *Corentin and *Tugdual. In the Middle Ages, there was a pilgrim's way called the *Tro-Breiz* leading to the seven shrines in succession, and traces of the route can still be identified.

A number of the early Breton saints were former warriors. The immigrants must have had to fight the Armorican tribes for their territory, and a pattern developed of fairly young fighting men, tired of bloodshed, going home to Wales to train in the monaster-ies, and then returning to Brittany to spread the gospel. When they were ready to establish monasteries of their own, they went to the Frankish kings to gain a title to their land. At first, the Frankish clergy distrusted them. About the time of St Remigius, who died in

533, the bishops of Rennes, Tours and Angers complained about the activities of two Celtic priests who were going 'from cabin to cabin' among the immigrants. They were celebrating the Eucharist on portable altars (which was a common practice), and were said to be accompanied by women whom they called *conhospitae*, who actually 'administered the chalice during the communion of the people'. Such innovations were profoundly shocking to the Frankish clergy. The incomers were also *fort peu episcopale*, inclined to ignore the Frankish bishops; but their theology was sound, and they became accepted. A few decades later, Childebert I, grandson of Clovis I whom Remigius converted, was generous in his hospitality and grants of land – provided that the Celtic clergy stayed in Brittany, and did not trespass into Frankish territory.

The Breton monasteries were to have only a limited span of life. In 914, Brittany was overrun by marauding Norsemen, and the monasteries were sacked. The monks were 'scattered to the four winds of heaven', as Professor Loth puts it. Those who could escape retreated into Frankish territory, taking with them their treasures – shrines, relics and records. A few went back to Brittany in 939, when the Saxon king Athelstan of Wessex helped the Franks to expel the Norsemen; but Athelstan was well paid in relics for his assistance, which suggests that most of the monasteries were empty, and explains why many relics of Breton saints found their way to Winchester, Glastonbury and other Saxon centres. The monasteries which did survive were gradually taken over in succeeding centuries by the Benedictines of Normandy or Anjou, or dwindled to the status of parish churches, until nothing remained of the Welsh colony but the names of the great saints.

Armel (Erzel, Ermel, Ermyn, Armagilus) (?532), 16 August, was a cousin of *Samson and *Cadfan who emigrated to Brittany with many kinsmen, probably during the Yellow Pestilence. The Breton chronicles record that he came from *Penohen*, like *Paul Aurelian, and this is probably Penychen, in the Taff valley. He founded and became abbot of two monasteries. At this time Judual, king of Brittany, was being held in Paris by the Frankish king Childebert I. Armel went to Paris, saw both kings, and was granted land for his monasteries. The monasteries became known as Plouarmel and Ploermel, both versions of Armel's name. His fame spread to Normandy, and was imported to England after the Norman Conquest. Henry VII invoked Armel's assistance during a storm off the Normandy coast, and was saved from shipwreck. He specified the saints to be represented on his own tomb in Westminster Abbey, and Armel is among them. Armel is also represented on Cardinal Morton's tomb in Canterbury cathedral. A stained glass window at Ploermel has scenes from his life.

Austell (Austol) (sixth century), 28 June, was *Mewan's godson, and possibly a relative of *Samson. He travelled with Samson from Wales through Cornwall to Brittany. He founded the church in the present Cornish town of St Austell, where the parish adjoins that of St Mewan. He seems to have made no other separate foundations. He went to Brittany with Mewan, and assisted in the foundation of his principal monastery, later known as Saint-Méen. He was also involved in the foundation of another monastery in the forest of Brocéliande. He stayed with Mewan, and died soon after him. They were buried in the same tomb, and venerated together at Saint-Méen.

Brieuc (Brioc, Breock, Briavel) (sixth century), 1 May, went to Brittany from Ceredigion (Cardigan) via Cornwall, where he is known as St Breock. A twelfth century Life claims that he was educated in Gaul. He spent four years studying in Paris, was priested there, and returned to Wales by ship, escorted by a school of dolphins and other great fish which terrified the sailors. He founded a monastery in Cardigan, and foundations have been attributed to him in both Cornwall and Brittany. In Brittany, there are many legends about him. When he arrived in Brittany, with his monks (sixty-eight of them according to one account, and eighty-four according to another), they were all arrested by the soldiers of the pagan Count Rigual, who gave orders to have them killed. But the count was suddenly seized by a violent attack of pain, which left him unable to move. He attributed this to his projected massacre of the monks, countermanded the executions, and sent for the newcomers. He had evidently come to Brittany himself in an earlier wave of immigration from Wales, because when he saw Brieuc, he exclaimed dramatically '*Mon cousin*!' Brieuc prayed over Rigual and gave him something to drink, and he recovered from what sounds remarkably like an acute attack of sciatica.

The count gave his cousin land, and Brieuc founded his abbey close to the count's headquarters at the place now known as Saint-Brieuc. It was hard work: the monks had to start by cutting down trees, rooting up bushes and tearing up brambles and tangled thorns to make a clearing. Perhaps the local people were hostile. They would have had good reason to be so: Brieuc is said to have stopped an outbreak of plague by his prayers. When the ships bearing new immigrants landed in Brittany, the established settlers must often have feared that they had brought the dreaded plague with them.

Brieuc was an abbot, not a bishop in the Continental manner: he did not have a diocese with fixed borders. There is a tradition that he was a man of great charity: he relieved a famine, healed the sick and gave to the poor. He is said to have lived to the age of ninety. In his old age, he 'began to devote himself constantly to contemplation, to persevere in long prayer with tears, to spend the night unwearyingly in vigils and holy meditation, and to wear out his body with fasts prolonged beyond what either nature or his advanced age could endure'. He was 'always intent on heavenly things: all earthly things had become to him of no account'.

Brieuc's emblem is a purse, and he is the patron saint of purse-makers, who were of some importance when people had no pockets.

Budoc (Buoc, Beuzac) (sixth century), 8 December. All Budoc's centres are close to the sea, and he is thought, on the strength of topographical evidence, to have travelled and worked with *Mawes. The town of Budock in Cornwall faces St Mawes across Falmouth harbour, while in Brittany, Budoc's island monastery is close to one founded by Mawes on a neighbouring island.

Though there is a good deal of documentation about Budoc's life in Brittany, it is remarkably uninformative. Much of it is taken up with legends about his mother (another princess said to have been thrown into the sea in a barrel when she was found to be pregnant: cp. the mother of *Kentigern), and some accounts are contradictory. The ninth century Life by *Winwaloe of Landévennes, who was his disciple, says that Budoc taught on the island of Laurea in south Brittany, where he himself lived. Budoc became abbot of Landévennes, and appointed Winwaloe as his successor. A slightly later Life, of *Maelor of Dol, written about 900, makes him Maelor's successor at Dol, and the eleventh century *Chronicles of Dol* call him 'archbishop of Dol'.

Budoc's entry in *The Oxford Book of Saints* suggests that there may have been two saints of the same name; but it is possible that a single St Budoc was successively abbot of Landévennes and Dol, since we know that *Samson of Dol sent missions to southern Brittany.

Carantoc (Carannog, Caredec) (?sixth to seventh century), 16 May, was the son of Ceredig, king of Ceredigion, and figures in Welsh folklore. Many of the Welsh saints trace their ancestry back to Ceredig. Carantoc was a young prince who went to live as a hermit, 'loving the heavenly King more than the earthly kingdom'. He went to Ireland, where his name is linked with that of *Cainnech. Llangrannog in Wales and Crantock in Cornwall are thought to bear his name. He was the leader of a group of Welsh monks who carried out a notable ministry in central Cornwall, and then went on to Brittany. Roscarrock mentions a Cornish church with his dedication and seven daughter churches in the same district. In Brittany, there are churches bearing his dedication at Carentec, south-west of St Pol-de-Léon, and Tregarantec, further west.

There is a story in the *Léon Breviary* which sheds some light on the question of skin diseases described as 'leprosy', and on the penitential practices of the Breton saints. Carantoc had a disciple named Tenenan or Tennoc, who was thought to be a leper. Carantoc prepared a hot bath, but Tenenan flatly refused to get into it. Carantoc told him that if he did not, he would never enter eternal life. Eventually Tenenan was induced to climb into the bath, Carantoc scrubbed him from head to toe, and the 'leprosy' was instantly cured. After this, Tenenan demanded that Carantoc should get into the same bath. He was hesitant, but finally agreed. When he stripped, he was found to be wearing seven iron belts about his body, and they all snapped in the hot water, and fell from him. After this, one monk cleansed and the other freed from penance, they praised God together.

There is also a pleasant story of a repentant serpent. When Carantoc prayed, 'it made a great noise like a calf running to its mother. And it bent its head before the servant of God like a servant obeying its master, with humble heart and downcast eyes.' Carantoc would not let the people kill it, but put his stole round its neck and led it 'like a lamb' out of the city, telling it not to come back.

The accounts of Carantoc's ministry in Brittany are very confused, and may involve references to two different saints. There are two Lives, but both are twelfth century, and somewhat suspect. However, the fact that Norman monks troubled to re-write his Life suggests that his ministry was of considerable local importance.

Congar of Brittany: there are thought to be three St Congars, all dating from the sixth century. *Congar of Wales (7 November) is noted earlier. The second is another Welshman, who carried out a ministry in Devon and Somerset, when the barriers between Cornwall and Wessex were breaking down. He is thought to have come from Llanwngar, near St David's. Bishop Asser, friend and biographer of Alfred the Great, mentioned his monastery at what is now Congresbury in the ninth century, noting that it was then derelict. His feast day is 27 November.

The third is a missionary also known as Doceo, who went from Cornwall to Brittany, and may have been the brother of *Kea. He is reputed to have worked under *Cadoc in Wales and with *Petroc in Cornwall. He could be the Breton saint Ingonger of the monastery of Llanivet, who died at Saint-Congard. This would place him in the early sixth century. His Breton feast day is variously given as 13 February and 12 May.

Corentin (Cury) (?sixth century), 12 December, was the founder of the church of Cury in the Lizard: an ancient cross marks the spot. He became a hermit in Brittany, and the people drew him out of solitude to become bishop of Cornouaille in south-east Brittany.

His Life was written in Brittany in the mid-ninth century. It lacks historical or biographical detail, but it is evident that like many of the saints of Brittany, he was a keen fisherman. It focuses on a Breton legend – the story of the miraculous fish which was said to have provided him with his daily food. He was said to cut a slice from it every day, and to find it whole again on the following day. This bears all the hallmarks of an ancient sun-legend which has been grafted on to the saint's life. A similar legend occurs in Wrdisten's Life of *Winwaloe.

*Padarn and *Malo are said to have visited Corentin in his hermitage at Douarnenez. He had nothing for them to eat except bread (having presumably consumed his daily slice of fish). He went to the spring to fetch water, and when he returned, the jug was full of eels, and the water had become wine. So they dined on eels in wine, evidently a princely dish. Like the story of *Brigid and *Ibar and the celebrated bacon sandwich, this story points to the duty of hospitality, and to the difficulties hermits must have had in providing food for their visitors.

Corentin's name occurs in a tenth century Winchester missal, and an early eleventh century litany at Canterbury. In the early 1640s, following a plague in the area, the Jesuit missioner Julian Maunoir, who was born in Brittany, carried out a remarkable religious revival in the Cornouaille region, with a devotion to Corentin as the first bishop. In 1890, a fresco was discovered at Breage (the mother church of the Lizard) showing him in cope and mitre, with a pastoral staff. The legendary fish is shown with him, and the fresco bears the inscription *Ste Quorentine ora pro nobis*.

Dogmael (Toel) (fifth to sixth century), 14 June, was a Welshman who seems to have spent most of his ministry in Wales. Numerous foundations in Dyfed are reputed to have been made by him, and St Dogmael's abbey near Cardigan is the best known. The monastic community at Caldey was a daughter house of this community. It seems that Dogmael went on to Brittany, because he is well known there, usually as Toel, and it is only in Brittany that he was traditionally invoked to help children to learn to walk.

Ernin (Ernan) (sixth century), 2 November. There are minimal records of a saint named Ernin or Ernan who came from the mainland opposite Anglesey, and lost his lands when they were permanently flooded by the sea. He and his brothers became monks at Bardsey. He is thought to be the same Ernin who later migrated to Brittany and settled near Carhaix. He lived as a hermit, and was buried at Locarn. A local chapel, which housed his shrine, was built at Locarn, and there is a fourteenth century statue of him by his well.

Gudwal (Gurval, Locoal) (sixth century), 6 June, is well known in the ancient Armorican litanies. In the Missal of St Vougay, he is cited third, immediately after *Samson and *Malo. He was probably Welsh, and went to Brittany via Cornwall, where he is thought to be the patron of St Gudwal. He founded the monastery of Plecit on what was then the island of Locoal (Locoal is a corruption of Gurval), in the inland sea between Vannes and Lorient in south Brittany. His monks made a home and a farm among the oak trees, and constructed dykes to keep out the tide and give them some protection in bad weather. He built up Plecit into a monastery of some 200 monks, and made other foundations in the area, with a more distant one in the forest at Guer where he lived with three of his priests in 'admirable sanctity'. The chapel of St Stephen at Guer is thought to have been his hermitage. In 959, when the monastery was under attack from 'barbarians and pagans', Gudwal's relics were taken for safety to Picardy, and then to the abbey of St Peter in Ghent. He is sometimes described as the bishop of Saint-Malo, but this is an error due to the fact that in medieval times, Guer came under the jurisdiction of Saint-Malo.

Gwen Teirbron (fifth to sixth centuries), 1 June, is sometimes described as the seventeenth 'daughter of *Brychan'. The *Book of Llan Dav* describes her as the twentieth. There are references to 'three-breasted Gwen Teirbron' in the Lives of the Breton saints, and she is so represented in Breton art. 'Three-breasted' was a common Breton phrase at the time for a woman who had two husbands and a child or children. We know that Gwen had two husbands. She and her first husband, Eneas Ludewig, who was Welsh, had only one child, *Cadfan. Her second husband was Fracan, cousin of the duke of Cornwall, and they had four children, of whom one was *Winwaloe, abbot of Landévennes, near Brest. Winwaloe's Life includes references to her, and she occurs elsewhere in Breton accounts as *la bonne dame Guen*.

The family went together from Cornwall to Brittany about 460. Gwen, who was Welsh, and evidently had family connections already established in Brittany, obtained a grant of land for a new colony, and others of the clan followed them. They seem to have lived a very hard life in their new territory, taming the wild horses in the woods, cultivating the coastal land, and defending themselves against the pirates who preyed on the coastal settlements. Two places commemorate their names: Plouguen (Plouvien) and Ploufragan, where Winwaloe was born.

Gwen was evidently respected as a notable Christian matriarch, the wife of a chief and the mother of saints. Baring Gould and Fisher say that most of her statues were destroyed on the orders of later clerics, who regarded them as 'somewhat outrageous and not conducive to devotion'.

Judicaël (658), 17 December, king of Brittany, was the elder brother of *Judoc. Their father Judual (see *Samson) had sixteen sons, and when he died, some of them disputed the succession. In about 636, attacked by the forces of his brother Saloman, Judicaël abandoned his claim to the throne, and took refuge in the monastery of Gaël, near Vannes. His spiritual director was *Mewan, who tried to modify the royal refugee's desperate and extreme penances. On one occasion in winter, he found Judicaël plunged in a frozen stream, with only his head showing through a hole he had made in the ice, and tried to counsel him away from these frenzied penitential exercises.

When Saloman died in about 630, the battle over the succession was over, and Judicaël was unanimously agreed to be the rightful heir. His family pleaded with him to return to secular life and to become king again. He decided that it was the right course to leave the monastery, and he married a modest wife who shared his desire to live simply and piously. They both gave generously to the poor and fasted, but they did not allow their courtiers to know of their penances and abstentions. Judicaël had a special goblet made with a cover, so that the nobles could not see that he was drinking water while they drank wine.

Judicaël was responsible for the foundation of several monasteries and churches, including the church of Notre-Dame-de-Paimpont, said to be built on a spot where the Druids had practised human sacrifice; but he still felt a pull to the monastic life, and a growing distaste for the worldly life of the court. At length he abdicated in favour of his brother Judoc, and re-entered the monastery at Gaël. He is said to have lived for another twenty years in the monastery before he died, and was buried next to his spiritual master, St Mewan. Judicaël is represented in art with a crown at his feet and a broom in his hand: symbols of the kingship he renounced twice, and the humble life he led in the monastery.

Judoc (Judicus, Josse) (668), 13 December, was the brother of *Judicaël of Brittany. When Judicaël abdicated to enter the religious life in about 636, he accepted the crown, but after some months he renounced it in the face of opposition from his brothers, and travelled with twelve companions on pilgrimages to Chartres, Paris and Amiens. He also visited Rome, and was ordained either in Rome or at the court of Haymon, count of Ponthieu. William Worcestre says that he was a secular priest, not a monk. He became a hermit in Ponthieu, 'at Braic on the river Authie' according to the chronicler Orderic Vitalis, at what is now the seaside resort of Saint-Josse-sur-Mer. There he lived a life of great austerity with one disciple named Wurmar or Wulmar. Twice they moved further into the forest to avoid the many visitors who came to ask for healing or counsel.

They stayed in the Braic district for eight years, living a very austere life, and Judoc earned a great reputation for his charity to the poor of the neighbourhood. He never refused them food as long as he had a scrap of bread left. There is a story that on one occasion, four hungry men came to his door in succession. Three times he halved his small piece of bread, until the piece remaining was too small to divide, and that he gave to the fourth. Then Wulmar, who had been understandably concerned at the disappearance of their small supply of food, saw four boats approaching along the river. They bore supplies, perhaps from Count Haymon. The legend grew up that the four hungry men had been appearances of Christ himself, testing the charity of his servant.

Judoc had the Celtic monks' love of animals. He 'fed birds of every kind, and little fishes from his hand as if they were tame creatures'. He built two wooden chapels in the forest, 'one for Peter who holds the keys of heaven, and one for Paul the great preacher (*magnilogo*)'.

In the eighth or early ninth century, the Emperor Charlemagne gave Judoc's hermitage to St Alcuin, the English scholar at his court, as a guest-house for English travellers. About 902, some refugees from Saint-Josse came to Winchester, bringing with them relics of their founder. Feasts of St Judoc were given a high rank at Winchester, and elsewhere in medieval England. Chaucer's Wife of Bath swears 'By God and by Seint Joce'. The name Joyce (for both men and women) is derived from 'Judoc'.

Judoc's cult spread to the Low Countries, where he is known as Joost, and then to Germany, Alsace, Switzerland, and Austria. His emblem is a pilgrim's staff, with a crown at his feet symbolizing his renunciation of royal power and honour, and sometimes crossed keys, indicating his pilgrimage to Rome.

Maelor (Maglorius) (sixth century), 24 October, was a cousin of *Samson, and like him, trained under *Illtud. He travelled to Cornwall and then to Brittany with Samson, became abbot of a monastery near Dol, and obtained the protection of the Frankish king Childebert. He was famed for his wise counsel, and people came great distances to consult him. He preached indefatigably, remedied abuses, and evidently became overwhelmed by the burdens of office. When Samson was on his deathbed, he nominated

Maelor as his successor. Maelor, not wishing to take on the responsibility, went to consult *Budoc, who told him roundly that it was his duty to accept; but he was evidently not cut out to be the abbot of a large monastery. Eventually the Count of Poitou gave him the island of Sark, where he could lead a quieter and more collected life. There he had a circle of a few monks, and helped the local people to defend themselves against Norse raiders and pirates. He was devoted to Budoc, and wrote his Life.

Malo (Maclow, Machutus, Malchus, Maclovius, Maclou) (sixth to seventh centuries), 15 November. Malo's many names indicate his importance in the development of the church in Brittany. There are at least four medieval Lives, and that by Bili, written in the ninth century, is thought to be based on older sources.

Breton Lives say that Malo was born in Ireland, and that *Brendan of Clonfert was his godfather, but Welsh sources say that he was born near Llancarfan in South Wales – it is said, in a monastery where his mother had gone for her Easter vigil. He was educated in the monastery school. His parents did not want him to become a priest, and for some time, he had to hide from them in 'the islands of the southern sea' (possibly the Bristol Channel). He left Wales during one of the periodic outbreaks of plague, and went to north Brittany, where he carried out missions in the Saint-Servan district, then called Aleth, and became bishop. He was a stalwart defender of the faith: the force of his character comes through the Latin accounts in spite of over-pious language and fanciful accounts of marvels, like riding on the back of a whale. He travelled tirelessly on horseback along the coast and up the Rance estuary, sweating profusely, and singing the psalms in a loud voice as he rode along. Like many of the Celtic monks, he could recite the whole Psalter from memory.

One story recounted by Bili illustrates both the kindness of his impetuous nature, and the opposition which the incomers often faced. Malo came of a wealthy family, and his parents gave him a group of attendants to serve him as long as he lived. He took them to Brittany. One, named Rivan, was set upon by local Armoricans, and pegged down on the sand as the tide rolled in. When Malo heard, he at once galloped down to the beach, to find the water already lapping round Rivan's body. He untied the serf, and because his arms and legs were numb (he must have been there for some time, waiting to drown), put him on his own horse for the return journey, and went on foot himself. The onlookers jeered to see the serf riding on horseback, and the master walking. Then Malo turned on the ringleader, cursing him and his descendants to the ninth generation.

Vehement as he was, he was often much resented for his rough tongue. His relations with the local chiefs were sometimes confrontational. When he solemnly denounced them after a quarrel over the insults offered to his monks, he and they were expelled, and he set off by ship with thirty-three monks for Saintes, scattering excommunications from the prow as they sailed up the river Rance. He refused to return until some years later when the people of his city begged him to do so. There was a severe and prolonged drought, and the town had come to the conclusion that this was because of their ill-treatment of their bishop; but Malo died before he could reach his monastery again.

Mawes (Maugdith, Maudez, Mauditus) (?sixth century), 18 November, is, like *Asaph and *Cadoc, credited with the miracle of carrying live coals to the water's edge to warm his freezing master without burning his apron. The penitential customs of the Celtic monks must have borne hard on the small boys who served them. When Mawes grew up, he was ordained, and became the friend and colleague of *Budoc. Their settlements are close together in both Cornwall and Brittany, and he settled in Brittany, on what is now called the Île Maudez on the Côte de Léon, where he became a celebrated scholar and teacher.

His eleventh century Breton Life records: 'In the time of Childebert, king of the Franks, a vast number of bishops and abbots crossed from the region beyond the seas to these parts.'

Curiously, Mawes is one of the few Celtic saints who is said not to have been kind to animals. He used to instruct his pupils at the water's edge, in an area where a great seal often came to swim. The 'bobbing about of the great head with its strangely human eyes' distracted the boys, and eventually the exasperated teacher flung a stone at it, hitting it on the head. The seal swam away. The chronicler piously interprets the incident to mean that the seal was actually the devil, come to trouble Mawes and to prevent him from passing on godly teaching to his students.

In Cornwall, Roscarrock saw 'a praty village or fischer town cawlid S. Maw's, with a chapel, a chair of stone and a well'. There is a well which is said locally to be that that of Mawes on the Île Maudez. His shrine was taken to Orléans in the tenth century, to prevent it from being destroyed by pirates.

Mawes has always been a popular saint both in Cornwall and Brittany. Invoking him is said to be efficacious in the cure of worms, the relief of headaches and (in Brittany) the healing of the *mal de S. Maudet*, a disease of the feet.

Mewan (Méen, Main, Mevennus) (sixth century), 21 or 25 June, was born in Gwent, and a cousin of *Samson of Dol. He entered Caldey during the short period when Samson was abbot of the community. Then he went with Samson, or followed him, on his missionary journeys to Cornwall and Brittany. He may be the deacon 'as yet in the flower of the age of youth', who accompanied Samson, but is not named. Among Mewan's friends and disciples was his godson, *Austell. The parishes of St Mewan and St Austell in Cornwall are close to each other.

In Brittany, Samson sent Mewan inland from Dol, into the forest of Brocéliande. He was given land at Gaël, and founded a monastery there. Later, Samson sent him further, to the south coast of Brittany, near Vannes, where he made another foundation which developed into the abbey of Saint-Méen. There he came into conflict with a brother of King Judicaël named Hoël. A peasant who could not pay the dues which Hoël demanded of him was thrown into a deep pit. Méen heard the man's piteous cries, and asked Hoël to release him, but the prince refused. Somehow the man escaped, and took refuge in the monastery. Mewan upheld his right of sanctuary, and hid him in the monastery church, but Hoël, furiously angry, broke the church door down, and seized the fugitive. Then Mewan confronted him with full prophetic force, and Hoël, instead of being impressed, roared with laughter ('*se prit à rire à gorge déployée*') and mocked the saint; but on his way back to his manor, his horse threw him, and he broke his hip. Mewan visited him and received his contrition, and he died three days later.

The dragon legend attached to Mewan's name may be a symbolic version of his victory over Hoël, but the Breton accounts say that incident occurred at Angers. Mewan intended to go to Rome, got as far as Angers, threw the dragon into the Loire, and then decided that it was God's will that he should return to his own monastery in Brittany.

Breton writers say that he died in his monastery among his brethren. Welsh accounts say that he returned to Wales in his old age, and died there. A cross in the churchyard of Llantwit Major (the site of Llantiltud Fawr) commemorates him, but his shrine is at Saint-Méen in Brittany. Wells and springs bearing his name became sites for medieval pilgrimages, where thousands of pilgrims came to be healed of skin diseases: one particular form of ulceration is known in Brittany as *le douleur de Saint Main*. In north Brittany, a wild flower which is a variety of scabious is still known as *l'herbe de Saint Main*.

Padarn of Vannes (Pattern, Paternus) (fifth to sixth centuries), 21 May, was a monk from Bangor Iscoed, the founder of the monastery of Llanbadarn Fawr, where he became abbot. He went to Brittany, and was consecrated at Vannes at a council of bishops in 467.

His canonization was confirmed by Pope Paul VI in 1964, and he is included in the Revised Roman Calendar as 'Paternus of Vannes'. Part of the Vatican interest in him in the 1960s may have been due to the necessity of distinguishing him from *Padarn of Wales (15 April) and Paternus of Avranches (16 April). The latter was born in Poitou and died in 564. Padarn or Paternus of Vannes was clearly an important missionary figure in south Brittany, and the investigation by Vatican scholars gives him a firm identity.

Paul Aurelian (Pol, Paulinus, Polinus, Peulinus) (*c.* 573), 12 March, was a disciple of *Illtud at Llantwit Major, founder of the monastery at St Pol-de-Léon, and a fellow-worker with *Samson in Brittany. 'Aurelian' was not his family name, and is in fact a misnomer: it means 'of Orléans' and the tag only became attached to his name much later. His relics were moved to Orléans for safety in the eighth century, and the people of Orléans contested their return to his own city of St-Pol-de-Léon. It is used here only for ease of identification.

Wrmonoc, a monk of Landévennes in Brittany, writing a Life based on older sources in the tenth century, states firmly that Paul Aurelian was the same saint as *Paulinus of Wales. He divides his account of Paul's career into two parts: first his ministry as a teacher of saints in Wales, and then his work as a monastic founder and bishop in north Brittany. He says that Paul came from *Penohen* in Wales (which is also said to be the birthplace of *Armel). He was under the direction of a priest named Hyldutus (Illtud), and studied with Samson, *Gildas and 'Daniel Aquaticus', who is evidently *David. After ten years in the monastery, he went to a 'desert place' on his father's land with twelve monks, and founded a monastery. Then they went to the kingdom of King Mark in Cornwall, and baptized him and his household. King Mark would have liked to keep them in Cornwall, but they sailed on to Léon in Brittany. The governor of Léon sent them to a Count de Guythère, whose estate was near Roscoff, and with his permission, they established a monastery on his land. Paul rid the region of a 'horrible' dragon (there is a place on the coast nearby still known as the Abyss of the Serpent, where the sea thunders and makes a strange noise). The people asked him to be their bishop. He fell to his knees, saying that he was not worthy of such a responsibility, but the count sent him to the court of Childebert, king of the Franks, where the king of Brittany, Judual, was an exile. Judual readily agreed to the monastery's possession of the land and revenues (which may have meant crops or rent from tenant farmers), and to Paul's consecration as bishop. On his return, the count and his entourage met him at Morlaix, and conducted him to his episcopal seat.

The present city of Saint-Pol-de-Léon is some five miles from Roscoff: its Breton name is Kastell Pol. Most writers on the Celtic saints have been dubious about the identification of the Welsh Paulinus with Paul Aurelian, but they may have underestimated the strength of the sixth century links between Brittany and Wales, which we now know to involve a number of Celtic saints of the period. Illtud was born in Brittany, and Paulinus was the brother of *Gwynllyw, who took his family to live there. *Cadoc, Gwynllyw's son, was born in Brittany. Paulinus was known as Paul Penychen, and Penychen was the name of the *cantref* which he ruled in Wales before he entered the religious life. *Penohen* looks very much like a tenth century Breton monk's attempt to record this unfamilar word which must have been passed on in crabbed manuscripts or by word of mouth for three hundred years by the time he recorded it. Paulinus may have taken his community to his relatives in Brittany during the wholesale emigration which followed the Yellow Pestilence. A problem is that Wrmonoc gives the name of Paul Aurelian's father as 'Perphius' or 'Porfius': the father of Gwynllyw and Paulinus was King Glwys; but the Breton chroniclers could hardly be expected to pass the name on correctly – or to be able to pronounce it.

Were Paulinus of Wales and Paul Aurelian the same person, or did Illtud have two disciples, both of whom trained under him at Llantwit Major, both scholars, both distinguished monastic teachers, both senior to Cadoc, David and *Teilo, and both named Paul? Dates are very difficult to establish, but the possibility that Paulinus and Paul Aurelian are the same person is supported by three dates which are as firm as anything we are likely to find in the sixth century: Paulinus was a senior cleric at the Synod of Brefi in 544 or 545, when he urged the assembled abbots and bishops to send for David, who had been his own student. The main attack of the Yellow Pestilence occurred about 547; Paul Aurelian died about 573, reputedly at a great age. Paulinus of Wales could have migrated to Brittany after the onset of the Yellow Pestilence, founded a new monastery and, as Paul Aurelian, carried out the ministry recorded of the Breton saint.

The Léon monastery became a celebrated one. Paul Aurelian administered his diocese for twenty-four years before finally retiring to the island of Batz, just off-shore, shortly before his death. He was buried in his monastery church. The granite former cathedral at St Pol-de-Léon houses his shrine, and claims his relics, eventually translated back from Orléans.

If Wrmonoc was right, accounts of Paulinus of Wales and Paul Aurelian should be read together as forming a record of one of the most influential leaders of the sixth century Celtic Church who had two distinct careers, one in Wales and one in Brittany.

Ronan of Locronan (dates unknown), 1 June, is the patron of Locronan in Cornouaille, Brittany. He is reputed to have made a daily penitential climb to a hill on the outskirts of the town, and this is still celebrated annually as the *Petite Troménie*. The *Grande Troménie* is held every sixth year (it was held in 1995 and 2001) and involves a 12 kilometer procession right round the hill, with the stations of the Cross. Baring Gould and Fisher (or one of them) evidently witnessed it, because they describe it in detail in *Lives of the British Saints*:

> The scene is wonderfully striking. The women are in white, with head-dresses of mediaeval cut; their gowns rich with embroidery and spangles. The procession winds about the mountain with fluttering banners and crosses gleaming in the sun; and the summer air, as it fans over the heather, comes laden with the scent of frankincense and snatches of song. The adjoining parishes arrive for High Mass in the morning, headed by drummers, and at the Sanctus, elevation and Communion, supplement the tinkling of the bell . . . (this is) Christianity in its most idyllic form.

Locronan was an important place of pilgrimage in the Middle Ages. There are several other saints named Ronan, including the Scottish bishop *Ronan of Kilmaronen.

Samson of Dol (*c.* 565), 28 July, is recognized as the chief of the 'Seven Saints of Brittany'. He was of Welsh origin, his father coming from Dyfed and his mother from Gwent. His parents offered him to *Illtud when he was very young, and he grew up in the monastery at Llaniltud Fawr. He was ordained priest by *Dubricius on 22 February 531. Illtud was present at his ordination, but not at his consecration as a missionary bishop, at which Dubricius officiated. Possibly he had died by that time. Dubricius wanted Samson to succeed him as abbot of Llaniltud Fawr, but Illtud's nephews, who were also monks in the same monastery, became jealous after their uncle's death. In the face of their hostility, Samson retired to the island monastery of Caldey off the coast of Dyfed (Pembrokeshire), and became abbot there, but it was not a happy move. His predecessor, *Pyr, had left Caldey in such a lax state that he was unable to control the monks and re-establish discipline. According to his Life by a monk of Dol, written between 610 and 615, they 'continued to enjoy feasts of plenty and flowing bowls' while he fasted and lived like a hermit. One account says that they tried to poison him. Samson left and went to Ireland, where he reformed a monastery, thought to be the religious house at Howth, and then joined a party of Welsh churchmen including *Paulinus, *Austell and *Mewan who were going to Cornwall on their way to Brittany.

Perhaps his reputation as a monastic reformer had preceded him. When he arrived near the monastery of Docco or Doceo in Cornwall (see *Congar), he sent word of his arrival, and a monk named Winniavus was dispatched to tell him tactfully that they would prefer that he went somewhere else. Winniavus explained:

> O most loving father, the thing that thou askest – that thou might stay with us – is not convenient, lest, for example, thou, who art better than we, shouldst be condemned by us, who are less worthy, and what is more proper, that we should be condemned by thee as we deserve. For I wish to you know this – that we come short of our former practice.

Samson took this broad hint, and moved on to spend some time in the Scilly Isles, where an island is named for him, and in Guernsey, where St Samson is the second port of the island, before founding his main monastery near Dol in Brittany.

When he and his party reached the coast of Brittany, they found it overgrown with brambles and infested with locusts. Samson is said to have interpreted the presence of the locusts as meaning

Locus sta (stay in this place) – which is poor Latin, and some commentators have dismissed it as a pun; but Samson's world knew nothing of the separation of philology, the forms of words, and semantics, the meanings of words. To them, the form and the meaning were inextricably linked, and capable of revealing the divine purpose.

Dol was then an island on flat marshlands, though the coastline has changed, and it is now about eight kilometres inland. Mont Dol, a large flat-topped rock, had been the site of Druid sacrifices, and Samson made that his hermitage. He seems to have settled there well before the Yellow Pestilence. *Teilo, who was his friend, went to visit him, and they planted an orchard together.

Samson made a journey to the royal Frankish court in Paris to plead for Judual, king of Brittany, who was still being detained there by Childebert I. There were some curious occurrences at court. The queen was determined that Samson should not take Judual back to Brittany. She became openly hostile, 'shamelessly bawling out to the saint in vile language which is not fit to be repeated', and ordered a hot drink to be brought for him. When he made the sign of the Cross over it, the vessel shattered. This was interpreted as meaning that the drink had been poisoned. Then she gave him a horse which reared and tried to throw him – though Samson was evidently a good horseman, for he managed to keep his seat. Finally (and here fantasy does seem to be taking over from probability) she loosed on him a lion which she kept in a cave; but he made the sign of the Cross again, and the beast fell dead at his feet. On the following day, Samson celebrated Mass. The queen turned her back on him and the altar, and talked loudly to her ladies. The Life from Dol says that eventually she repented, fell at Samson's feet, and was forgiven; but another Breton Life suggests a more dramatic finale: she had a violent nose-bleed, and died soon after. Even without those moralistic flourishes, the story suggests a very tense situation at the Frankish court; but Childebert, who welcomed Christian missionaries to his borders, and seems to have received a constant stream of them from Brittany, reassured Samson by releasing Judual and confirming the grant of land for the monastery at Dol.

Samson may have had quite close relations with the Frankish clergy. He is probably the *Samson peccator episcopus* who signed the acts of an episcopal council in Paris in 557. He is described in Breton accounts as archbishop of Dol. The Life from Dol is embellished with legends which also occur in the Lives of other saints: a dove perches on Samson's shoulder at his ordination (like *David) and he captures a dragon with his stole and throws it over a cliff (like Mewan and *Paul Aurelian). These stories may have rational twenty-first century explanations, but they serve symbolically to emphasize the importance of his work and the reverence in which he was held by his successors.

Dol was overwhelmed by a catastrophic tidal wave in 709, and there is now no trace of the monastery. Samson's relics were taken to Canterbury and Ely in the time of King Athelstan of Wessex.

St Samson presiding at a Council of Prelates:
stained glass window at Dol

Tudwal (Tugdual, Tual) (sixth century), traditionally 1 December, now 30 November in the Revised Roman Calendar, was an abbot of Welsh origin. Three places on the Lleyn peninsula in North Wales bear his name, including Ynys Tudwal, a small island now uninhabited, which is thought to be the site of his hermitage. He went to Brittany with a party of monks and members of his own family, including his mother and sister, and became known as *Pabu* or Father over a wide area round Saint-Pol-de-Léon, as a result of his missionary activity. The land for a monastery near Tréguier was granted to him by the local ruler, Deroc, who was of his own kin, but he travelled to Paris to have the grant confirmed by King Childebert I. Childebert insisted that he should become the bishop of Treher (Treguier). His monastery became known as *Lan Pabu*, Father's church or cell, which led to a legend that he became pope.

Tudy (Tudec) (sixth century), 11 May: the parish of St Tudy in Cornwall claims to be the site of his first monastic foundation. He went to south Brittany with *Mawes, and was his 'faithful companion in labour and in the service of God'. He founded a monastery on what is now the Île Tudy, carrying out missionary work in the Quimper district. He is said by some sources to have been the companion of *Brieuc, and also to have made foundations in north Brittany.

There is no separate Life of Tudy, and information about him has to be gleaned from the Lives of other saints – Mawes, Brieuc and *Corentin. There is an interpolated story in the thirteenth century copies of the Life of Corentin that the people of Cornouaille sent Tudy, Corentin and *Winwaloe to St Martin of Tours, to ask which should be their bishop. Tudy was commended for his learning and honesty, Winwaloe for his eloquence and piety, and Corentin for 'great sanctity by the inspiration of the Holy Ghost'. There are objections to this story (not least the fact that all three lived in the sixth century, while Martin of Tours died in 397). The point appears to be in the description of how Corentin was appointed bishop, and he blessed the other two, appointing them to be abbots under his jurisdiction – thus justifying the decision to bring Loc-Tudy under the jurisdiction of the bishops of Quimper. Since Martin of Tours died in 397, this appears to be a distinctly unskilful invention.

Winwaloe (Guénole, Guingalois, Onolaus) (sixth century), 3 March, was the son of *Gwen Teirbron and her husband Fracan, cousin of the duke of Cornwall, born after they emigrated to Brittany. He was educated by *Budoc on the island of Laurea, and became his disciple. He had a great desire to go to Ireland, and discussed the matter with '*quelques marchands bretons-cambriens*' (one of the few references we have to the traders whose activities must have kept open the sea-routes between Brittany and the Celtic lands to the north); but he decided that it was not God's will that he should take so long a voyage. He subsequently became a hermit on the isle of Tibidy before joining with a group of monks to found the monastery of Landévennes in a populated valley near Brest. Budoc appointed him abbot of Landévennes, and he later wrote his Life of Budoc.

Winwaloe, whose Life is written by a monk named Wrdistan of Landévennes, was greatly admired for his asceticism, which rivalled that of the early Irish monks. He was accustomed to recite the entire Psalter with his arms outstretched in the form of a cross 'standing motionless or kneeling' – not, admittedly, in icy water, but holding this position must have been a painful penance in itself. He ate a little cheese on Saturdays and a few small fishes on Sundays, but otherwise lived on herbs and vegetables. This was rare among the Celtic monks of Brittany. Most of them were keen fishermen, and ate fish regularly. Winwaloe drank only water or cider made of wild apples. Wine, except for the Eucharist, was unknown in his monastery. He never wore wool or linen, his clothes being made of goat's hair. He slept in the clothes he wore during the day, on a hard bed, with a stone for a pillow and no covering save birch bark fibre.

The other personal scrap of information we have about Winwaloe suggests that he had a very trusting nature. One of his monks asked leave to go home, saying that his mother was dying. He took a holiday, and eventually returned to the monastery, giving the excuse that his mother had been dead when he reached his home, but that he had been able to perform a miracle and revive her by earnest prayer. Winwaloe appears to have been satisfied by this explanation, though it seems that the chronicler had his suspicions.

When he was dying, Winwaloe called the monks together to talk to them about his successor. He had evidently thought long and carefully about his experiences as abbot, and he recommended them to find a new abbot who would be 'as sweet as honey and as bitter as absinthe'. He is said to have died while standing at the altar at the end of Mass. There are many dedications to him in Brittany under different versions of his name.

The monks of Landévennes fled from the Norsemen in 915, taking his shrine to Montreuil, where it remained at the church of Saint-Sauve until the French Revolution.

8

Travellers in Europe

While the Celtic Church developed its own distinctive traditions, it always had links with the Church on the mainland of Europe. *Patrick, *Ninian and probably *Dubricius had been trained in the Roman tradition. Devotion to the Desert Fathers and to St Martin of Tours became part of the Celtic heritage. If the practices of the Church in the regions to which they travelled in Europe were different from their own, this does not seem to have greatly concerned the Celtic monks, or to have been regarded as a threat to their own traditions. For many of the travellers, known as *peregrini*, the main purpose of travel was penance, the deliberate rejection of the ties of home and extended family. 'Exile for Christ' was the aim of many Celtic travellers, particularly those from Ireland, who travelled most widely. It was expressed by *Columbanus in one of his sermons:

> Let us concern ourselves with heavenly things, not human ones, and like pilgrims, always sigh for our homeland. It is the end of the road that travellers look for and desire, and because we are travellers and pilgrims through this world, it is the road's end, that is of our lives, that we should always be thinking about. For that road's end is our true homeland.

Their home was not Ireland, but heaven; and to reach it, they crossed the sea into unknown territory; but there were other motives, too. Some groups of Irish monks (the travellers were nearly all Irish) developed friendly links with monasteries in the territory of the Franks. Some Celtic monks must have been motivated by curiosity and a sense of adventure. Some set out on pilgrimage to the Holy Land, though probably only a few actually reached the places they had learned about in their studies of the Bible. In the sixth and early seventh centuries, most of them travelled by sea. It was only when the Great Paschal Controversy developed towards the end of the seventh century that the Irish travellers, concerned at the mounting criticism of their customs on the Continent, began to go down the Rhine and through the Alpine passes to investigate the causes of their differences. Fra Anselmo Tommasini claims to have identified over 220 Italian parish churches dedicated in the name of Irish saints, and hundreds more chapels and shrines. Whether the *peregrini* were seeking mortification, adventure or devotional understanding (or perhaps all three), they were ready both for mission and for pilgrimage.

Columbanus (who is here referred to by the Latin form of his name rather than by the Irish form 'Columban', to avoid confusion with *Columba of Iona) must have been one of the earliest of these long-distance travellers. He took the tradition he had learned from *Comgall at Bennchorr first to the Vosges in south-east Gaul and then to Bobbio in Lombardy, making no concessions to the territorial claims of Continental bishops, but being respectful of the authority of the pope. His letters to Gregory the Great show a great desire for knowledge about Scripture and the traditions of the Church, and he asks the pope's prayers. For his part, Pope Gregory, unlike some of his successors, seems to have shown a sympathetic understanding of the Celtic position. Through Columbanus and his group of clergy, the faith and discipline of Bennchorr were to influence the work of many Continental monasteries.

*Gall accompanied Columbanus as far as what is now German-speaking Switzerland, where he remained, and set up a monastery of his own. *Fintan of Rheinau compiled a calendar which ensured that the names of Celtic saints such as Patrick, *Brigid, and Columba took their place in Continental lists of saints, and eventually found their way into the Revised Roman Calendar. *Kilian and *Donat both became involved in high-level Continental diplomacy. *Ferghil became virtual bishop of Salzburg, to the distress of St Boniface, who accused him of unorthodox cosmological speculations. *Fursey and his colleagues took the gospel to East Anglia, and were encountered there by St Augustine's missioners in the 630s. The body of the mysterious *Cathaldus still lies in the cathedral at Taranto, in the foot of Italy, in its silver shrine.

Much of what has been written about the travelling Irish monks is devotional literature rather than sound history; but there is enough historical information for us to see why, by the ninth century, Charlemagne's biographer was moved to complain that there were 'too many Irishmen' at the Frankish court. Their devotion, their physical endurance and their fighting instincts (one contemporary wrote of Columbanus 'hurling the fire of Christ wheresoever he could, without concerning himself with the blaze it caused') became quite literally the stuff of legends.

Cathaldus of Taranto (?Cathal) (seventh or eighth century), 10 May, may be one of the most travelled of the travelling monks, but the evidence is distinctly shaky. Tradition in Taranto is that he came from the monastery school at Lismore, south of Cashel in southern Ireland, and arrived in this city on the 'in step' of Italy on his way to the Holy Land. The cathedral is dedicated in his name, and possesses a silver reliquary said to contain his relics; but the only basis for the tradition is that of a tomb discovered in Taranto in 1071. It included with the body a small cross of Irish workmanship, inscribed *Cathaldus*, of the sort which it was assumed might have headed a Roman bishop's crozier. Additions were twice made to the inscription: in the eleventh century, *Rach* was added after *Cathaldus*; and in the twelfth century *au* (*av* in Latin) was added to *Rach*. It was subsequently assumed that 'Cathaldus' was a bishop, and 'Rachau' the name of his see.

There was no previous tradition of a bishop named Cathaldus in Taranto. The city was destroyed, and its inhabitants massacred, by the Saracens in 927. For forty years after that, it remained desolate, and it is understandable that shrines and religious traditions could have been lost by the time it was rebuilt. When the tomb of Cathaldus was rediscovered in the eleventh century, the Benedictines in the Norman kingdom of Sicily, which included southern Italy, inspired great devotion to him. He is shown in mosaics at Palermo and the great basilica at Monreale in Sicily. There is a painting of him in the Church of the Nativity at Bethlehem – commissioned by the Norman archbishop Drogo of Taranto and approved by the Norman patriarch Raoul of Jerusalem; but the earliest account of his supposed Life, written by an Italian monk named Petrus de Natalibus, did not appear until as late as 1382.

Efforts to identify the 'diocese of Rachau' proved inconclusive. It has been suggested that it could be the name of his birthplace or his monastery, possibly Rachaa in Co. Tipperary, or Rahen in south Meath, and that he was a missionary from one of the Irish monastic centres on the Continent. He is venerated locally as bishop of Taranto. Cardinal Baronius included his name in the Roman Martyrology, and dated his death to the year 160, but this is much too early for any traveller from the Irish monasteries. The story of Cathaldus reminds us how thin is the dividing line between saving the tradition of a lost saint, and what Fr Hippolyte Delehaye, the celebrated Bollandist critic, calls the 'manufacture' of a saint.

San Cataldo, as he is called in Italy and Sicily, is invoked against drought, tempest, plague and other calamities only too common in the region. No great interest was taken in this wandering saint in Ireland until 1746, when he was associated with a claim that the diocese of 'Cashel of the kings' should take precedence over the diocese of Armagh in the north.

Columbanus (Columban) (*c.* 543–615), 23 November, was born in Leinster. We know nothing of his parentage, but there is a story that when he decided to go away to study, his mother threw herself across the threshold to prevent him from leaving. He stepped over her, and went on his way. Columbanus was always single-minded. He went to the monastery of Sinell, a former disciple of *Finnian of Clonard, as a student, and then entered Bennchorr, where he became a monk. He developed into a notable scholar, versed in the Latin classical authors, as well as the Latin Fathers, and wrote a commentary on the Psalms, which has not survived. He was a teacher at Bennchorr for a time before he undertook 'exile for Christ' about the year 573.

He and his party went to Gaul via Cornwall and Brittany. He is thought to be St Colomb of Cornwall, and St Conlomb of a village near St Malo. At this time, Clovis's empire of the Franks had disintegrated as a result of warfare between his sons and grandsons. Clovis (d. 511) had adopted Christianity as a result of the influence of his wife, St Clotilde, but by the time Columbanus arrived there, Frankish society had reverted to paganism, magic and witchcraft. Ritual murder and the breaking of oaths were common. Columbanus's *Penitential* reflects the prevalence of all these practices, and forbids them, prescribing severe penalties for those who practise them. When the Irish group first arrived, they suffered such privation that they had nothing to eat for nine days except leaves from the trees; but when he heard of their arrival, King Sigebert, ruler of Austrasia and Burgundy, welcomed them, and gave them an old Roman fort at Annegray, in the wooded foothills of the Vosges mountains. They established their first monastery, and many came to join them. Another monastery was established some eight miles away, at Luxeuil, and a third at nearby Fontaines. There Columbanus wrote his Rule and the *Penitential*, modelled on the system at Bennchorr. It was based on the principles of obedience, silence, abstinence, poverty, and chastity, with a strict keeping of the monastic Hours.

He preached in the surrounding villages with much force and conviction, and taught auricular confession and penitence, not then practised in Continental monasteries, and some neighbouring monasteries adopted the practice. Columbanus and his monks maintained the Celtic tonsure, which would have made them look odd in the eyes of the Gallic clergy. They kept to their own monastic organization, annoying the Gallic bishops, who expected to control the monasteries within the boundaries of their dioceses; and they kept the Celtic date of Easter. The Easter question early became a matter of controversy in Gaul, and was debated at the Synod of Mâcon (583) by some fifty bishops.

Columbanus wrote to Pope Gregory the Great in 600, asking for guidance on a number of questions, such as whether deacons or men who had bought their priesthood could become bishops, and what was to be done about monks who left their monastery without permission. Pope Gregory sent a copy of his *Pastoral Care* to 'the priest Columbus' in 591, and commended him to the care of the abbot of Lérins.

Columbanus had a very warm and friendly personality, which made him both human and animal friends. It is said that on one occasion, he was walking in the woods, debating whether he would rather be attacked by men or by animals, and deciding that it would be better to be attacked by animals, because men were capable of sin and animals were not. At this point in his meditations, he was surrounded by a pack of wolves. He stood absolutely still. The wolves snuffled around him for some time, found no cause for alarm, and went away. He turned a bear out of its cave so that he could meditate, but the bear came back, and became his friend. He had a pet squirrel which would jump on to his hand.

With humans, he was less fortunate. Quarrels with Theoderic of Burgundy sparked by Theoderic's grandmother, Brunichild, who was jealous of the influence of the Irish monks, led to their expulsion, though the Frankish monks they had taught were allowed to stay. The Irish party was harried about the kingdom. They went to Tours, praying at St Martin's sepulchre, but were unable to find a place where they could settle anywhere in the conflict-ridden kingdoms of Clovis's successors. Eventually they sailed down the Rhine to Bregenz on Lake Constance, rowing themselves in a small boat. A poem by Columbanus describes the 'wind-driven squalls' and 'despair's dark storms', on what was clearly a desperate journey in the depth of winter.

*Gall remained in what is now Switzerland with some of the party. There is some mystery about the parting between Gall and Columbanus. It seems that Gall was suffering from a fever, and pleaded that he was too ill to travel; but Columbanus thought that he was malingering, and finally pressed on without him. Columbanus and the main party went on to Milan, where they were called to the court of the king and queen of Lombardy. This was to cause some problems, because the royal couple were Arians. The Arian party in the Church, which was then strong on the Continent, held that Christ was the first creation of God, but not co-equal with the Father. Columbanus and his monks were inevitably accused of unorthodox beliefs, though, like all the Celtic monks, they were firmly Trinitarian. Columbanus wrote in some indignation to Gregory the Great's successor, Pope Boniface IV, in 612 or 613, strongly defending the practices of the Celtic Church:

> For we are the disciples of Saints Peter and Paul and all the disciples who by the Holy Spirit wrote the divine canon. No one of us has been a heretic, no one a Jew, no one a schismatic . . . the Catholic faith is maintained unchanged.

Despite her Arian leanings, the queen, Theodolinda, was a devout Christian, and with her support, the Celtic party settled at the ruined church of St Peter at Bobbio, in a pass in the Apennines between Genoa and Piacenza. There Columbanus founded his most celebrated monastery, which was to have a profound effect on monastic development and learning in northern Italy and beyond. Nearly one hundred monasteries strongly influenced by the system at Bobbio have been identified. Jonas, who entered the monastery three years after Columbanus died in 615, was commissioned by the next abbot to write his life. Many people who knew Columbanus were still alive, and contributed. Among them was Gall, to whom he had sent his pastoral staff as a token of forgiveness and friendship.

The church at Bobbio still contains the altar which Columbanus used and his shrine, together with the shrines of three of his staunchest followers, Attala, Bertulf and Cummian. His knife and bell, and a wooden cup said to have been sent to him by Pope Gregory the Great, are kept in the sacristy.

Donat of Fiesole (Donatus) (876), 22 October, lived after the Irish Church had finally accepted Roman jurisdiction, but he is included here because his life illustrates the respect in which the Irish travellers came to be held in Italy. He was a scholar and teacher who became bishop of Fiesole. He left Ireland 'because of the attacks of evil men', probably the Vikings, and went on a pilgrimage to Rome in about 852. On the way home, he and his companions got as far as Fiesole, some five miles north of Florence, when they encountered a crowd debating the election of a new bishop. At that time Fiesole, which is now not much more than a village, was the larger city of the two, and the cathedral seat. After much discussion, Donat found himself elected bishop. Perhaps he was a compromise candidate to whom the crowd turned when unable to agree on a local candidate.

As bishop, he became a powerful landowner with a responsibility for military affairs. He gave his support to Lothair, king of Italy, and his son Louis II, who succeeded him in 844, helping to rally resistance against the Norsemen (who had sailed up the Arno and sacked Fiesole in 825, destroying all the episcopal records) and against the Saracens who were attacking in the south of Italy. He turned out to be a brilliant statesman, adjudicating in a dispute between the bishops of Siena and Arezzo with the king and the pope, and advising the papacy on diplomatic and political issues.

Donat was a trusted courtier, given the right to hold his own court and levy taxes. Under his guidance, Florence became a centre of Irish ecclesiastical scholarship. Louis II carried on the educational work of his father by founding nine major educational establishments, and Donat's school became the nucleus of the University of Florence.

Donat modelled his Latin style on Virgil, and taught both grammar and poetry himself. He also created a centre for Irish pilgrims on their way to Rome, and introduced a devotion to *Brigid of Kildare, which may account for her popularity in Italy. According to his epitaph (which he wrote himself shortly before he died) his episcopacy lasted forty-seven years. He was buried in his cathedral at Fiesole.

Ferghil of Salzburg (Virgil) (784), 27 November, was an 'exile for Christ' who exercised an outstanding ministry for some forty years in Germany, and was finally consecrated as the bishop of Salzburg. It has been suggested that he was educated by *Samthann, chiefly on the grounds that he introduced her cult into the Salzburg diocese. Nothing seems to be known of his Irish antecedents, and he was not the Ferghil who became abbot of Aghaboe, and whose death is recorded in the *Annals of Ulster* in 789, though they have often been confused.

Ferghil went to the Frankish territories in the time of Pippin the Short, and spent two years at Pippin's court. Pippin had been dealing with an insurrection in Bavaria, and when it was quelled, he sent Ferghil as his emissary to the court of Duke Odilo. The mission was a success, and Odilo was converted to Christianity. He made Ferghil abbot of St Peter's monastery, and virtually bishop of Salzburg; but St Boniface (*c.* 675–754), the Wessex missionary who became known as 'the Apostle of Germany', was strongly opposed to his consecration. Boniface, with his noble Anglo-Saxon monks, had evangelized the small German dukedoms all down the Rhine, acquiring influence and authority as far south as Hesse and Thuringia, and in 752, the pope commissioned him as archbishop, with the power to appoint bishops in this territory and beyond. Whether Boniface blocked Ferghil's consecration because of Ferghil's typically Irish disregard of ecclesiastical boundaries or his Celtic practices is not clear, but the grounds of the objection were novel: Boniface sent messages to the pope alleging that Ferghil had unorthodox views on cosmology.

The only evidence available on this unusual debate comes from papal letters to Boniface, and perhaps it is hardly fair to judge Ferghil's concepts from these; but he was said to have believed that there was another world of people under the earth, and another sun and moon ('*quod alius mundus et alii homines sub terra sint, seu sol et luna*'). These ideas were common enough in his day. There were many speculations about what lay beyond the boundaries of the known world. Dante was to develop a somewhat similar theme in his *Purgatorio* in the thirteenth century, though he had the advantage of believing that the world was round, and not flat. Some commentators have suggested that Ferghil was reverting to an ancient Celtic belief in an underground fairyland, but we have only Boniface's view of the matter, mediated through the (probably uncomprehending) papal secretariat in Rome.

Perhaps Rome did not take the matter too seriously, for after Boniface's death in 754, Ferghil was formally consecrated bishop of Salzburg. He is one of the few Irish saints to have been formally canonized. The *Liber Confraternitatis S. Petri Salzburgensis* was compiled at Ferghil's suggestion, and contains the names of a number of Irish saints – including that of Samthann, who was then not widely known on the Continent. St Alcuin of York (735–804), who went to the court of Charlemagne, wrote a poem on the litanies in use in Salzburg and the relics in the cathedral, and this is generally accepted as a better source of information about Ferghil than an unsatisfactory twelfth century Life.

Fiacre of Breuil (Fiachra) (670), 30 August. This Fiacre has to be distinguished from Fiacre of Ullard (8 February). Though comparatively little known in Ireland, he inspired much devotion in France, where both the great seventeenth century ecclesiastical philosopher Bossuet and St Vincent de Paul are known to have made pilgrimages to his tomb. He left Ireland in search of solitude, landed in Normandy, and found his way to Meaux, where the bishop, St Faro, offered him a dwelling in the forest of Breuil, in the province of Brie. There is a story that the bishop offered him as much land as he could turn up in a day, and that instead of digging the soil, he merely turned over the topsoil with his staff – but similar legends are told of a number of other saints, and perhaps the pioneers learned this useful trick from each other.

Fiacre cleared the land, made himself a cell with a garden at the spot which later developed into the village of Saint-Fiacre, Seine et Marne, and became renowned for his skills in growing vegetables, plants and herbs, which is why he became the patron of horticulturists and market gardeners.

It is said that he 'received kindly all that came to him', but this only applied to men. He adamantly refused to meet women, or to allow them within the bounds of his hermitage. Even in the seventeenth century, when Queen Anne of Austria, wife of Louis XIII of France, wished to pay him honour, she stopped at the curtilege, and did not enter, in deference to his views. One story told in France to account for this extreme misogyny (though perhaps only by the strong anti-clerical element) is that he had a venereal disease for which the woman was held to blame, and this set him against all women. So he also became the patron of men with syphilis, and was long invoked for cures.

French hackney carriages became known as *fiacres* because they plied for hire from the Hotel Saint-Fiacre on the rue Saint-Martin in Paris, where his portrait hung over the door in the nineteenth century. The term is still sometimes applied to taxis.

Fintan of Rheinau (878 or 879), 15 November. Fintan was born in Leinster, captured and carried off as a slave to the Orkneys by Vikings. He managed to escape, and spent some two years as a follower of a bishop in Scotland. Then he resolved to make a pilgrimage to Rome to visit the tombs of the Apostles Peter and Paul. On the way back, he encountered a group of hermits on the island of Rheinau in the Rhine near Schaffhausen, and settled there for twenty-two years or more as a solitary.

Fintan has been credited with the compilation of the celebrated *Sacramentary of Zurich*, a Mass Book which is now a treasure of the Zurich City Library, but it is now thought that this was not his work. He certainly owned a copy of the *Sacramentary*, and he added to it a Calendar which contains the names of Irish saints. This may have contributed to the spread of devotion to them along the Rhine valley.

Gall (Gallech or Callech) (*c.* 550–640), 16 October, probably came from Leinster. He was a monk at Bangor under *Comgall and *Columbanus, and went with Columbanus to Gaul. After their expulsion from Gaul, he went with the party led by Columbanus as far as what is now Switzerland, where they encountered a hospitable hermit called Willimon, and acquired land for a monastery at Tuggen, by Lake Zurich, and a smaller site at Bregenz on Lake Constance. At Bregenz, Gall found the people worshipping bronze images, and he broke them in pieces and threw them into the lake. There seems to have been a rift between Columbanus and Gall. Whether it started with fishing (according to the monk Jonas, Columbanus prided himself on his fishing skills, but Gall caught more fish), or whether it was basically a disagreement about their future plans, is uncertain. Columbanus decided to move on to Lombardy, but Gall and a few of the monks stayed. Gall pleaded a fever. One account says Columbanus thought he was malingering, and lacking in obedience. He forbade him to say Mass again while he, Columbanus, lived. Before Columbanus died at Bobbio in 615, he asked for his pastoral staff to be sent to Gall as a sign of forgiveness.

King Sigebert offered Gall a bishopric if he would return to Luxueil, but he stayed in his quiet hermitage. He did not found the monastery of St Gall, which was a later Benedictine foundation. He was never an abbot or a bishop; but he was listed in ancient martyrologies, and his shrine (identified by his unusually large bones) was kept at St Gall until it was destroyed at the time of the Reformation.

In Alsace, folk-myths developed in connection with Gall's feast day, the date of which, 16 October, made it a suitable marker for harvesting. It was the recognized date for bringing cows down from the pasture and stabling them for the winter; the date when the first flakes of snow were expected in mountainous areas; and the right time for picking apples. A French rhyme says,

> *Au jour de saint Gall, crac!*
> *La pomme doit être au sac.*

Gunifort of Pavia (?eighth century), 22 or 26 August. The body of Gunifort or Bonifort, 'accoutred in the uniform of a soldier, pierced with arrows, and enclosed in a superb urn', lies in the church of St Gervase and St Protus in Pavia. He and his brother Gunibald, with two sisters whose names are not recorded, are said to be Irish (*genere Scotii*). They had been persecuted in their own country, and went to the Continent as missionaries. All four witnessed to their faith in Germany. The sisters were killed there, and Gunibald was beheaded. Gunifort, mortally wounded, escaped to Pavia. He was cared for by a pious matron, but died three days after his arrival.

This story raises two immediate questions. If the four were Irish, why do the only names we have sound Anglo-Saxon? And what persecutions were they taking flight from? There were no religious persecutions in Ireland. A possible answer to the first question is that the group had been carrying out their mission in Germany, and may have adopted or been given new names there because their own were unpronounceable. A possible answer to the second is that, though there was no specifically religious persecution in Ireland, there were other kinds of violence: they may have been escaping from clan warfare, or from raids by the Norsemen.

Mgr Tommasini comments that all we have is a body in a shrine, the remains of an unknown *pellegrino* who, like most of his kind, was probably Irish.

Kilian (Cilian, Chilian) of Würzburg (?689), 8 July, may have come from Mullagh, where the church bears his dedication, but nothing is known for certain until he arrived with a party of eleven monks at the mouth of the Rhine. He sailed up the Main to Würzburg, where he converted the local ruler, Duke Gozbert, and then visited Pope Conon in Rome at some time in his brief pontificate (686–7).

Kilian spent two years in Rome. He returned to find a very difficult situation in Würzburg. While he had been away, Duke Gozbert had married his brother's widow, which was then against canon law. Kilian denounced both duke and duchess, and assassins (employed it is said by the duchess) killed him and two monks, Colman and Totnan or Dothan.

In 752, Kilian's relics were solemnly translated to Würzburg cathedral by the Anglo-Saxon St Burchard, and a cult developed. Kilian appears in the *Martyrology of Tallaght*, so the story was evidently taken back to Ireland, and hymns and folk-songs were composed in honour of the saint who sacrificed his life by upholding canon law.

Pellegrino (?seventh or eighth centuries), feast day unknown, is described in a document dated 1 August 1110 in the archives of the diocese of Lucca. His full title is Pellegrino delle Alpe di Garfagnano. This 'St Pilgrim' is said to have been the son of a Christian king named Romanus. He renounced the throne, gave his wealth to the poor, and went to the Holy Land. After visiting the Holy Places, he spent forty years in the desert, and then went to preach at the court of the Sultan. He was scourged and imprisoned, but managed to escape and reached Italy. He lived in a hollow tree, high in a pass in the Apennines on the border between Tuscany and Lombardy.

There he eventually died at the age of 97 years, 9 months and 23 days.

While the details of this story are fairly obviously fictional, the outlines may well be true. There were rich young men who renounced their heritage and set out for the Holy Land. Most of them were Irish. A number of them seem to have stayed in Italy as hermits rather than going home. Tommasini estimates that he has identified twenty with no name other than *San Pellegrino* in northern Italy alone.

Ursus (?late sixth century), 1 February, was an Irishman who settled in the Val d'Aosta in northern Italy, and preached against the Arians (see *Columbanus). He built a collegiate church of St Peter, and was known as 'the Apostle of the Valdostani'. He probably adopted Roman practices in the matter of the tonsure and the date of Easter, because he was appointed archdeacon of Aosta, and was clearly acceptable to the diocese.

The city of Aosta has a gate known as the *Porto di San Orso*, and until the seventeenth century, there was a hospital of the same name, which finally fell into disuse. The church remains, and is now dedicated in the names of St Peter and St Ursus. Ursus distributed wooden clogs to the poor, and the clergy of his foundation kept up this practice for centuries after his death. A market in wooden utensils and implements has traditionally been held on the site.

Ursus founded churches along the valley of the Cogne on a Roman road, and his name is well known in the Hautes Alpes. 'Ursus' is probably a nickname: there were bears in the mountains in his time.

9

Northumbria and Anglo-Saxon England

The Celtic foundations in Anglo-Saxon England were the last missions of the Celtic Church to be established, and the first to yield to the jurisdiction of Rome. The mission from Iona lasted only thirty years – from the time when *Aidan brought the Columban Rule to Lindisfarne in 635 to the time of the Synod of Whitby; but in that time it extended far beyond the kingdom of Northumbria into central and eastern Britain, made Celtic monks of Anglo-Saxons as well as Irish immigrants, and established a high reputation for learning and evangelism. It also brought the Celtic Church into direct confrontation with the power of Rome. At the Synod of Whitby, the two sides met in a dramatic climax, and the Celtic cause was lost.

The story is told in considerable detail (though with divided loyalties) by the Venerable Bede. 'Venerable' means respected, and does not refer to his age. He was an old man when he wrote his *Ecclesiastical History*, but when he was young, he must have had first-hand knowledge of the bitterness and turmoil which followed the decision that the Northumbrian monasteries should accept the Roman jurisdiction. He was born in 673, and entered the monastery at Monkwearmouth (a sister foundation to Jarrow) at the age of seven. He was taught to condemn those who 'failed to keep the correct date of Easter'; but he was a Northumbrian, and an intelligent observer. He must have met many older monks who found obedience to Rome hard, because their hearts were still with Celtic values and Celtic practices. Bede saw the issues quite clearly. He writes:

Aidan, who was the first bishop [of Lindisfarne], was a monk,

Northumbria and the South

and had always lived according to monastic rule . . . hence all the bishops of that place (Iona) exercise their episcopal functions in such a way that the abbot, who they themselves have chosen by the advice of the brethren, rule the monastery, and all the priests, deacons, singers and readers, and the other ecclesiastical grades, together with the bishop, keep the monastic rule in all things.

Though Bede knew this, he wrote in the Roman idiom, not the Celtic idiom, referring to Celtic abbots as bishops, and assuming areas of episcopal jurisdiction similar to those of the Roman Church, though he must have known that they did not exist in the Celtic Church. He is a good and conscientious historian, and he strives to be fair, but he cannot accept the Celtic frame of reference, because he had been taught from his early years not only that it was out-dated, but that it was morally wrong.

How the kingdom of Northumbria came to accept the Celtic way of faith, and how it later rejected it at the Synod of Whitby, is one of the great stories of the Church in the British Isles.

In the seventh century, Christian mission was still primarily a matter of converting pagan kings or chieftains. If they and their households accepted Christian baptism, the nobles and all their followers automatically followed suit. Angles and Saxons had migrated to Britain in large numbers, settled, and coalesced into five major kingdoms: Kent, the kingdom of the West Saxons, the kingdom of the East Saxons, Mercia and Northumbria. Of these, Northumbria was the largest.

The first Christian missionaries from Rome were sent by Pope Gregory the Great in 597. Gregory was an enthusiast, and a planner. He had petitioned his predecessor for permission to lead the mission himself, and only his own election to the pontificate prevented him from doing so. The story that he saw some fair-haired Christian slaves in the market in Rome, and that this was the inspiration behind his plans, was widely current in the Middle Ages, and may have some truth behind it. He is said to have commented, '*Non Angli sed angeli*', and when told that they came from Deira, said that he would rescue them *de ira* – from the wrath of God. This is precisely the kind of word-play which Gregory indulged in – like *Samson of Dol and many other clerics of the time, he saw divine instructions where later generations would see only an accidental similarity in word-forms. Gregory took a leading part in formulating the plans for the mission, dividing the territory of the Angles and Saxons into two provinces, Canterbury and York, each with twelve dioceses. So little was known about this distant and pagan land that the only maps available in Rome were those which had been drawn up before the withdrawal of the Roman legions nearly two hundred years earlier.

The mission consisted of some thirty or forty Italian monks, led by Augustine, prior of Gregory's own monastery of St Andrew-on-the-Coelian-Hill in Rome. He was perhaps not the most flexible of leaders for such an enterprise. He had already acted as the papal representative in Constantinople, where he refused to learn Greek, and insisted on conversing with the Eastern clergy only in Latin. That enterprise had not been a success. Now he and his party regarded the prospect of going to the former Britannia with frank horror. Bede says that they 'were appalled at the idea of going to a fierce and pagan nation, of whose very language they were ignorant'. They took a ship as far as Marseilles, but when they landed in Frankish territory, their hearts failed them, and Augustine went back to Rome to ask Gregory to call off the mission. The pope ordered him back, commending the party to the bishop of Arles, and eventually they crossed France and reached the English Channel. They would have learned a good deal about Kent and London from merchants in the trading ports there, and they were able to begin negotiations with Ethelbert, king of Kent.

Ethelbert was the *bretwalda* or overlord of eastern England as far north as the Humber. He had married a Frankish princess named Bertha, who was a Christian, and one of the conditions of the marriage was that she should be free to keep her own faith. With her had come a Frankish bishop, Ludhiard, and attendant clergy. They worshipped in an old church, St Martin's, Canterbury, which had been built during the Roman occupation, but Ethelbert remained a pagan. He agreed to receive the Roman mission, but he was apprehensive. He insisted that his meeting with them should take place in the open air, since he was fearful that they would exercise magical arts against him (magical arts were believed only to be effective in closed spaces). Evidently Bishop Ludhiard had not succeeded in teaching him much about Christianity.

The meeting took place on the Isle of Thanet. The monks approached the royal party 'carrying a silver cross as their standard, and the likeness of our Lord and Saviour painted on a board'. Augustine preached through his Frankish interpreters, the monks sang a litany, and the king received them hospitably, offering them a house in Canterbury and provisions. There they settled, worshipping in St Martin's, and eventually the king and his court were converted and baptized.

Stage One of Pope Gregory's plan had been achieved. Augustine went back to Arles to be consecrated 'archbishop of the English nation'. The pope sent him many detailed instructions about how to proceed, and in 601 granted him the *pallium*, the traditional lamb's-wool collar confirming his status as archbishop, with a second group of clergy. The leader of the second party was Paulinus. Though the mission in Kent became well established, it did not grow as quickly as Pope Gregory had hoped. A separate mission was sent to Wessex in 635, under Birinus, and though the East Saxons accepted Christianity, and there was a bishop of London (then wholly on the north bank of the Thames), much of East Anglia, the Midlands and the north remained pagan. There was Celtic Christianity in Wales and western Scotland, but it was of an unfamiliar kind, organized on monastic lines, and owing no allegiance to Rome. Augustine attempted to come to terms with the Welsh abbots, whom Bede calls 'the British bishops' (see Chapter 5), but they withdrew, offended at what they regarded as his lack of courtesy and proper Christian humility. About 605, his successor, Laurence, 'sought to extend his pastoral care to the original inhabitants of Britain, and to the Irish of Ireland'. He wrote to the Irish clergy, complaining about the unsociable behaviour of Bishop Dagan, who refused to eat with Roman clergy (see p. 45), and the activities of *Columbanus in Gaul, and he also sent a 'dignified letter' to the 'British bishops', urging them to accept Catholic unity; but he received no encouragement from either. If he was writing to bishops under the impression that they were superior to abbots, and hectoring both groups about the 'correct date of Easter', this is hardly surprising. It was a dialogue of the deaf.

The claim that the archbishop of Canterbury was 'archbishop of the British nation' had not been fulfilled, and it was not until some twenty years later that an opportunity occurred for expansion to the north. The means, as in Kent, was a royal marriage. In 625, King Edwin of Northumbria wished to make an alliance with Kent and the East Saxons, whose territory stretched up to the Humber, for security against the fearsome Penda of Mercia. The alliance was to be sealed by a marriage which made the two parties kin. Edwin, who was a widower, proposed to marry Ethelburga, a Christian princess of Kent. He was told that 'it was not permissible for a Christian maiden to be given in marriage to a heathen husband, lest the Christian faith and sacraments be profaned by her association with a king who was wholly ignorant of the worship of the true God'.

Edwin seems to have been a reasonable man. He agreed that Ethelburga and her court should have complete freedom of worship in their own manner, and also to accept the Christian faith 'if on examination, his advisers decided that it appeared more holy and acceptable to God than their own'. Paulinus and his clergy accompanied the princess and her court on her journey north. They must have worked very hard. Bede says that Edwin 'found it difficult to bend his proud mind to accept the humility of the way of salvation, or to acknowledge the mystery of the life-giving Cross'. The task took two years, but in 627, the king and all his household were baptized, including the young *Hilda. Edwin's arch-Druid, Coifi, is said to have become so convinced a Christian that he took a lead in destroying his own temples. Paulinus was consecrated as bishop of York – Eboracum, the old Roman capital of the north.

Pope Honorius I sent a letter of approval and encouragement to King Edwin, and granted Paulinus a status equal in authority to that of Augustine in the south. A wooden church was built at York, and the walls of a more permanent stone building in the Continental manner were beginning to rise round it six years later. Then disaster struck: Edwin was attacked by a coalition between two pagan kings, Penda of Mercia and Cadwalla of Wales, and killed in battle. In a gruesome gesture of hatred, the invaders left his head for the survivors to find in his church at York. Many thousands of Northumbrians were massacred by Cadwalla and his forces. The queen and her court, with Paulinus and his clergy, escaped by sea, sailing back to Kent. Paulinus never came north again. He stayed in the south, and became bishop of Rochester.

A year later, the Christian prince *Oswald of Northumbria defeated the invaders at Hexham, and took the throne. He became master of Bernicia (roughly covering present-day Northumbria and the Scottish Lowlands) and Deira (roughly equivalent to the four counties of Yorkshire). He was also overlord of the Scottish kingdoms of Dalriada (Galloway and Dumfries) and Pictland. Christianity was re-established; but this time it was 'Irish' Christianity, not the Roman version. Oswald, exiled as a child, had spent his formative years in exile on Iona, and he sent for a mission from Iona, not from Canterbury. *Aidan of Iona headed the new mission – and significantly, made his headquarters not in the old Roman capital of York, but on the deserted island of Lindisfarne, opposite the king's castle at Bamburgh, over a hundred miles further north. His monastery (a ramshackle affair by Roman standards) became the centre of wide-ranging missions.

The arrival of the Celtic monks in Northumbria must have caused alarm in Rome. Pope Honorius I was strongly opposed to the Celtic system, and a letter which he sent to the clergy of Ireland in 633 is frankly contemptuous:

> He earnestly warned them not to imagine that their little community, isolated at the uttermost ends of the earth, had a wisdom exceeding that of all churches ancient and modern throughout the world, and he urged them not to keep a different Easter, contrary to paschal calculations and the synodical decrees of all the bishops in the world.

The travelling Irish monks on the Continent, with their disregard of the authority of bishops and their curious haircuts, were only a comparatively minor irritant; but the establishment of this 'little community' in the former Roman province of Britannia, replacing the pope's own appointed bishop to whom he had sent full authority, was a very different matter. Northumbria was a large and powerful kingdom. Monasteries were set up there, and became centres of learning – notably the great double monastery at Whitby, where Hilda, a member of the royal house, became abbess, presiding over the training of the next generation of missionary monks. Northumbrian influence spread in central Britain. By the mid-650s, Mercia and East Anglia had both made alliances with Northumbria, and both accepted missions from Lindisfarne, led by *Cedd, which had a considerable success. An Irish monk named *Fursey founded a monastery in East Anglia, near modern Yarmouth, and some of his monks carried out missions as far south as modern Chichester. The influence of Celtic Christianity spread to all parts of the British Isles. The Roman clergy of the Canterbury province came face to face with these strange monks from 'the uttermost ends of the earth' who simply ignored Rome's peremptory claims to primacy.

In Ireland, the Great Paschal Controversy was raging. In 621, *Cumian Fota, abbot of Durrow, had taken a group of Celtic clergy to Rome, and came back convinced that the Celtic Church should submit to Roman authority. He was rebuked for this view by Segene, abbot of Iona, and other senior abbots, and Segene wrote to the pope, defending the Celtic system, and asking for tolerance. He pointed out that the followers of the Celtic Rite and the followers of the Roman Rite were all Christians, and he pleaded that they might co-exist without bitterness.

The answer from Rome was a decided negative. Successive popes wrote to bishops and abbots in Ireland and Iona (evidently

Celtic Cross at Stonegrave Minster, North Yorkshire

still unable to comprehend the very different structure of the Celtic Church), urging them to give up their unorthodox system; but, though some monasteries in southern Ireland accepted Roman jurisdiction, the northern Irish monasteries, Iona, and the developing Celtic Church in Britain still held out for their own distinctive system.

As abbot of Lindisfarne, Aidan had the friendship and support of King Oswald. On Oswald's death, the kingdom of Northumbria was again divided, between Oswy of Bernicia and *Oswin of Deira. Oswin was also close to Aidan, but Oswy and Oswin came close to war, and in 651, Oswin was killed by Oswy's men. The news of Oswin's death may have contributed to Aidan's own death only a few days later. Oswy then took over Deira, re-uniting Northumbria. With that military and political coup, and Aidan's death, the situation changed radically.

Oswy was a Celtic Christian, but his queen, Enfleda, was a daughter of Edwin. She had been baptized by Paulinus with the rest of his household, and retained her allegiance to the papacy and the Roman jurisdiction. The result was that the clergy of the king's court were Celtic, while the clergy of the queen's court were Roman. It was this problem which led to the final confrontation of the two systems at Whitby in 664.

Aidan (651), 31 August, led the second expedition of Celtic monks to Northumbria. Bede tells how the first expedition was a failure. It was a considerable undertaking, because it involved taking the Columban Rule to Angle-land, part of the former Roman province of Britannia, and to non-Celtic peoples. Though *Oswald, the young king, had lived on Iona during his exile, and followed the practices of the Celtic Church, it was a new kind of mission. The first leader, 'a man of austere disposition', returned to Iona to tell the community that the English were 'an ungovernable people of an obstinate and barbarous temperament'. The monastic system he urged upon them was too rigorous for the Northumbrian laity; and perhaps language had something to do with his problems, for the Iona monks spoke Irish and wrote Latin, while the Northumbrians spoke only their own Germanic tongue. At the community meeting where the matter was discussed, the monks sat in silence until Aidan spoke up, saying that the missioners had been too harsh with these unfamiliar people, and that they should have given them 'the milk of simple teaching' rather than the rigours of the monastic rule. He was sent in charge of the second mission in 635.

Oswald probably already knew Aidan from his time on Iona. The two became firm friends. Oswald understood that the monks must have a place of solitude for prayer and meditation, and assisted them in building their simple huts and oratory on Lindisfarne, now known as Holy Island, two miles from the mainland, but accessible on foot at low tide. They were within sight of Bamburgh, the small walled city where the king had his castle, and under the protection of his forces. Aidan would dine with the king, eating sparely, and then withdraw across the causeway to his own quiet place. When he went on missions in the surrounding countryside, the king, who was bilingual after his period of exile, often went with him, translating for him until he had mastered the new language for himself.

Aidan was a sociable man, who liked to travel on foot, and spoke to anyone he met. He took the gospel to rich and poor alike, telling them to say their prayers and to follow Christ's commandments; but if wealthy and powerful people did wrong, he was outspoken in reproving them. He used the money he was given by the nobility to ransom slaves, mostly war captives, and send them home again. He founded churches and monastic schools on the mainland, and started a school of his own for twelve boys, two of whom were the brothers *Cedd and *Chad. He kept in touch with the hermits who came to settle in the Farne Islands, further out in the North Sea than Lindisfarne. He encouraged women in the religious life, visiting small communities regularly, and acting as friend and spiritual director to *Hilda, who eventually became abbess of the double monastery at Whitby. He was strongly opposed to slavery, and spent much time and effort in ransoming captives and sending them to their homeland.

Penda of Mercia ravaged the Northumbrian countryside, destroying villages and ordering the beams and thatched roofs from the houses to be stripped and piled against the stone walls of

Bamburgh before being set on fire. Aidan saw the smoke and the flames from Lindisfarne, and prayed for his friends. The wind changed, and the city was saved.

Aidan was at Lindisfarne for sixteen years in all, nine with Oswald, who died in 642, and seven with *Oswin of Deira and Oswy of Bernicia after the kingdom was subdivided. Though he stayed at Lindisfarne, he seems to have had a much closer relationship with Oswin than with Oswy, across the causeway in Bamburgh. The two kings became enemies, and in the summer of 651, they came close to battle. Oswin, realizing that Oswy's forces were stronger than his, disbanded his army at Catterick, and headed back towards York. He was killed in an ambush by Oswy's men on 20 August. Aidan died only eleven days later, on 31 August. He is said to have died standing up and leaning against a post in a royal residence near Bamburgh. Possibly he had just heard the news of Oswin's death at Oswy's court, and the shock killed him. The culmination of the rivalry between the two kings in the murder of Oswin must have been an event he had worked and prayed long and hard to avoid.

Bede, who greatly respected Aidan, says of him, 'He never sought or cared for any worldly possessions, and loved to give away to the poor who chanced to meet him whatever he received from the king and wealthy folk.' When Aidan died, he had no personal possessions except his church and a few fields round it. His body was taken back to Iona for burial, but his frugal lifestyle, his generosity and his gentle holiness left an enduring mark on the Church in Northumbria.

Begga (Begha, Begu, Bez, Bee) (*fl*. 680), 31 October, is said to have been an Irish girl, who went to Northumbria and was consecrated as a virgin by *Aidan. According to the *Breviary of Aberdeen*, she ruled a small community and handed it over to the abbess *Hilda of Whitby after praying to be freed from the burden of government. In some reference books, her date of death is given as 660, but Bede mentions her as a younger nun, one of the community at Hackness in North Yorkshire, some thirteen miles from Whitby, who had a vision of Hilda's death on the night when it occurred in 680.

Melvyn Bragg's novel *Credo*, of which Begga is the heroine, gives her a part in the great events of 664 at Hilda's monastery. The real Begga is thought not to be the Irish nun for whom St Bee's Head, Cumbria, is named.

Boisil (Boswell) (*c.* 661), 23 February, trained in Ireland, and went to the monastery at Melrose, on the banks of the Tweed. As prior of Melrose, he became *Cuthbert's teacher. He had a great knowledge of the Scriptures and was an enthusiastic and effective missioner. Cuthbert accompanied him on many of his journeys in the locality, and became greatly attached to him. When he heard that Boisil had caught the plague, he went to him and stayed with him, ignoring the risk. Together they read St John's Gospel until Boisil was too ill to read any longer. Cuthbert caught the plague, but recovered, and after Boisil's death, he was elected his successor.

Bede refers to Boisil as 'a priest of great virtues and prophetic spirit' and as 'God's beloved priest'. The town of Boswell in Roxburghshire bears his name, as did several churches on the Scottish border until the time of the Reformation. Part of his eighth century shrine is kept at Jedburgh.

Caedmon (680), 11 February, was a cowherd on the estates of the monastery at Whitby who was discovered to have a gift for composing sacred poetry and songs. His story gives a revealing picture of the monastery at work, and the quality of its theological teaching.

Caedmon told the steward of his visions, and the steward told the abbess *Hilda. The abbess saw the cowherd, and asked him if he wished to become a monk. When he agreed, she directed that he should be received into the clergy school, and such was the quality of his spiritual understanding that 'his teachers became his hearers'. Whitby was a royal monastery, and the community's willing reception of one of their own illiterate labourers not merely as a monk but as a teacher says much about their openness to the Holy Spirit.

It seems unlikely that Caedmon ever learned enough Latin to

compose in that language, but he composed in the vernacular (perhaps with the help of scribes) a volume of poetry on biblical and sacred themes, and the monastery praised God for his gifts.

Bede says that he 'stored up in his memory all that he was taught, and like one of the clean animals chewing the cud, turned it into such melodious verse that his delightful readings turned his instructors into auditors'. The account of what Caedmon was taught indicates thorough biblical teaching in the clergy school:

> He sang of the creation of the world, and the whole story of Genesis. He sang of Israel's exodus from Egypt, the entry into the Promised Land . . . the Lord's Incarnation, Passion, Resurrection and Ascension into heaven, the coming of the Holy Spirit, and the teaching of the Apostles. He also made poems on the terrors of the Last Judgement, the horrible pains of hell, and the joys of the Kingdom of Heaven.

It was chiefly through Bede's account of him that Caedmon became known as 'the father of English poetry' though nearly all his work has been lost, and many of the poems later attributed to him were written by others. Only one fragment has been recognized as authentic:

> Now we must praise the ruler of heaven,
> The might of the Lord and his purpose of mind,
> The work of the glorious father.
> For he, God eternal, established each wonder,
> He, holy creator, first fashioned the heavens
> As a roof for the children of earth.
> And then our guardian, the everlasting God,
> Adorned this middle earth for men.
> Praise the almighty king of heaven!

Caedmon's songs were used for evangelism among the laity, who knew no Latin. Bede went to the monastery at Monkwearmouth as a boy in the year Caedmon died at Whitby. He must have heard much about the gifted cowherd who became a monk, and probably sang his songs. Caedmon's gift must have appealed to the Irish bardic heritage of the Lindisfarne monks, and his compositions made their teaching easier. In an age when most people were unlettered, the elements of the faith had to be memorized, and the regular metre of his poetry made it much easier to remember than prose.

Cedd (Cedda) (664), 26 October, and his brother *Chad, were among *Aidan's first twelve boys at Lindisfarne. They had at least two younger brothers who also became Celtic priests. Cedd was sent to head a mission to Mercia in 653 when Peada, Penda's successor as king of Mercia, accepted Northumbrian overlordship, and asked for a mission from Lindisfarne to evangelize his people. *Finan, Aidan's successor as abbot of Lindisfarne, baptized Peada, and Cedd headed a team of four priests who were so successful in Mercia that Sigbert, king of the East Angles, also asked for a mission.

Like Northumbria, the kingdom of the East Angles was large and unwieldy. To the south of its territory was the kingdom of the East Saxons, which stretched south to the Thames. London, then wholly on the north bank of the Thames, was its major city. Like Northumbria, this kingdom had received a Roman mission which had failed. While Augustine was archbishop of Canterbury, the East Saxons acknowledged Ethelbert of Kent as their *bretwalda* or overlord. Mellitus had been consecrated bishop of London with full papal approval, and the first St Paul's was his church; but after the death of the Christian king in 616, the pagan princes demanded the 'white bread' of the Eucharist, which they believed to have magical properties, but refused to be baptized. Mellitus was driven out, and the Roman clergy had been unable to re-establish the diocese.

Cedd and his colleagues came into this territory from the north, avoiding the Roman bishopric of London; but they established Celtic monasteries in the Thames estuary, at Tilbury and Bradwell-on-Sea. They carried out preaching tours, built churches, and ordained many priests. Cedd was consecrated by the Celtic Rite as missionary bishop of the East Saxons. The activities of his clergy inevitably brought them into direct confrontation with the Roman clergy of London and southern Britain, and caused concern in papal circles.

Cedd's brother Caelin was chaplain to the sub-king of Deira, and Cedd himself was one of the influential seniors of the Lindisfarne community. On one of his visits to Lindisfarne, he was offered land for a monastery in Northumbria. He chose a site 'among some high and remote hills, which seemed more suitable for the dens of robbers and haunts of wild beasts than for human habitation' at what is now Lastingham in North Yorkshire. He purified the site by spending Lent there alone in prayer and fasting. Each day, Bede tells us, he took only 'a morsel of bread, a hen's egg and watered milk'; but ten days before Easter, he was called urgently back to court, and he left another brother, Cynibil, to complete the fast for him.

At the Synod of Whitby, Cedd acted as an interpreter between the Roman party and King Oswy and his noblemen, who spoke only the Northumbrian dialect. The Synod took place in September, and in November, he caught the plague, which was still raging in Northumbria. He went back to Lastingham to die, and some of his monks, who had gone there to be with their father in God, also caught the plague, and died with him. After his death, Chad took over the monastery.

Finan of Lindisfarne (661), 17 February, was *Aidan's successor as abbot of Lindisfarne. Bede says that he was 'learned and prudent'. He was a staunch upholder of the Columban Rule of Iona, and sent *Cedd and other monks as missionaries to Mercia and the kingdom of the East Saxons. He built a wooden church on Lindisfarne, constructed of oak, with a roof 'thatched with reeds after the Irish manner'. It seems that Aidan's other-worldliness had been so great (and perhaps his link with *Oswald so strong) that he had not embarked on this task. It must have become increasingly necessary for the monks to have a place of worship of their own during Oswy's reign, when the Lindisfarne monks no longer had the same close link with the king, and the queen Enfleda and her court followed the Latin Rite.

In response to pressure from the queen and her advisers, Finan agreed to allow Wilfrid, who was one of his monks, to go to Rome and explore contacts with the papacy. Bede calls Finan 'a hot-tempered man whom reproof made more obstinate'. With hindsight, one can see that the abbot's position was a very difficult one. Personal loyalty to Aidan, who died in 651, and was universally beloved, must have concealed tensions both in the monastery and in the court which came to the surface after his sudden death; and Finan faced mounting hostility from the queen's court.

Finan struggled for ten years, supporting his missionaries in their work in the Midlands and East Anglia, and finding his rule at Lindisfarne increasingly threatened. He died before the Synod of Whitby was convened. Possibly the Roman party waited until after his death before embarking on the final confrontation, for he was a doughty opponent, and perhaps more learned than *Colman, who succeeded him.

Fursey (Fursa) (650), 16 January, founded a monastery in Ireland, but left it because the crowds who flocked to see him disturbed his devotions. With two companions, Dicul and Maeldubh, he set out for the land of the Angles and Saxons about 630 or soon after, as 'a pilgrim for Christ'. Presumably he knew of the Roman mission under St Augustine in 597, but neither the Roman mission nor the mission from Lindisfarne had reached East Anglia by the time he arrived. Fursey made contact with King Sigbert of the East Anglians, who had been an exile in Gaul.

Sigbert must have been aware of the differences between Celtic and Roman practices, because he also welcomed a Burgundian bishop named Felix, who died in 647. Felix established a Roman diocese named Dunwich, but this has now disappeared under the North Sea as a result of coastal erosion. All the records were lost, and the only remaining trace of his mission is the name of the port of Felixstowe. Sigbert seems to have thought that there was room for both Celtic and Roman missioners in his large, predominantly pagan, kingdom. He gave Fursey land at Burgh Castle, near modern Yarmouth, where he founded a small monastery. Fursey and his community stayed there for twelve years, following the

Celtic Rite. Felix was a faithful missioner, and evidently tolerant about the Celtic monks and their ways. The Roman clergy who came to the area respected Fursey for his devotion and his visions: he was given to sitting out in the biting East Anglian winds wearing only a thin shirt, and sweating with the power of his spiritual experiences. Bede says of him:

> There came out of Ireland a holy man called Fursa, renowned both for his words and actions, and remarkable for his singular virtues, being desirous to live like a stranger for our Lord, wherever an opportunity should offer . . . he saw the angels chanting in heaven, and a vision of hell in which he saw four fires – the fire of falsehood, the fire of covetousness, the fire of discord and the fire of iniquity.

When Sigbert was killed by the pagan Penda of Mercia, Fursey and some of his monks went to the Frankish kingdom of Neustria. He left one of his brothers, Foillan, in charge of the Norfolk monastery, and at least one other Irish monk, Ultan (not Ultan of Arbraccan), went to join him. In Neustria, Fursey had the protection of Echinoald, the mayor of the palace, and established a new monastery at Lagny-sur-Marne.

After Fursey's death, Echinoald had his body translated to Péronne, which became known as *Perrona Scottorum* (Péronne of the Irish) and a great centre for Irish monks on the Continent. Ultan went there, and became abbot. Fursey's shrine is said to have been the work of St Eloi (Eligius, *c.* 588–660), a celebrated metalworker who also made the shrines of St Denys of Paris and St Martin of Tours.

Of Fursey's companions, something is known of the activities of Dicul and Maeldubh. Dicul (Dicuill, Deicola) (625), 18 April, went on to evangelize the South Saxons, and founded a monastery at Bosham, near Chichester, with five or six monks. Later Wilfrid of Ripon, during his travels, discovered this small group of Celtic monks still keeping to their old ways in what by then was solidly Romanized territory. Dicul has suffered from confusion with Deicolus or Desle (18 January), who went with *Columbanus as far as France, and stayed there to found the abbey of Lure. Maeldubh went to Wessex, and founded a monastery at Malmesbury, where St Aldhelm (639–709) is said to have studied for a time.

Though little appears to be known about the work of these small Celtic groups in the Anglo-Saxon kingdoms, their existence does suggest that some attempt was made at evangelism from Ireland, and that the Roman clergy may have encountered Celtic monks quite early in their own mission.

Hilda (614–80), 17 November, was of the royal house of King Edwin of Northumbria, the daughter of his nephew Hereric. She was baptized with his household by Paulinus of York when she was thirteen years old, but grew up in the Northumbrian court of *Oswald, in the Celtic tradition.

Bede says that she lived to be sixty-six years old, and that her life was divided into two equal parts – thirty-three years in which she lived the life of a Christian noblewoman, much given to charitable work, and thirty-three years in the monastic life. She intended to join her sister Hereswitha, who had entered the royal monastery of Chelles in the Frankish kingdom, but she was still on the first stage of her journey when *Aidan called her back, and persuaded her to stay in Northumbria. He seems to have under-taken her spiritual direction personally, and with much care, making regular pastoral visits to her and her companions. She spent a year with a few young women in a place on the banks of the river Wear, following the Columban Rule, before he sent her to become abbess of a small monastery at Hartlepool. After several years during which she was 'instructed by learned men' she was sent to found a double monastery at Whitby. Double monasteries headed by noblewomen (who often had experience of administering large estates) were not uncommon on the Continent at this time: the pattern was followed in a number of Benedictine houses. The nuns were enclosed, and spent their lives in prayer and study, while the monks celebrated the Eucharist, heard confessions, and dealt with external relations. In some, the monks laboured in the fields, did all the heavy work, and provided subsistence for the nuns. In others, the heavy labour was carried out by serfs, as it sometimes was in Ireland; but Hilda's monks were scholars, and her monastery had no serfs. She had a paid work-force. The monastery at Whitby was economically self-sufficient. It employed many artisans and craftsmen – stone-masons, builders, blacksmiths, wheelwrights, fishermen, hunts-men, shepherds and others, so that Hilda was responsible for a large work-force as well as for the management of a monastic institution.

There was a theological school at Whitby, and its students included five future bishops. The monastery had its own great library. Copying manuscripts was a major activity for the monks and nuns, the tanners providing the vellum and the beekeepers providing the wax for writing-pads and candles. Manuscripts were borrowed from other monasteries, and a remarkable library was built up, including all the New Testament and much of the Old Testament in Jerome's version.

Hilda accepted the Roman jurisdiction after the Synod of Whitby in obedience, but found it hard (see Chapter 10). She remained as abbess for a further sixteen years. She was ill for the last seven years of her life, suffering from an undulant fever and increasingly severe internal pains. It is thought that she may have been suffering from tuberculosis. Bede says that she taught her community 'to serve God obediently when in health, and to render thanks to him faithfully when in pain or bodily weakness' until 'she joyfully welcomed death, or rather, in the words of our Lord, passed from death into life'.

Oswald (604–42), 5 August, whom Bede calls 'the most Christian king of Northumbria', was exiled as a boy during the reign of Edwin. He spent seven formative years on Iona, and returned in 634 to claim his throne a convinced and practising Christian of the Celtic Rite. On the night before battle with the invading forces of Penda of Mercia and Cadwalla of Wales, he set up a cross, and called on his troops to pray for victory. They were probably mainly pagan at that time, but his action had a profound effect. Cadwalla, a heathen who was responsible for massacres and burning villages, was killed at Hexham, and Penda's forces were driven out.

After he secured his throne, Oswald united the kingdoms of Bernicia and Deira under his rule. He sent to Iona for a mission, and after a false start, welcomed *Aidan and his party of monks, giving them Lindisfarne, close to his own castle at Bamburgh, as a monastic base. He and Aidan were personal friends, and he gave the monks every support possible. He had learned the Irish language during his time on Iona, and often accompanied Aidan on his preaching journeys on the Northumbrian mainland, interpreting for him. He was killed in battle against Penda at Maserfield, Shropshire, in 642 at the age of thirty-eight.

Oswald was a devout man, generous to the sick and the poor. He subsequently became a national folk-hero, celebrated as a warrior-saint and a martyr, and inspired many church dedications. There is a painting of him by Tiepolo in the National Gallery in London.

Oswin (651), 5 August, king of Deira, was of the royal line of Edwin, and cousin to *Oswald and his brother Oswy. Bede says that Oswin was 'a man of very handsome appearance and lofty stature, pleasant in speech and courteous in manner, a man of great holiness and piety'. Bede gives a vivid description of the occasion on which Oswin tried to persuade *Aidan to accept the gift of a horse. He says that, though Aidan usually travelled on foot, the king thought he might need a horse in emergencies, for long journeys, or to cross rivers. (One can almost hear the king arguing his case.) The horse was a splendid beast, with rich trappings. Aidan gave it to the first beggar who came along asking for alms. When Oswin, exasperated, asked why he had done this, Aidan asked him if the foal of a mare meant more to him than a child of God. They went in to dinner, and the king, who had been hunting all day, stood warming himself by the fire, turning over in his mind what Aidan had said. Then he unbuckled his sword and knelt before Aidan, asking his forgiveness, and saying that he would never refer to the matter again. Aidan immediately stood up and raised the king, assuring him that he had a high regard for him, and that he must sit down to his food without further regrets. Oswin 'sat down and began to be merry', but Aidan grew sad, and when he was asked why, said, 'I know that the king will not live very long, for I have never before seen a humble king. I feel that he will soon be taken from us, because this nation is not worthy of such a king.'

Relations between Oswin and Oswy deteriorated, and by the beginning of August 651, they were close to war. Oswin, realizing that Oswy's forces were superior to his own, disbanded his army at Catterick, and headed back towards York. He was betrayed and killed at Gilling, where thick forest provides the ideal conditions for ambush, only some twenty-five miles from home. Bede says that Oswy 'most treacherously murdered him'. Oswy then took over the kingdom of Deira, uniting it again with Bernicia.

Oswy has never been regarded as a saint in either the Roman Catholic or the Celtic tradition.

10

Whitby and After

The Roman cause had powerful allies in Northumbria. In 653, two years after the death of *Finan, Queen Enfleda persuaded the king and *Colman, the new abbot of Lindisfarne, to allow two young noblemen, Wilfrid and Biscop, to make a journey to Rome. Wilfrid was in training at Lindisfarne, and one of the monastery's best students. Biscop, who was in attendance at the royal court, was also seeking to enter monastic life, but could not decide whether to follow the king's way or the queen's way. The two went to Canterbury before crossing the Channel. They separated at Lyons, but both went to Rome, and spent much time in Frankish monasteries on the way there and back. They encountered a splendour and a power which deeply impressed them. Both eventually returned to Northumbria as monks and priests, ordained in the Roman Church, experienced in the practices of Continental monasticism and strongly advocating the superiority of the Roman system over the simple, homespun ways of the Celtic monks.

By the time Wilfrid returned to Northumbria, Oswy's son Alchfrid, who followed his mother's persuasion, had become sub-king of Deira. A monastery at Ripon had been given to *Eata and *Cuthbert, but Alchfrid appointed Wilfrid as abbot and Wilfrid instituted the Latin Rite. Eata and Cuthbert soon left, and Bede says that they were 'thrown out'. Ripon became a centre of Roman influence as Wilfrid commissioned an Italianate church built by Continental stone-masons, decorated it with paintings, crucifixes and other sacred objects, and instituted Gregorian chant.

The issue came to a head in 664 at the Synod of Whitby. The immediate cause was the fact that this was a year in which the Celtic Church and the Roman Church had observed different dates for Easter. As Bede explains, this created problems in the Northumbrian court. 'Easter was . . . kept twice in the same year, so that when the king had ended Lent and was keeping Easter, the queen and her attendants were still fasting and keeping Palm Sunday.'

This disparity must have caused much irritation and misunderstanding on both sides. The basis of the two practices was both complicated and obscure. In the days of the early Church, Easter had been celebrated at the time of the Passover, which occurred on the fourteenth day of the first lunar month of the Jewish year, Nisan; but this could occur on any day of the week, and the custom developed among Christians of celebrating Easter Day on the following Sunday. This practice was endorsed at the Council of Nicaea in 324–5. If Nisan 14 fell on a Sunday, some Christian congregations celebrated it on that day, but others, wishing to distinguish the day of the Resurrection from the Jewish Passover, celebrated it on the following Sunday. Easter Day could therefore fall anywhere between Nisan 14 and Nisan 20 according to the first group (the practice followed by the Celtic Church) or between Nisan 15 and Nisan 21 according to the second (the practice followed by the Roman Church). The two dates coincided except when Nisan 14 fell on a Sunday, when the Celtic Church celebrated Easter on that day, while the Roman Church celebrated Easter on Nisan 21, a week later.

This problem had been 'patiently tolerated' for the first ten years of Oswy's reign, but patience was evidently wearing thin. Pressed by his queen and his heir, Oswy agreed that the time had come to resolve it. After much discussion, a great synod was called at Hilda's monastery at Streanashalch (usually referred to by its more manageable Danish name of Whitby) in September.

There had been a summer of tribulation. There was an eclipse of the sun on 3 May, and the *Annals of Tigernach* record an earthquake in Britain. The plague came back suddenly during the summer months, and spread from the south to the north, causing many deaths. Bede says that 'many nobles and lesser folk' fled to Ireland. No doubt all these events were seen as portents of divine disapproval, and increased the anxiety to achieve a settlement at

Whitby. This single decision was the fulcrum on which the fate of the Celtic Church depended.

Abbot Finan of Lindisfarne had died in 661. His successor, Colman, was fairly new in office, and harassed by the dissension at court. It fell to him to lead the Celtic party at the Synod. The Roman party was led by Bishop Aghilbert, a Frankish cleric who had become bishop of Dorchester. Since he had no knowledge of the Northumbrian dialect, Aghilbert delegated the task of putting the Roman case to Wilfrid of Ripon, newly returned from the Continent, and armed with all the latest arguments for his cause. The Synod was attended by many clergy, princes and noblemen. The abbess *Hilda was present, and 'the venerable bishop *Cedd', acting as interpreter.

Colman of Lindisfarne opened the proceedings. The main point of his argument was that he was loyal to the teaching of Iona, which he believed to be scriptural. If Bede gives a fair summary of his speech, it was a fairly short one; but this is not certain: Bede does say that he adduced 'other arguments', but does not say what they were. Perhaps they were never taken down by the scribes who must have been frantically scribbling on their wax pads, or perhaps they were subsequently erased; but Wilfrid's arguments are given in considerable detail. Wilfrid was young, intelligent, incisive, and very well informed on the Roman view from his own travels in Gaul and Italy. His speech, which Bede reproduces, stressed his superior knowledge of the practice in 'Africa, Asia, Egypt, Greece, and throughout the world wherever the Church of Christ has spread'. He contrasted this with the 'stupid practice of those Irishmen and their partners in obstinacy, the Picts and Britons, who inhabit a portion of these the two uttermost islands of the ocean'.

Colman was stung, and they began a hot and wordy debate. Then Colman made a mistake. He evidently intended to point out that many of the Eastern Churches also refused to conform to the Roman date of Easter, and he cited as an example Anatolius, patriarch of Constantinople.

Do you maintain that Anatolius, a holy man highly spoken of in Church history, taught contrary to the Law and the Gospel when he wrote that Easter should be kept between the fourteenth and the twentieth days of the moon? Are we to believe that our most reverend father Columba and his successors, men so dear to God, thought or acted contrary to Holy Scripture when they followed this custom?

Citing Anatolius of Constantinople was a fatal error. Anatolius, who died in 458, had been a strong supporter of the independence of his own patriarchate from the Roman jurisdiction, and had written works with which Colman was evidently familiar; but Wilfrid knew, as Colman did not, that under extreme pressure, Anatolius had finally bowed to the authority of Pope Leo the Great – and had therefore agreed to observe the Roman date of Easter. Wilfrid pounced, and at that moment, Colman was defeated.

Wilfrid went on to speak slightingly of '*your* Columba' in terms which can only have been deeply wounding to the Lindisfarne monks who knew that he had once been one of their company, before making a powerful appeal to the authority of St Peter. Peter, first bishop of Rome, he argued, had kept the Roman date of Easter, based on the Jewish calendar calculations for the date of the Passover. He ended with Christ's words as reported in the Gospel according to Matthew (though not the other three Gospels): 'You are Peter, and upon this rock I will build my Church, and the gates of Hades shall not prevail against it; and I will give you the keys of the kingdom of heaven' (Matt. 16:18).

There must have been a silence after these tremendous words. King Oswy asked Colman if Christ had given a similar authority to *Columba, and Colman had to admit that he had not. The question was put to the great gathering of clergy and nobles, whether they should follow the Roman way. Bede says that '[a]ll present, high and low, signified their agreement, abandoning their imperfect customs' and 'hastening to adopt those they had learned to be better'. Oswy gave the judgement for Wilfrid and Rome. The curious thing was that neither Wilfrid nor anybody else had been able to claim that St Peter or his Master ever said a word about 'the correct date of Easter'.

Eddius Stephanus, Wilfrid's chronicler, who was present, says that Oswy smiled as he gave his judgement. Was it a smile of relief that his immediate domestic difficulties were solved? Or a propitiatory smile directed at Colman? Perhaps it was a compound of the two. Bede says that Oswy loved Colman, and he seems to have done his best to alleviate the great sorrow and great confusion which followed his judgement. He did decree that Lindisfarne should be exempted from the new Roman jurisdiction, and be left free to follow its Celtic practices; but Colman and the Irish monks were in obedience to the abbot of Iona, and their mission was over. They were recalled to Iona. With them went a strong contingent of Anglo-Saxon monks under *Gerald of Mayo, who preferred exile to the acceptance of what they regarded as alien ways.

Pope Vitalian sent King Oswy a letter expressing his delight at the Whitby decision:

We know how you have been converted to the true and apostolic Faith by the guiding hand of God, and trust that, as you now reign over your own nation, so you will one day reign with Christ. Your nation is fortunate to have a king . . . (who) labours day and night to lead his people to the Catholic Apostolic Faith, and to save his own soul. Who can help being glad at such encouraging news?

To Queen Enfleda, 'our spiritual daughter', he sent a cross 'made from the fetters of the blessed Apostles Peter and Paul', with a golden key.

In Northumbria, the former leaders of the Celtic Church struggled to cope with the new situation. Eata became abbot of Lindisfarne, with Cuthbert as prior. Tuda was appointed bishop of York, but died within a year of the plague, as did Cedd. Alchfrid of Deira appointed Wilfrid bishop of York, and Wilfrid promptly claimed episcopal jurisdiction from the Humber to the Firth of Forth. He went to the Frankish kingdom for his consecration, where he was carried shoulder-high in a golden chair in a procession which included six bishops. He stayed on the Continent so long that Oswy tired of waiting for him to return, rescinded his son's decision, and appointed *Chad in his place. Wilfrid promptly appealed to Rome, arguing that Chad's consecration was invalid, but matters dragged. The archbishop of Canterbury, Deusdedit, had died, and a new nominee, Wighard, was sent to Rome for consecration, but died there before the ceremony could take place. Eventually Pope Vitalian asked the abbot of a Greek monastery near Naples to take on the responsibility, but he refused, saying that one of his monk-scholars, Theodore, was better suited to the office.

So Greek Theodore became archbishop of Canterbury. It proved to be an inspired choice. Theodore had experience of the rift between the Eastern Church and the Roman Church, which helped him to understand the Celtic problem. He was a man of rare energy, despite his sixty-five years, and of considerable administrative ability; but changes came slowly. Theodore not only had to wait four months for his hair to grow: he had to be given holy orders in the Latin Rite – successively made deacon, ordained priest and consecrated archbishop. Biscop was in Rome at the time. He had studied at the great Continental monastery of Lérins, which had adopted the Benedictine rule, and had taken the name of Benedict in religion in addition to his own Saxon name. As Benedict Biscop, he accompanied Theodore on his way across Frankish territories to Canterbury. The party stayed at a number of monasteries on the way, learning their ways and their problems, so that Theodore was thoroughly versed in the practice of the Roman Church by the time he arrived in Canterbury.

The new archbishop had problems to settle in the south. He did not finally go north to sort out the tensions and bitterness which followed the Whitby decision until 669. Then he acted decisively. The enormous Northumbrian diocese was divided into four, and Wilfrid, whose ambitions do not seem to have impressed him, was sent to the small and comparatively obscure diocese of Hexham. Wilfrid appealed to Rome, but though the papacy supported him, the kings of Northumbria did not, and he spent most of the rest of his life in fruitless trips to Rome, finally dying at Oundle. Chad's consecration was found to be uncanonical, but Theodore ordered his reconsecration, and sent him to be bishop of Mercia. Eata was made bishop of Lindisfarne, and Cuthbert of Hexham in Wilfrid's absence; but Eata was old and tired. In the end, they were able to exchange appointments, so that Cuthbert, who was younger and more active, could go to Lindisfarne.

Hilda, who remained as abbess of Whitby for a further sixteen years, was obedient to the Latin Rite. She was a princess of the royal house, and she had been baptized according to that Rite by the Roman Paulinus with the rest of King Edwin's household half a century earlier, so that was not too painful a transition; but she was also the spiritual daughter of *Aidan, the friend of Cuthbert, and the spiritual mother of the Celtic monks. The link between Whitby and Lindisfarne was a close one. She must have felt the new dispensation acutely, particularly when Wilfrid claimed authority over her monastery. If Lindisfarne was exempt from his intervention, Whitby was not. Wilfrid's departure to the Continent for his consecration must have eased a very difficult situation, and she supported Archbishop Theodore when he made fresh appointments in 669. She left no writings, but she must have made her views very clear to Theodore, and they were well known in Rome. A papal letter written to King Alchfrid during Wilfrid's time in Rome describes how Wilfrid 'came in person with an appeal to the Apostolic See', and refers to 'the holy abbess Hilda' and Theodore jointly as his 'adversaries'.

Hilda lived to see five of her former students become bishops: Bosa of York, John of Beverley, Oftfor of Mercia, John of Hexham and another Wilfrid, known as Wilfrid II, who went to York after Bosa. Benedict Biscop, abbot of Monkwearmouth, whose ambitions were less extensive than those of Wilfrid I, founded the monastery at Jarrow, where Bede was to struggle some sixty years later to set the story down for posterity.

Adamnan (Adomnan, Cain Adomnain) (*c.* 627–704), 23 September, was the fifth abbot of Iona, and biographer of his kinsman *Columba. He was an outstanding scholar. His Life of Columba is modelled on the Lives of the Desert Fathers, particularly Antony and Evagrius. It is full of affection and understanding for the founder of the Iona community, and was to serve as a model for many Lives of the Irish saints. It was widely circulated (which meant widely copied) both in Britain and on the Continent.

Despite his attachment to the Celtic Church, Adamnan slowly became convinced that the future of Iona and Lindisfarne depended on joining the Roman Church and not in opposing it. He was greatly interested in the Holy Land, and when he heard that a Frankish bishop named Arnulf, who had been in Jerusalem, was in Britain, he invited him to Iona. He and his monks eagerly listened to Arnulf's accounts of the Church of the Nativity and the Church of the Holy Sepulchre. Adamnan subsequently wrote his own account of the Holy Places, *De Locis Sanctis*, which Bede ranked as 'beneficial to many, particularly to those who, being far from these places where the patriarchs and prophets lived, know no more of them than they can learn by reading'.

As nominal superior of Lindisfarne, Adamnan visited the monastery twice. On the first occasion, his main purpose was to ransom some Irish prisoners held in Northumbria. On the second, he also visited Monkwearmouth, where Benedict Biscop had founded his monastery in 684. Like Wilfrid, Benedict Biscop had build a stone church in the Italianate manner, and he had gone to great lengths to bring to it all the colour and vitality of which the Continental Church was capable. He visited Rome repeatedly, and spent much time in Continental monasteries, collecting manuscripts, statues, pictures, altar furnishings, relics and sacred objects of all kinds. Wilfrid had brought back an expert in Gregorian chant, Eddi or Eddius Stephanus, who later wrote his Life; but Benedict Biscop went one better, and brought back John the Chanter, a cantor from St Peter's, Rome. The warmth and drama of Roman liturgical practice at its best were imported to replace the bleak simplicity of Celtic worship.

Adamnan visited Monkwearmouth towards the end of his life. The contrast with the liturgical practice of Iona must have struck him forcibly. Benedict Biscop had died, and Ceolfrid, abbot of Jarrow, had also become abbot of Monkwearmouth. It was Ceolfrid who finally convinced Adamnan of the need for Iona to change to the Roman system. Adamnan went back to convince his monks, but failed to do so. Iona did not finally give up its independence until 716.

Aebbe (Ebba) (683), 23 August, was the sister of Oswy and *Oswin of Northumbria, and a contemporary of *Cuthbert and Wilfrid. She remained on excellent terms with both. She became abbess of a monastery at what is now St Abbs' Head, and later of the double monastery at Coldingham (see *Hilda for double monasteries). Cuthbert used to visit her, and she made him a present of a linen cloth which was eventually used as his shroud; but she also managed to remain on good terms with Wilfrid during his time at York. She supported him against her nephew, King Egfrid, in a difficult controversy. Queen Ethelburga had been married to Egfrid against her will and remained a virgin, claiming that she had a prior commitment to the religious life. Aebbe gave Ethelburga sanctuary in her own monastery. Wilfrid supported her, and Egbert imprisoned him. Later Egbert visited Coldingham with his new queen, who became ill. Aebbe told him roundly that the queen's illness was a punishment for his treatment of Wilfrid. Wilfrid was released, and the queen apparently recovered.

A monk named Adamnan (not Adamnan of Iona), who had committed some great sin and lived a penitential life in consequence, visited Coldingham towards the end of Aebbe's life. It seems to have been a large and impressive establishment; but 'when he saw its buildings towering up, the man of God burst into tears'. When his companion enquired the reason, he prophesied that 'the time is near when all the public and private buildings that you see in front of you will be burned to ashes'. When this was reported to Aebbe, she summoned Adamnan, who told her that he had seen the life of her monastery in a vision. 'Nowhere have I found anyone except yourself concerned with the health of his own soul. All of them, men and women alike, are either sunk in unprofitable sleep or else awake only to sin.' Vigils, prayers and study were neglected, the monastic cells were used for eating, drinking and gossip, and the nuns, many of them from noble families, spent too much time in making themselves fine clothes 'either to adorn themselves like brides or to attract strange men'. This may have been part of the growing worldliness which Bede says invaded the monasteries after the relaxation of Celtic discipline. Adamnan comforted the abbess, telling her that the catastrophe would not happen in her time; but five years later, after her death, the monastery caught fire, and was burned down. Bede uses this as an example of Divine retribution.

Chad (Ceadda) (672), 2 March, was the brother of *Cedd and a student and disciple of *Aidan. Bede calls him 'a holy man, modest in his ways, learned in the Scriptures, and careful to practise all that he found in them'.

He spent some time in an Irish monastery, but came back when Cedd died, to succeed his brother as abbot of Lastingham. Wilfrid was appointed bishop of Northumbria and went off to the Continent for his magnificent consecration; but he stayed there so long that King Oswy's successor, Egfrid, who inclined to the Celtic cause, assumed that he had no intention of returning, and appointed Chad in his place. Chad was duly consecrated, but there was some difficulty in finding three bishops to carry out the ceremony. The archbishop of Canterbury, Deusdedit, had recently died, and the only bishop available whose consecration was recognized by Rome was Wini of Wessex, who had recently been accused of simony. The other two bishops were probably Cornish bishops, who still did not conform to 'the correct date of Easter', and so were not recognized in Rome. Wilfrid returned to claim his diocese, and alleged that Chad's consecration had been dubious, if not uncanonical. Chad meekly said that he had never thought himself worthy to be a bishop, and thankfully retired to Lastingham; but when Theodore, archbishop of Canterbury, finally came north to adjudicate in a very difficult and tangled situation, Wilfrid was moved to the small and relatively obscure diocese of Hexham, and Chad was re-consecrated as bishop of Mercia, where his brother Cedd had carried out the first mission.

The story of how Chad, loyal to the memory of Aidan, insisted on going about on foot, and how the exasperated Theodore, who was convinced that he could not cover a large diocese with territorial boundaries without more efficient transport, actually hoisted him on the back of a horse, is a revealing sidelight on the basic difference between the Celtic and the Roman systems. In the three years of his episcopacy in Mercia, Chad founded a monastery at Barrow, Lincolnshire, and one close to the site of the present

Lichfield cathedral. At Lichfield, the monks suffered from the plague, and Chad died from it. The monks were deeply impressed by his holiness. There were stories of visions in which angels were seen taking his soul up to heaven, and miracles of healing were reported at his shrine. The *Lichfield Gospels* are thought to have been compiled by his monks in his memory.

Colman of Lindisfarne (?676), 18 February, was the third abbot-bishop of Lindisfarne, and the leader of the Celtic party at the Synod of Whitby. A man of strong loyalties, he was ill-prepared for the conflict with Wilfrid. In his speech to the Synod, his appeal to the authority of the patriarch Anatolius of Constantinople was based on the patriarch's early writings, which defended the Eastern Church against the claims of Rome; but he evidently did not know (as Wilfrid did) that Anatolius, who died in 458, had been forced to fight charges from Rome of irregular consecration and heresy. Pope Leo the Great set out the papal view of the nature of Christ in the so-called 'Tome of Leo', and Anatolius circulated this to all his metropolitan bishops for their approval before finally accepting it. Pope Leo made it clear that he still had reservations about the consecration of Anatolius, but accepted him 'rather in mercy than in justice'. As a consequence, Anatolius in his final years kept 'the correct date of Easter' in the Roman manner.

Colman's unfortunate choice of an authority – there were others he might have cited if he had thought of them in the heat of the moment – left him open to Wilfrid's attack. His appeals to the authority of *Columba received little better treatment, for Wilfrid implied that he too was irregularly consecrated, and possibly a heretic.

Colman and the Lindisfarne monks were decisively defeated – their traditions swept aside, and a new and unwelcome authority imposed on their monastery. Colman left Northumbria with 'all the Irish he had collected at Lindisfarne' and some thirty Anglo-Saxon monks. They went back to Iona, and then back to Ireland, where Colman founded a new monastery on Inishboffin, an island off Galway. The Anglo-Saxons broke away and founded a monastery of their own under *Gerald of Mayo.

Colman died in comparative obscurity. The date of his death is not certain, and it could have occurred anywhere beyond 672 and 676. Bede praised the new Irish monastery of the Anglo-Saxon monks, but studiously avoided reference to Colman and the Irish monks. Alcuin was later somewhat more generous, saying that Colman and his community were distinguished by their learning 'among a very barbarous nation'.

Cuthbert (*c.* 687), 20 March, came from the Scottish Border country, probably the Lammermuir Hills, which in his time were part of the kingdom of Northumbria. He was fostered with a holy widow named Coenswith, whom he called 'mother', and to whom he had a deep devotion. Though many of the Celtic monks, like *Aidan and *Chad, insisted on going about on foot, he usually rode on horseback, which suggests that he came from a noble family. On one occasion when he was travelling and had no food, his horse nosed around in the thatch of a deserted cottage, and found some bread and meat left by a shepherd, 'half a loaf still warm and some meat wrapped in the cloth, enough for one meal'. Cuthbert ate half – and gave the other half to the horse.

When he was seventeen or eighteen, he entered monastic life. He chose to go to Melrose, on the banks of the river Tweed, to study under *Eata the abbot and *Boisil the prior. Perhaps they had visited Coenswith, and he already knew them. He arrived still in secular dress, and carrying a spear. Boisil was standing at the monastery gate when he arrived. When Cuthbert had given up his horse and spear, he went into the church. Boisil followed him and said, 'Behold the servant of the Lord.' Boisil and Eata were Cuthbert's teachers, and he was to form strong attachments to both, accompanying them on their journeys, learning from them how to carry out his own ministry. He did not stay within the monastery walls, but scoured the countryside, talking to people as he met them. Since *Columba's time, many parts of the Border country had relapsed into superstition and idolatry in an attempt to ward off the recurrent epidemics of the plague. Cuthbert would range far and wide, sometimes leaving the monastery for as much as a month at a time, visiting villages 'whose barbarity and squalor daunted other teachers' according to Bede.

Eata was given a site for a monastery at Ripon, and took Cuthbert with him; but when Alchfrid of Deira appointed Wilfrid as abbot, they left. Bede implies that this was Wilfrid's decision, not theirs. Feelings between Roman and Celtic monks were evidently running high. Shortly before the Synod of Whitby, Boisil caught the plague. Cuthbert stayed with him in his last days. Boisil asked if he would read a book to him, '[o]ne that can be got through in a week', and Cuthbert chose St John's Gospel. He caught the plague from his teacher, but recovered. He succeeded Boisil as prior of Melrose, and went to the Synod later that same year, in that capacity. Some time after the Synod, when Eata had jurisdiction over Lindisfarne as well as Melrose, Cuthbert was sent to Lindisfarne as prior, to bring the monastery into conformity with the Latin Church.

Cuthbert seems to have convinced the monks that much of the argument was about externals, and not about the essentials of faith. He persuaded them to observe the Latin date of Easter, and to adopt the Latin tonsure; but Lindisfarne continued to follow the way of Celtic spirituality, adapting the new Benedictine rule to the existing Columban rule. The Lives of Cuthbert tend to omit dates, but he is thought to have stayed at Lindisfarne for about twelve years. This must have been a time of great strain for him. Bede says: 'At chapter meetings, he was often worn down by bitter insults, but would put an end to the arguments simply by rising and walking out, calm and unruffled.'

There was a price to pay for this appearance of calm. It was during this period that a monk discovered that Cuthbert went down to the sea at night, 'going out into the deep water until the waves rose as far as his neck' and spending 'the dark hours of the night watching and singing praises to the sound of the waves'. Perhaps he was not sleeping much. It was this monk who reported that when he finally came ashore, two otters (or seals) came and dried his feet with their fur, to warm him. He must have been on good terms with the creatures of the deep, and perhaps found them better company than his distressed and bickering monks.

Cuthbert's decision to become a hermit has to be seen in the light of the confusion and discord on Lindisfarne in the years following the Synod of Whitby. After a time on an island close to the coast, he chose the island of Inner Farne far out to sea. Bede says that there were evil spirits on Farne, and Cuthbert defeated them; perhaps he was more concerned with his own internal spiritual struggles. The Lindisfarne monks rowed out and built him huts on the Celtic pattern, surrounded by a high wall of the kind constructed by the Desert Fathers of Egypt, so that he could see 'nothing but the heaven which he desired so ardently'. Bede, in his Life of Cuthbert, which he calls his *libellus*, his little book, describes it in detail, closely paralleling a passage in the Life of St Antony by Evagrius:

> It is a structure almost round in plan, measuring four or five poles from wall to wall, the wall itself on the outside is higher than a man standing upright, but inside he made it much higher by cutting away the living rock, so that the pious inhabitant could see nothing except the sky from his dwelling, thus restraining both the lust of the eyes and of the thoughts, and lifting the whole bent of his mind to higher things.

When the monks dug a well for Cuthbert, clear water filled it. He sowed wheat, but it would not grow. In the second year, he sowed barley, and obtained a good crop. After that, he lived on barley bread and water, saying, 'I would rather return to the monastery than be kept here by the labours of others.' He had arguments with the birds, which ate his seeds until he told them firmly to stop, and expelled the ravens which pulled the thatch from the roof of his cell, until one came back, dejected, hanging its head and croaking mournfully, when he forgave them. He lived with the cormorants and the eagles, the seagulls, the puffins and the eider ducks – ever since known as 'Cuddy's ducks' in his memory – in what has now become a National Trust bird sanctuary.

Many people came to see him on Inner Farne. He built a small guest-house for visitors, and at first came out to greet them and wash their feet, but there were so many that he had to give up this hospitable practice. Later visitors found that the window on his small cell was kept shut when they were on the island, and only opened to give them a blessing on their departure. He remained in close communion with God, away from the world, until he was appointed bishop of Lindisfarne. The monks rowed out to Inner Farne to take him back to the monastery for his consecration and, 'compelled to submit to the yoke of episcopacy', he left his retreat in tears.

Two years later, when he knew that he had a mortal illness, he went back to his hermitage. There he endured storm and tempest and great physical pain. Some of the monks were with him when he died. He asked to be buried on the island, but they pleaded that they should be allowed to take his body back to Lindisfarne, and his shrine, now in Durham cathedral, is still a place of pilgrimage.

Drithelm (Drythelm) (*c.* 700), 1 September, is a late example of Celtic vision and Celtic practice in Northumbria. He was a layman with a wife and children, living at Cunningham. He fell ill, and was thought to have died in the night; but at daybreak, he revived, 'to the great consternation of those weeping about the body', and told the mourners that he had 'truly risen from the grasp of death'.

'A handsome man in a shining robe' had led him to a dreadful valley, with burning fires on one side, and raging hail and bitter snow on the other. In it, men's souls were hurled from side to side, escaping from the terrible heat only to be engulfed by the terrible cold, and back again. He began to think that this was hell; but his guide led him further to a great dark pit with a foul stench, where exultant devils seized human souls, writhing, howling and lamenting, and cast them into the pit.

Drithelm thought that they would seize him; but suddenly he saw 'a bright star rising in the gloom'. It was his guide, who led him to 'an atmosphere of clear light, a meadow filled with flowers where happy people in white robes sat'. He began to think that this was heaven, but he was led on through 'the abodes of blessed spirits' to a place so beautiful that 'even the wonderful light that had flooded the flowery meadow seemed thin and dim when compared with that now visible'. Before he could enjoy the sights and scents and sounds of this wonderful place, his guide led him back along the road. He explained that the first place Drithelm had seen was purgatory, where the souls of those who had 'delayed to confess and amend their wicked ways, and who at last had recourse to penitence in the hour of death' were punished for their sins until the Day of Judgement; but they could be helped by the prayers, alms and fasting of those still living. The dark pit was the mouth of hell, where those were consigned who were eternally damned. The flowery meadow was the place where those who had done some good during their earthly lives, but were not yet perfect, stayed to await the Day of Judgement; and the place where he heard 'the sounds of sweet singing, with the sweet fragrance and glorious light' was the entry to the Kingdom. Then Drithelm came to himself, but he knew not how.

He gave away his money – one-third each to his wife, his children and the poor – and entered the monastic community at Melrose, which still maintained many Celtic practices. There he followed the Irish penitentials, standing in the river even when 'the half-broken cakes of ice were swirling around him which he had broken to make a place to stand'. When people asked how he could stand the cold, he said simply, 'I have known it colder.' When he was asked how he could bear it, he said, 'I have known greater suffering.' So he 'tamed his aged body' to be ready for the blessings of heaven.

Drithelm's vision became well known. He would not tell his story to 'apathetic or careless-living people', but he told it to the king of Northumbria, and it became immensely popular in medieval England – so much so that it rivalled the popularity of Bede's own *Ecclesiastical History*.

Though it has been almost forgotten since the publication of Dante's *Divina Commedia*, it may well have been an inspiration to Dante – and much later for Cardinal Newman's poem *The Dream of Gerontius*.

Eata (686), 26 October, was one of the first twelve boys taught by *Aidan at Lindisfarne (with *Cedd and *Chad). He entered the monastery at Melrose, and became abbot. *Boisil was his prior, and between them, they trained *Cuthbert, who was greatly

devoted to them both. When he and Cuthbert were at Ripon and
Wilfrid was appointed abbot, Bede says that the two went as far as
receiving the Roman tonsure in their efforts to come to terms with
him, but this proved impossible.

After the Synod of Whitby, Eata accepted the Latin Rite. Bede
says that before *Colman left Lindisfarne for Ireland, he asked
for Eata's appointment as abbot in his place. In 678, under the re-
organization ordered by Archbishop Theodore, Eata was appointed bishop with jurisdiction over the whole of Bernicia, roughly
modern Northumbria and part of the Scottish Lowlands. Cuthbert
was appointed bishop of the small diocese of Hexham; but Eata
was an old man, and managed to plead his age in order to exchange
dioceses, so that his younger and fitter pupil could go back to
Lindisfarne. In these rapid moves, one gets a sense of the Celtic
monks' anxiety to make sense of the somewhat arbitrary decisions
of their new Roman masters, and of Eata's personal concern for
Cuthbert and his ministry.

Eata died a year later at Hexham, and was buried there. Bede
calls him 'a gentle man, and greatly revered'.

Gerald of Mayo (732), 13 March, was one of the group of thirty
Anglo-Saxon monks who accompanied *Colman of Lindisfarne
when he returned to Ireland after the Synod of Whitby. They were
unwilling to accept the Latin Rite, and wanted to remain part of the
Celtic Church.

They settled on the island of Inishboffin in Galway, but disputes
arose between the Irish monks and the Anglo-Saxon monks. The
Anglo-Saxons complained that the Irish 'went wandering', preaching round the countryside during the summer months as was their
practice, and the Anglo-Saxon monks had to do all the work of the
monastery, including gathering the harvest, without them. Colman
tried to resolve the dispute, but eventually settled the English
monks at Mayo, where their monastery became known as 'Mayo
of the Saxons', with Gerald as abbot. Mayo of the Saxons developed
a great reputation for learning, and later Alcuin of York corres-
ponded with the abbot. Gerald is thought to have been responsible

for the foundation of the abbeys of Tempul-Gerald in Connacht and Teaguena-Saxon.

The *Litany of Irish Saints* from the twelfth century *Book of Leinster* records 'Three thousand and three hundred with Gerald the bishop and fifty saints of Luige of Connacht, who occupied Mag Eo of the Saxons'.

Epilogue

The end of the independent Celtic Church came slowly and unevenly to the Celtic lands. In Northumbria, Archbishop Theodore, despite his sympathetic treatment of the Lindisfarne monks, acted to eradicate continuing Celtic practice. The Anglo-Saxon Synod of Hertford in 672 accepted his *Penitential*, which decreed the excommunication of all those who did not recognize Roman jurisdiction or conform to Roman practice, and swept away the traditions of the Celtic saints. When this was implemented, not a single dedication to *Aidan of Lindisfarne was left in the whole of Northumbria.

Lindisfarne acted to preserve its own traditions. Within two decades of *Cuthbert's death, two monks, Aedfrid and Aelfrid, had composed the manuscript known as the *Lindisfarne Gospels* 'in honour of God and St Cuthbert'. This document forms our chief artistic inheritance from the Celtic monks of Northumbria, and vividly evokes their world. Aedfrid, the calligrapher, was a trained scribe. He probably borrowed a copy of St Jerome's text of the Gospels, which was highly prized, from the library at Monkwearmouth, and copied it in its entirety in the elegant insular majuscule script, more complex than the uncial script used at Monkwearmouth and other Roman monasteries. Aelfrid was the illustrator. His work has earned him the title of 'the first personality in British art history', and has provided inspiration for many later artists and craftsmen. It shows a rare combination of observation and artistic skill, and brings to life Cuthbert's companions on Inner Farne – the ravens, the puffins, the cormorants, the seagulls, the eider ducks – even an elongated cat which runs the whole length of a page, its head between its claws at the foot of the page, ready to pounce. The work is so extensive and so beautifully executed that many commentators have doubted whether its 225 vellum pages could all be the work of two men, but it is now established that it all came from their hands in years of painstaking labour.

Aedfrid became bishop of Lindisfarne in 698. He may have been a young monk at Lindisfarne or Whitby at the time of the Synod of Whitby, and must surely have known Cuthbert personally. In addition to his work on the *Gospels*, he restored Cuthbert's oratory on Inner Farne, and, as bishop, invited Bede to write his *Life of Cuthbert*. When he died, he was buried with Cuthbert.

Danish raids on Lindisfarne increased in intensity in the eighth century. Alcuin of York (737–804) wrote to King Ethelred, 'The church of St Cuthbert is spattered with the blood of the priests of God, stripped of all its furnishings, exposed to the plundering of pagans.' In 793, the Danes sacked Lindisfarne, and killed many of the monks. Those who escaped took with them Cuthbert's shrine and the *Lindisfarne Gospels*. Though they later went back for a time, the monastery, which had become wealthy under Roman jurisdiction, was again a tempting target for raiders, and in 875, they had to leave for good. They wandered about for some years, and then settled at Chester-le-Street, where a monk named Bifrid enriched the cover of the *Lindisfarne Gospels* with gold and jewels. Their treasures stayed in the keeping of the monks when they moved to Durham in 995. Their order was replaced by Benedictines after the Norman Conquest, but Cuthbert's shrine and the *Gospels* remained in the new stone cathedral built by the Normans. The shrine of St Cuthbert is still there, but the *Gospels* were seized by Henry VIII's Commissioners in 1539. The valuable cover was ripped off, and the manuscript was sent to London, where it was eventually acquired by the seventeenth century antiquary and bibliophile Sir Robert Cotton. It is now in the MSS Cotton Collection in the British Library.

In Ireland, *Adamnan strongly advocated the Roman case at the Synod of Birr in 697, but the monasteries of Northern Ireland did not submit to Rome until 715. Dublin became a Viking bishopric, but it seems that most diocesan sees were not set up in Ireland until after the Norman Conquest. *Declan's Ardmore tried to claim diocesan status, but nothing more was heard of the claim after 1210. *Ciaran's Clonmacnoise suffered from the expansion of the neighbouring diocese of Clonard, and by 1516, its cathedral was 'roofless and ruinous' according to an eye-witness. *Kevin's Glendalough was taken over by Dublin in 1216. The estates of *Ailbe's monastery at Emly were given to the archbishopric of Cashel. At Lorrha, the nave fell into ruins, only the chancel remaining in use. Since the Reformation, most Celtic and Roman Catholic monastic sites in Ireland have been occupied by Protestant churches. Very few medieval parish churches are still in use; but many of the early sites are still places of pilgrimage or tourism, and the 'rounds' on saints' feast days are often performed.

Iona's acceptance of Roman jurisdiction was inevitable once Ireland had submitted. It came in 716, some time after Adamnan's death. The last independent abbot was Dunchad, who approved the change shortly before his own death. Bede says that he 'adopted the Catholic way of life' as a result of a mission by Egbert, by that time the bishop of Lindisfarne, and a convinced supporter of the Roman system; but the loss of support from the Irish clergy must have been a powerful factor. Bede notes that Dunchad taught his monks 'to observe our chief solemnity in the Catholic and Apostolic manner, and to wear the symbol of an unbroken crown', but it is doubtful whether the immediate changes went beyond the essential ones of the date of Easter and the tonsure. Because of the ravages of the Danes, the Iona community abandoned its island site some time between 807 and 814, and the monks went to Kells, which was downgraded to the status of a parish church in the twelfth century.

Wales held out for another half century. According to Nennius, who was his disciple, Elfoddw, the senior abbot of Gwynedd, negotiated the final submission of the Welsh clergy in 768. A note in the *Annals of Britain* reads: '768: Easter is changed among the Britons, Elbogudus, a man of God, emending it.' Elfoddw or Elbogudus became bishop of Gwynedd, but he had difficulty in convincing the other Welsh bishops, as it is recorded that they 'did not concur therein'. The date of Easter was not altered in South Wales until

777, and the controversy rumbled on. In 847, some clerics were still 'proceeding to profess themselves diligent readers of S. Chrysostom and resisting the Archbishop of Gwynedd's authority'. Elfoddw lived to argue with his opponents for forty years, 'migrating to the Lord' in 809.

In the northern parts of the kingdom of Northumbria, now part of Scotland, the king of the Southern Picts, Nechtan IV, had agreed to adopt the Roman system as a result of Abbot Ceolfrid's advocacy from Monkwearmouth, and the Celtic monks were expelled in 713. This must have been another reason for Iona's capitulation, as the monks in Scotland represented its last foreign mission. A new bishopric was set up at *Candida Casa*, with two bishops known as *Pect-helm*, Guardian of the Picts, and *Pect-wine*, Friend of the Picts. The Celtic Church continued in some areas. King Kenneth I (Kenneth Mac Alpin), who united the Picts and the Scots in 843, and is described as 'the first King of Scotland', had Celtic monks at his court at Dunkeld, though there were Roman monks in Edinburgh. Perhaps Kenneth was named for *Cainnech, friend of *Colomba. As late as 1070, when Margaret, a grand-daughter of Edmund Ironside, married Malcolm Canmore, king of Scotland, there were still many 'Culdee' or 'Keledai' hermits, living as solitaries or in small groups. Margaret's Benedictine spiritual director, Turgot, says that they did not keep Lent or Easter; they kept the Sabbath on Saturday, and worked on Sunday; and they stood for worship, refusing to kneel. Many of them could not read or write, and the liturgy had become corrupted. Possibly Turgot exaggerated: he found Scotland a wild and uncouth country after the court of Edward the Confessor, and had no patience with what he regarded as unorthodoxy. If the Culdees had lapsed from the original asceticism of the *Céili Dé*, it is necessary to remember that by Turgot's time, they had received no support from Ireland, Iona or Lindisfarne for over three centuries. A Benedictine mission was dispatched to Scotland. The Culdees were called together, and the queen explained to them the error of their ways, her fearsome and warlike husband acting as her interpreter, for she spoke no Gaelic. With some grumbling, most of the Culdees complied with the Latin Rite, though some of them insisted on keeping to their old practices.

In 705, according to Haddan and Stubbs, Aldhelm, bishop of Sherborne, persuaded 'the Britons subject to Wessex' (probably most of Devon) to adopt the Roman Easter. Pressure from Wessex continued, and in 815 and 835, Egbert of Wessex overran Cornwall. From that time until about 900, Cornwall was a separate principality, but formally subject to the Saxon Church. Cornish resistance, both military and ecclesiastical, proved hard to eradicate, and it was not until 926 that the last 'British bishop' (or abbot) submitted, and was re-consecrated as bishop of Bodmin.

In Brittany, the invasions of the Norsemen in the eighth century and the plundering of monastic sites by Athelstan in the ninth led to the almost total devastation of the monasteries, only a few precious manuscripts and relics reaching the safe havens of French monasteries – which proceeded to lay claim to them.

The Celtic lands were not easily conquered. It was not until the reign of Edward I (1239–1307) that major political resistance was subdued, and with it the older ecclesiastical system finally erased. Even when the territory was neatly carved up into dioceses, and powerful bishops sought to impose orthodoxy within their boundaries, the fact remained that the Roman ecclesiastical system was essentially urban. In mountainous and marshy regions, remote from highways and cities, memories were long, and the old ways lingered on.

The adverse effects of accepting control by the Roman Church were very clearly seen and argued by Bede in the early eighth century. In an almost elegiac passage in his *Ecclesiastical History*, he laments the drowning of the primitive New Testament simplicity of the Celtic Church and their love of poverty in a flood of worldliness and luxury. He describes the 'fragility and austerity' of the Lindisfarne monks:

When they left the seat of their authority there were very few buildings except the church – indeed, no more than met the bare requirements of a seemly way of life. They had no property except cattle, and whenever they received any money from rich folk, they immediately gave it to the poor, for they had no need to amass money or provide lodging for important people, since

such visited the church only to pray or to hear the word of God
. . . for in those days, the sole concern of these teachers was to
serve God, not the world, to satisfy the soul, not the belly.

This contrasts sharply with the picture he draws of the abuses of
the monastic system in Northumbria shortly before his own death
in 735. He writes in a letter to Egbert, archbishop of York, of
'deformed people' who have secured charters from noblemen and
ecclesiastics and set up establishments which have 'none of the
reality of a monastic way of life'; of secular intervention in monastic affairs, of rapacity and the buying of privilege, of ignorance and
the failure to teach the young men, of 'the attractions of a loose
way of life' for people he regards as false monks. He pleads with the
bishop to see that they are transformed by synodical authority
'from impurity to chastity, from vanity to truth, from intemperance
and greed to continence and holiness of heart'. Of course not all
monasteries were of this kind, but there is no doubt that Bede felt
the monastic system itself was under threat.

Despite his zeal for 'the correct date of Easter', Bede evidently felt
acutely the destruction of cherished traditions as the hallowed
memories of the old Celtic saints were suppressed or distorted. All
the same, the picture is not a simple one of total loss. Bede identified the need for change when he said that the Celtic Church was
'fragile'. It was unstructured, its buildings were temporary, and its
practice was designed primarily for monks, not lay people. A more
efficient and comprehensive structure was needed as Christianity
replaced paganism, and it was perhaps inevitable that it should
come from Britain's European neighbours. Though the geographical position of the British Isles makes its inhabitants extremely
wary of Continental innovations, they were (and still are) too close
to Europe to remain entirely detached.

The Roman system of territorial administration by bishops
became more feasible in the former Celtic lands as cities and roads
developed. The Celtic system, based on coastal monasteries, had
originally been a matter of practical necessity rather than of princi-
ple. The great heritage of the Continental Church brought in
much of spiritual value – artistic treasures, paintings, statues,

ivories, music and drama, all to glorify God. These innovations carried spiritual dangers, but also broadened opportunities for worship. Celtic worship was monastic and essentially verbal, based on the recital of psalms, biblical passages and long lists of saints, reinforced by extreme penitential practices learned from the Desert Fathers. Now there were new visual and emotional aids to faith, vital for the understanding of secular clergy and laity.

With all its admirable qualities, the Celtic system had to give way to change; but it had made a distinctive and lasting contribution to Christian spirituality.

Notes on Sources

In the distant world of the Celtic saints, the *Scotii* are Irish, the 'British' are Welsh, Brittany is a Welsh colony, and England does not yet exist as a political entity. The Roman occupation of the neighbouring lowlands of Britain is a memory, but still a powerful one. The main sources of knowledge about the Christian faith are the writings of the great Eastern Fathers of the Church, and the claims of the papacy in Rome to supremacy over other Christian Churches are not taken as seriously as Rome expects. From a standpoint in the early twenty-first century, it takes quite an effort of imagination to enter into that world, and to see the lives of the Celtic saints from something approaching their own perspective.

Not all writers on the subject have appreciated this difference of perspective. For this reason, the quotation of a source in the References which follow does not necessarily imply endorsement of the whole text. The circumstances in which particular sources were written are often important in assessing whether what they say is reliable.

The most important finding of the past thirty years is the understanding of the importance of the sea-routes followed by the Celtic peoples, which has revolutionized assessment of their movements and their missions. The result of this finding is that almost everything written about the Celtic saints before the early 1970s is now likely to be dated, mediated through the conventional understanding of earlier generations, which we now know to have been mistaken in important respects.

Simon Winchester's *The Map That Changed the World* (2001) describes the basis of this change. It came, not from theologians or from historians, but from a geologist named William Smith. His map of the British Isles was published in 1815. The original now hangs in Burlington House in London's Piccadilly, and it shows very clearly how the rock formation of the Celtic lands differs from that of the rest of Britain. This explains much about their separate development; but the message took a long time to permeate the academic community. It was not until 1923 that Sir Cyril Fox, Director of the National Museum of Cardiff, produced his book *The Personality of Britain*, which made a clear distinction between the topography of the Highland Zone and the Lowland Zone. Detailed maps showing archaeological finds from the Mediterranean and the Middle East in the Celtic lands proved the importance of the trade routes from the Neolithic period onwards. Professor Emrys Bowen of University College, Cardiff, applied these new concepts to the travels of the Celtic saints in a number of papers in academic journals before publishing his seminal study *Saints, Seaways and Settlements in the Celtic Lands* in 1969. This conclusively established the strength of Eastern Mediterranean influence on the Celtic Church, and stressed the importance of shipping routes to both patterns of settlement and patterns of mission.

Professor Bowen describes how the early Celtic monasteries were usually sited in 'estuarine locations'. Estuaries provided shelter for trading ships, and settlements grew up around them. More recent historical and archaeological studies have confirmed his analyses, and there is plenty of evidence in the ancient Lives of the saints once one is alerted to looking for it. Understanding of the seaborne lines of communication – so different from the land-based lines of communication in the Romanized Lowland Zone – fundamentally changes the parameters of study. The references which follow draw wherever possible on the early Lives of the Celtic saints and on recent analyses, rather than on works published in the long centuries when land travel across Britain and a short sea-route to the Continent were assumed to be the norm.

The early Lives are a very mixed collection: some are in the original Celtic languages, some in Latin, and some of the Breton Lives in French. Latin and French Lives have been consulted in the original, but those in Celtic languages have necessarily been read in translation, and in edited versions. Over the centuries, some of these have been subjected to re-translation, editing and glosses. For example, the *Nova Legenda Anglie*, a collection of ancient Lives, consists of John of Tynmouth's *Sanctilogium Angliae*, dating from the second quarter of the fourteenth century, which had already been through the hands of many scribes by the time it was compiled. It was edited by Nicholas Capgrave in the fifteenth century, re-edited by Wynkyn de Worde in 1516, and edited once more by Carl Horstmann in 1901. The final version is still useful, but it contains the mistakes and misunderstandings of many generations.

Since the Reformation, the Roman Catholic Church has been the chief guardian of the records of the saints. The sixteenth century Protestants who looted shrines and plundered monastic libraries in Britain and western Europe destroyed many of the documents which had survived the destruction of the Vikings and later men of battle, so that Rome became the chief repository of what remained. The standard collections of early Lives of the saints are those contained in the sixty-four large volumes of the *Acta Sanctorum*, begun by the Jesuit Society of Bollandists in the 1670s. Most volumes were compiled in the seventeenth and eighteenth centuries. The last volume (November) was completed by the Bollandist scholar Fr Hippolyte Delehaye in 1941, and the December volume has never been published. Some of the better-known Celtic saints are included, though often in the bowdlerized version re-written by Norman scribes in the eleventh and twelfth centuries. In retrospect, one can have some sympathy for the unfortunate scribes who were expected to produce clear and unambiguous accounts useful to their bishops. They were working on copies of texts which were already some five or six hundred years old, and had been re-copied many times before. If they sometimes borrowed a miracle from Saint A and attributed it to Saint B, or suppressed the record of Saint C in order to enhance the reputation of Saint D, they had to cover the sheets of vellum at all costs. If they assumed a Roman pattern of ecclesiastical jurisdiction where it demonstrably did not exist, and Latinized Celtic names which they found unfamiliar or unpronounceable, thus causing confusion over names and identities, they at least kept some of the traditions alive. However, they did produce distortions, many of which have been passed on to subsequent scholars, and formed the basis of centuries of Catholic tradition. Any mention of Celtic bishops, dioceses, croziers, cathedrals, visits to Germanus of Auxerre or visits to Rome before 700 ought to alert the modern reader to possible bias. This does not mean that the accounts can be dismissed out of hand, but it does mean that biases have to be identified and acknowledged.

The Society of Bollandists is still active in Brussels, and their journal, *Analecta Bollandiana*, regularly published, is the source of many scholarly papers and reviews, most of them in Latin or French. Other standard Roman Catholic sources are the *New Catholic Encyclopaedia*, fourteen volumes published in 1967 in English, with later supplements, and the *Biblioteca Sanctorum*, twelve volumes published between 1960 and 1970 in Italian.

The most up-to-date and accessible source for English readers is the twelve-volume edition of *Butler's Lives of the Saints* published in 1998–2000, which takes account of much recent scholarship, and includes considered assessments of such outstanding Celtic figures as Patrick, Columba, Aidan and Cuthbert. Cardinal Basil Hume, who loved the saints, is said to have had a particular devotion to Aidan of Lindisfarne.

The primary interest of Roman Catholic scholars has naturally been in those saints recognized and venerated within their own Church, but David Hugh Farmer's *The Oxford Dictionary of Saints*, available in several editions and regularly updated, includes many Celtic saints not listed in the other standard works.

The chief Anglican writers on the saints are Sabine Baring Gould (1834–1924), the author of 'Onward, Christian Soldiers', and John Fisher. Their *Lives of the British Saints* (1907–13) is now distinctly dated, but it contains many odd and unusual bits of scholarship as well as some idiosyncratic interpretations.

Knowledge of the ancient Irish Lives has been greatly enriched by the work of Charles Plummer, whose *Vitae Sanctorum Hiberniae* (1910) has become a standard work on the subject. The two main volumes are in Latin. Plummer's *Lives of the Irish Saints* consists of one volume in Irish and one in modern English. J. F. Kenney's *Sources for the History of Ireland* (1929) is primarily an updating of Plummer's work, and has been updated once more by Dr Ludwig Bieler, the German classical philosopher and linguist who arrived in Dublin in 1941. Dr Bieler repaid his adopted country for its hospitality with several books on the Irish saints, and a stream of scholarly papers.

Publications from the Irish University Press and the University of Wales Press are of a high academic standard, often by scholars who combine the ability to read the original Irish or Welsh with a knowledge of the terrain and its history, and a sense of kinship with their subjects.

Scotland, Cornwall and Brittany have been less fortunate. Knowledge of the Scottish saints would all but have disappeared had it not been for the labours of Bishop Alexander Forbes (an Episcopalian) whose *Kalendars of Scottish Saints* (1872), based largely on the *Aberdeen Breviary*, restored knowledge of many saints who had sunk under successive waves of Calvinist disapproval. Much of what we know about the saints of Cornwall comes from tenaciously held traditions in villages, from place-names, and from local historians or even visitors. William Worcestre of Norwich made a two-week visit to Cornwall in September 1478, talked to clergy, collected ancient church calendars, and produced an interesting but unsystematized account of what he found. The bibliographer and antiquary John Leland visited Cornwall about 1540, and added further material. In the reign of Elizabeth I, Nicholas Roscarrock, who was brought up in the manor house of Roscarrock in the parish of Endellion in Cornwall, read and edited what Worcestre and Leland had written, and added much from his local knowledge. Roscarrock became a Catholic at Oxford. In 1680, he met Lord William Howard in the Marshalsea Prison, where they were both imprisoned as 'dangerous Papists', and he spent the last twenty-six years of his life in Lord William's household at Naworth, near Carlisle, writing his *Lives of the Saints*. He had the assistance and encouragement of his patron and his friend Mr Camden, a fellow bibliophile. Sir Robert Cotton, whose Cotton MSS are now the pride of the British Library, was Lord William's son-in-law. Roscarrock's intention was to write a series of works on the saints of the British Isles, but this was never completed, and only his *Lives of the Saints of Cornwall and Devon* have been republished.

Canon Gilbert Hunter Doble of Truro rescued many Cornish saints from obscurity in a series of pamphlets published by local printers. Most of these were re-published in *The Saints of Cornwall*, a five-volume edition edited by Donald Attwater in 1950–60. The others are now difficult to track down, but will be found in the British Library. Doble claimed many saints better known in Wales or Brittany as 'Cornish saints', and Baring Gould complained that, though he had corrected many errors in the earlier Lives, he had introduced some unwarranted enthusiasms of his own. (Doble repaid the compliment by pointing to Baring Gould and Fisher's own idiosyncrasies.) Like Roscarrock, Doble was inclined to over-stress the Cornish element in the accounts of these travelling saints, largely ignoring their subsequent careers in Brittany. His *Lives of the Welsh Saints* is a more sketchy book than the Cornish Series, which was clearly a labour of love. In 2000 Nicholas Orme, who edited Roscarrock's work, produced a more accurate and up-to-date account of the Cornish saints, but this is primarily based on the evidence of Wessex church records, which may be biased by the interests of the Benedictines. It also includes many entries (such as those on the Apostles and the Archangel Michael) which refer to saints who have dedications or place-names in Cornwall, but are clearly not of Celtic origin.

Monsignor Le Grand's *Les vies des saints de la Bretagne Armorique* is a two-volume edition of ancient Lives, only slightly tinged with Francophile sentiments, and evidently representing years of labour in searching and identifying scattered documents. Though it bears some anxious corrections made by a canon of Quimper who edited the work in 1901, it still displays a complete lack of geographical grasp in its treatment of '*Bretagne insulaire*', by which the original scribes meant Britain-across-the-water-from-Brittany. The settlers in Britanny often used place-names from home for their new settlements, much as settlers in North America, centuries later, established New York or London, Ontario. One of the names they used was *Cornouaille* – now well known as the region of southern Brittany for which Quimper is the capital, but originally a form of 'Cornwall'. It is disconcerting for those who study the ancient Breton Lives to find how many of the saints are said to have been born in *Cornouaille* until they discover not only that the chroniclers were referring to Cornwall across the water, but that they had absolutely no grasp of the topography of the lands from which their ancestors had come. *Cornouaille* was used to refer to modern Devon and Cornwall (the ancient kingdom of Dumnonia), and sometimes to the whole of Wales. The writer of the Life of Brieuc makes this clear when he explains that he is referring to *Cornouaille insulaire*, not *Cournouaille Armorique*, and adds that by his time, it had become known as the *Principauté de Walles*. Other Lives claim that Samson and Dubricius were both archbishops of 'Yorkh', and locate this city in the 'province' of Winchester – presumably in 'Walles'. But in spite of these shortcomings and the overlaps and gaps caused by lack of communication across what is now the English Channel, Le Grand's *Lives* do provide additional evidence on some of the key saints. He is commendably free from the mental constructs of some other French writers on the subject, who are as cavalier in their assumptions about the Frenchness of seventh and eighth century Brittany as many Victorian and Edwardian historians are about the Englishness of Ireland, Wales and Scotland.

Most of these English historians are much more at home with the history of Roman Britannia and that of England after the time of the Anglo-Saxon settlement than with the Celtic fringe. They are properly sceptical of the writings of Nennius, the ninth century Welsh writer who recorded the Arthurian legends, and of their subsequent elaboration by Geoffrey of Monmouth (*c.* 1100–54). Geoffrey, who was archdeacon of Llandaff, refused to reveal his sources; and since he traced the genealogy of the kings of Britain back to the Trojans as well as introducing obviously fictitious accounts of the Druids and their dealings with the Romans, the suspicion arose that his sources were non-existent, or at best tainted. Both Nennius and Geoffrey write in the tradition of heroic romance which stretches from the bards to the troubadours. The result is entertaining, but no more reliable than a Hollywood epic on the period.

Much confusion has arisen from the fact that up to the ninth or tenth century, the Britons were the *Brythons*, the people of Wales, and not the people of a homogeneous Britain. Gildas, whose *De excidio Britanniae* referred to the havoc wrought on the coasts of Wales and Cornwall by the Norsemen, has often been taken for an 'English' historian, and criticized by later historians because the horrors he described were not found in the records of Lowland Britain. The *Dictionary of National Biography*, which includes some Celtic saints in the original edition of 1895–1900, is a compilation from many different hands, and while some of the entries are sound, others are now very dated. They often seem to be based on the assumption (common to Victorian and Edwardian Englishmen as well as the older Roman Catholic writers) that the only way from the British Isles to the continent of Europe involved a crossing via the Channel ports.

Haddan and Stubbs, pillars of the mid-Victorian History establishment at Oxford, are reliable on solid fact, but capable of some odd interpretations. For instance, they blame the Welsh abbots (Bede's 'British bishops') for their refusal to accede to the demands of Augustine of Canterbury in 603, and accuse them of causing 'schism' in the Church; and there is a vague reference to 'Welsh bishops' as being 'not diocesan, but presiding over monasteries and educational establishments' which suggests that the authors had not grasped the status of Celtic abbots which Bede described so clearly. Volume I was principally the work of A. W. Haddan, a Fellow of Trinity College, Oxford. William Stubbs, his collaborator, was Regius Professor of Modern History in the University. Oxford traditionally dates 'Modern History' from 1485, but even so, he was well out of his period. (This will not surprise those historians who are aware that in the celebrated *Stubbs' Charters*, he described Magna Carta in lyrical terms as the source of English liberalism and democracy.)

Many books have been written about the saints of a single Celtic country, whether Ireland, Scotland, Wales, Cornwall or Brittany, which largely ignore the strong links between the Celtic lands and the wandering habits of the saints, and assume the national frameworks of the writers' own day. Even standard sources like Bishop

Forbes' *Kalendars of Scottish Saints*, Canon Doble's *The Saints of Cornwall* and Monsignor Le Grand's *Les vies des saints de la Bretagne Armorique* include many saints who were not native to the countries concerned, and spent most or all of their ministries elsewhere. The result is a good deal of overlapping, much duplication, and often contradictory accounts. This creates what are known as 'doublets' – one saint may appear to be two different people in different settings, or two saints may be combined into one. Confusion over names, which appear in different forms in different languages, makes the task of identifying the people concerned even more difficult.

For the Northumbrian mission, we have only one reliable primary source: the Venerable Bede, who, apart from his obsession about 'the correct date of Easter' and his slightly questionable dates, is a very sound and conscientious historian. (His exact dates are questionable because he started the year from September, and not from January, so we are not quite sure whether the Synod of Whitby, which was convened in that month, should be dated to the year 664 or 665.) The other main source for the Synod of Whitby is the Life of Bishop Wilfrid by Eddius Stephanus; but this is a very partial work, written to justify and promote the ambitious Wilfrid, and lacking Bede's objective judgement. Eddi, to give him his original Saxon name, was an expert in Gregorian chant, trained in Rome, and very different from the rough-hewn 'Eddi, Wilfrid's priest' of Kipling's charming but misleading poem.

Nobody seems to have written a systematic account of what happened to the Celtic Church after the Synod of Whitby. The story has had to be patched together from brief references in works on other subjects. It seems that after the formal submission of the Irish Church in 715, the movement survived unacknowledged in lonely and remote monasteries and hermitages until the Celtic lands were thoroughly subjugated by Edward I in the thirteenth century.

In working through the sources, the individual scholar has to exercise his or her own judgement about what is possible, what is probable, and what is simply mistaken or alleged in order to support partisan interests. Generations of scholars have contributed to this process (sometimes adding fresh errors as they proceed) and it is to be hoped that the work of sieving the evidence will continue. There is still much to be done to get the story straight.

Abbreviations

AA.SS.	*Acta Sanctorum*, 64 vols., Antwerp, Rome and Paris from 1643. Page numbers may vary slightly in different editions: each volume has an alphabetical index.
Adamnan, *Columba*	*Adomnán's Life of Columba*, trans. and ed. Richard Sharpe, 1995.
Anal. Boll.	*Analecta Bollandiana*, Brussels, 1852–.
Annals of Ulster	*The Annals of Ulster*, ed. S. MacAirt and G. Mac Nioccaill, Part 1, text and translation, Dublin, 1983.
Bede, *H.E.*	Bede, *Historia Ecclesiastica*, trans. and ed. L. Sherley-Price as *Bede's Ecclesiastical History of the English People*, 1990 edn, rev. R. E. Latham and D. H. Farmer.
Bieler	L. Bieler, *The Irish Penitentials*, Dublin, 1963.
B.G.F.	S. Baring Gould and J. Fisher, *Lives of the British Saints*, 4 vols., 1907–13.
B.T.A.	*Butler's Lives of the Saints*, ed. H. Thurston and D. Attwater, 4 vols., 1953–4.
Butler 2000	*Butler's Lives of the Saints*, ed. Paul Burns, 12 vols., 1998–2000.
Cambro-British Saints	W. J. Rees, *Lives of the Cambro-British Saints*, Welsh Manuscripts Society, Llandovery, 1853.
Celt and Saxon	K. Jackson, P. Hunter-Blair, B. M. Colgrave et al., *Celt and Saxon: studies in the Early British Border* (1963).

Carmina Gadelica	*Carmina Gadelica: hymns and incantations*, trans. and ed. A. Carmichael, 2 vols., 1900, repr. 1928.
Chadwick	Myles Dillon and Nora Chadwick, *The Celtic Realms*, 1967.
Cormac Bourke	*Studies in the Cult of St Columba*, ed. Cormac Bourke, Dublin, 1977.
D.A.C.L.	F. Cabrol and H. Leclercq, eds., *Dictionnaire archéologique et de liturgie*, Paris, 1907–36.
D.C.B.	*The Dictionary of Christian Biography*, ed. W. Smith and H. Wace, 4 vols., 1877–87.
D.H.G.E.	*Dictionnaire d' histoire et de géographie ecclésiastique*, ed. A. Baudrillart et al., Paris, 1912.
D.N.B.	*Dictionary of National Biography*, ed. L. Stephen et al., 1885– .
Doble, *Cornish Saints*	G. H. Doble, *The Saints of Cornwall*, ed. Donald Attwater, 5 vols., 1950–60: a compilation of pamphlets in The Cornish Saints Series, nos. 1–48, various printers and places of publication.
Doble, *Welsh Saints*	G. H. Doble, *Lives of the Welsh Saints*, Cymmrodorion Society, London, 1971.
Eddius Stephanus	*Eddius Stephanus, The Life of Bishop Wilfrid*, ed. B. M. Colgrave, 1972, paperback edition, 1985.
E.H.R.	*English Historical Review*, 1886– .
Félire	*The Martyrology of Oengus the Culdee*, trans. and ed. Whitley Stokes, 1905.
Gildas	*The Ruin of Britain, Gildas's De excidio Britanniae*, trans. and ed. Michael Winterbottom, 1978.
Gougaud	L. Gougaud, *Les saints irlandais hors d'Irlande*, Louvain/Oxford, 1936.
Haddan and Stubbs	A. W. Haddan and W. Stubbs, *Councils*

	and Ecclesiastical Documents relating to Great Britain and Ireland, 3 vols., 1869–71, new edn ed. F. M. Powicke and C. R. Cheney, 2 vols., 1964.
Heist, *V.S.H.*	*Vitae Sanctorum Hiberniae,* trans. and ed. W. W. Heist, 2 vols., Brussels, 1965.
Irish Saints	D. Pochin Mould, *The Irish Saints,* Dublin, 1964.
Kenney	J. F. Kenney, *Sources for the Early History of Ireland: Ecclesiastical,* New York, 1929, revised by L. Bieler, Dublin, 1966.
K.S.S.	A. P. Forbes, *Kalendars of Scottish Saints,* Edinburgh, 1872.
Le Grand	A. Le Grand, *Les vies des saints de la Bretagne Armorique,* 2 vols., Rennes, 1636. 5th edn, Quimper, 1901.
Leland	*The Itinerary of John Leland,* ed. L. Toulmin-Smith, 5 vols., 1964–9, vol. 1. (The 2-volume edition, ed. John Chandler, omits most of the information about saints.)
Mayr-Harting	H. Mayr-Harting, *The Coming of Christianity to Anglo-Saxon England,* 1972.
Menzies	Lucy Menzies, *The Saints in Italy,* 1924.
N.C.E.	*The New Catholic Encyclopaedia,* 14 vols. plus appendices, New York, 1967.
Nennius	Nennius, *Historia Britonum,* trans. and ed. A. W. Wade-Evans as *Nennius's History of the Britons,* 1938.
N.L.A.	*Nova Legenda Anglie,* ed. C. Horstmann, 2 vols., Oxford, 1901.
O.D.S.	D. H. Farmer, *The Oxford Book of Saints,* 3rd edn, 1992.
Orme	Nicholas Orme, *The Saints of Cornwall,* 2000.

Plummer, *Lives*   *The Lives of the Irish Saints*, trans. and ed. Charles Plummer, vol. 2 (selected Lives only: vol. 1 is in Irish), 1922, 2nd edn 1968.

Plummer, *V.S.H.*   *Vitae Sanctorum Hiberniae* (Latin), ed. C. Plummer, 2 vols., 1910, 2nd edn, 1968.

Rhygyfarch   A. W. Wade-Evans, trans. and ed., *The Life of St David*, Gregynog, Wales, 1914, repr. 1923, 1927.

Roscarrock   *Nicholas Roscarrock's Lives of the Saints of Cornwall and Devon*, ed. Nicholas Orme, 1992.

R.S.   Rolls Series, *Rerum Britannicum Medii Aevi Scriptores*, HMSO, 1858– .

Saints, Seaways   E. G. Bowen, *Saints, Seaways and Settlements in the Celtic Lands*, Cardiff, 1977 (1st edn 1969).

Sharpe, *M.I.S.*   Richard Sharpe, *Medieval Irish Saints*, Oxford, 1991.

Stanton   R. Stanton, *A Menology of England and Wales*, 1892.

Stenton   Frank Stenton, *Anglo-Saxon England*, Oxford History of England, 3rd edn, 1971.

Tommasini   A. M. Tommasini, *The Irish Saints in Italy*, 1937.

Tripartite Life   *The Tripartite Life of Patrick*, ed. W. W. Stokes, 1887.

Wade-Evans, *V.S.B.*   A. W. Wade-Evans, *Vitae Sanctorum Britanniae et Genealogiae*, Cardiff, 1944.

Worcestre   William Worcestre, *Itineraries*, ed. J. H. Harvey, 1969.

References

Names of authors not followed by titles are biographies of the saint who is the subject of the reference.

Preface

Saints, Seaways, chs. 1–3, pp. 1–80; Cyril Fox, *The Personality of Britain* (1943, repr. 1947); T. O'Loughlin, 'Living in the Ocean', in Cormac Bourke (ed.), *Studies in the Cult of St Columba* (Dublin, 1997), pp. 11–23; Barry Cunliffe, *Facing the Ocean: the Atlantic and its Peoples* (2001); Mayr-Harting, chs. 5–6, pp. 78–102; Chadwick, chs. 1–4, pp. 1–91; Haddan and Stubbs (1964), 1, pp. 3–40.

1. Palladius and Patrick

Introduction: Prosper of Aquitaine: *Butler 2000*, June, pp. 188–9; Pope Celestine: *Butler 2000*, July, pp. 217–19; Palladius: Bede, *H.E.*, bk 5, ch. 24; *D.N.B.*, 15, pp. 112–13; *Butler 2000*, July, p. 43; the four 'Palladian bishops': Plummer, *V.S.H.*, 2, p. 45.

Patrick: Ludwig Bieler (trans. and ed.), *The Works of St Patrick* (1953) and *Studies on the Life and Legend of St Patrick* (1986); A. B. A. Hood (trans. and ed.), *St Patrick: his writings and Murchiu's Life* (1978); R. P. C. Hanson, *The Life and Writings of the Historical St Patrick* (1983); Sharpe, *M.I.S.*; David Dumville (ed.), *St Patrick 493–1993* (1993); E. A. Thompson, *Who was St Patrick?* (1985); D. R. Howlett (trans. and ed.), *The Book of Letters of Saint Patrick the Bishop* (1994); *Irish Saints*, pp. 272–9; W. S. Kerr, *The Independence of the Celtic Church in Ireland* (1931), p. 17.

Asicus: *Irish Saints*, pp. 30–1; *Butler 2000*, pp. 190–1.

Attracta: T. O'Rourke, *The History of Sligo*, 2, pp. 366–78; *Irish Saints*, pp. 31–2.

Gobnet: *Irish Saints*, pp. 192–5; *O.D.S.*, p. 207; Heist, *V.S.H.*, under 'Vita S. Abbani'.

Loman: B.T.A., 1, p. 356; *O.D.S.*, p. 302, suggests that he may be confused with a seventh century bishop of Trim of the same name. See *Butler 2000*, Oct., pp. 68–9.

Macanissey: *AA.SS.*, Sept., 1; Kenney, p. 350; *Butler 2000*, Sept., p. 25.

Macarten: *O.D.S.*, p. 308; *Irish Saints*, p. 213; Heist, *V.S.H.*, pp. 343–6; E. C. R. Armstrong and H. J. Lawlor, *The Domnach Airgid* (1917–19), pp. 96–126; Kenney, p. 350.

Mel: *Irish Saints*, p. 245; B.T.A., p. 262 (brief mention in *Butler 2000*, Feb., p. 67); *D.N.B.*, 13, p. 216; *O.D.S.*, p. 338.

Mochta: *Annals of Ulster*, p. 71; Adamnan, *Columba*, pp. 104–5, 244; Heist, *V.S.H.*, pp. 394–400; *Butler 2000*, Aug., p. 186; *O.D.S.*, p. 341.

2 Ireland: the Monastic Founders

Introduction: L. Gougaud, *Christianity in Celtic Lands*, trans. Maud Joynt (1932); Kathleen Hughes, *Early Christian Ireland* (1972); Nora Chadwick, *The Age of the Saints in the Early Celtic Church* (1961); Myles Dillon and Nora Chadwick, *The Celtic Realms* (1967, repr. 2000), quotations pp. 176–7; Kathleen Hughes and Anne Hamlin, *The Modern Traveller in the Irish Church* (1977); Ian Bradley, *The Celtic Way* (1993, repr. 2000); J. F. Webb and D. H. Farmer (eds.), *The Age of Bede* (1988), pp. 13–14; R. van de Weyer, introduction to *Celtic Fire: an anthology of Celtic Christian Literature* (1990, repr. 1997), pp. 1–12.

Ailbe of Emly: Plummer, *V.S.H.*, 1, pp. 44–64; B.G.F., 1, pp. 128–36; *D.N.B.*, 6, pp. 783–4; Kenney, pp. 314–15; *Butler 2000*, Sept., p. 106; Joseph O'Neill, 'The Rule of Ailbe of Emly', *Erin*, 3 (1907), pp. 92–115.

Brigid: *AA.SS.*, Feb., 1 has Brigid's Life by the monk Cogitosus; Kenney, pp. 356–63; Sharpe, *M.I.S.*, p. 391. Modern Lives by A. Knowles (1927); A. Curtayne (1931, new edn 1954); F. O'Briain (1938). See also *Irish Saints*, pp. 41–7; N.L.A., 1, pp. 153–60; N.C.E., 2, p. 803, and 8, p. 178; D.H.G.E., 10, cols. 715–19; *D.N.B.*, 2, pp. 1248–50; *Butler 2000*, Feb., pp. 1–5.

Buite: Plummer, *V.S.H.*, 1, pp. 87–97; Kenney, p. 373; *Irish Saints*, pp. 48–50.

Ciaran of Clonmacnoise: Plummer, *V.S.H.*, 1, pp. 200–16; *Irish Saints*, pp. 71–6; R. A. S. MacAlister (trans.), *The Latin and Irish Lives of Ciaran* (1921); *The Rule of Ciaran* (Irish text), ed. J. Strachan (1905); *D.N.B.*, 4, pp. 350–2.

Ciaran of Saighir: Plummer, *V.S.H.*, 1, pp. 217–33; Kenney, pp. 316–17; P. Grosjean in *Anal. Boll.*, 59 (1941), pp. 217–71; *Irish Saints*, pp. 76–9; *D.N.B.*, 4, pp. 350–2.

Colman of Dromore: *AA.SS.*, June, 2; Heist, *V.S.H.*, pp. 357–60; B.G.F., 2, pp. 162–4; *Irish Saints*, pp. 85–9; *O.D.S.*, pp. 105–6; *Butler 2000*, June, p. 59.

Comgall: *AA.SS.*, May, 2, 580–6; Adamnan, *Columba*, bk 1, p. 49, bk 2, pp. 13, 17; J. Ryan, *Irish Monasticism* (1951); L. Gougaud, *Christianity in Celtic Lands* (1933); Plummer, *V.S.H.*, 2, pp. 3–21; A. Gwynn, 'The Irish Monastery of Bangor', *Irish Ecclesiastical Records*, November 1950, pp. 385–97; *Irish Saints*, pp. 125–32; *Butler 2000*, May, pp. 52–3.

Conleth: *Irish Saints*, p. 132; *Butler 2000*, May, p. 20; *D.N.B.*, 2, pp. 1248–50.

Declan of Ardmore: P. Power (trans. and ed.), *The Life of St Declan of Ardmore and the Life of St Mochuda of Lismore* (1914); Plummer, *V.S.H.*, 2, pp. 32–59 has the Irish Life of Declan in Latin, as has *AA.SS.*, July, 5. There are manuscript copies in the Royal Irish Academy and the Bibliothèque Royale in Brussels. See also *Irish Saints*, pp. 137–42; *O.D.S.*, pp. 129–30; *D.N.B.*, 5, pp. 717–18; Kenney, pp. 312–13; D. O'Conchuir, *The Pilgrim Round of Ardmore* (2000).

Enda: Plummer, *V.S.H.*, 2, pp. 60–75; Heist, *V.S.H.*, pp. 670–5; *Irish Saints*, pp. 167–9; *O.D.S.*, pp. 157–8; J. Fahy, *A History of Kilmacduagh* (Dublin, 1893), pp. 54–5; *D.N.B.*, 6, pp. 783–4.

Erc of Slane: Worcestre, pp. 114–15; *B.G.F.*, 2. pp. 459–63; Doble, *Cornish Saints*, 1, pp. 95–6; *O.D.S.*, p. 160; Orme, pp. 116–17.

Finnian of Clonard: Heist, *V.S.H.*, pp. 96–107; Irish Life in W. Stokes, *Lives of Saints from the Book of Lismore* (1890), pp. 75–83 and 222–30; *N.L.A.*, pp. 444–7; Kathleen Hughes, 'The Historical Value of the Lives of Finnian of Clonard', *E.H.R.*, 69 (1954), pp. 353–67; Bieler, pp. 74–95; L. Beiler, 'The Office of St Finnian of Clonard and St Ciaran of Duleek', *Anal. Boll.*, 72 (1954), pp. 347–62 and 75 (1957), pp. 337–9; *D.N.B.*, 7, pp. 39–41; *D.H.G.E.*, 7, pp. 167–75, under 'Finden'; *N.L.A.*, 1, pp. 444–7.

Finnian of Moville: Kenney, p. 391; *Irish Saints*, pp. 169–71; *N.C.E.*, 5, p. 828; *O.D.S.*, p. 190; *Butler 2000*, Sept., pp. 88–9.

Fintan of Clonenagh: *AA.SS.*, Feb., 3; *D.N.B.*, 7, pp. 41–2; Plummer, *V.S.H.*, 2, pp. 96–106; *O.D.S.*, p. 180; *Butler 2000*, Feb., p. 171.

Ibar: There is no known ancient Life of Ibar, though he figures in the Lives of Declan, Brigid and other Irish saints. Kenney, pp. 310–11; *Irish Saints*, pp. 195–6; *Butler 2000*, April, p. 164; *B.T.A.*, 2, p. 151; P. Grosjean, 'Deux textes inédits sur Ibar', *Anal. Boll.*, 77 (1959), pp. 426–50.

Ita: *Irish Saints*, pp. 196–9; Plummer, *V.S.H.*, 2, pp. 116–30; Robin Flower, *The Irish Tradition* (1947) has a metrical version of her hymn; *D.N.B.*, 10, pp. 514–15.

Jarlath of Tuam: *Irish Saints*, p. 199; *O.D.S.*, p. 251; *Butler 2000*, June, p. 63.

Liadain: *Irish Saints*, p. 204.

Monnena: *AA.SS.*, July, 2; Kenney, pp. 366–71; Sharpe, *M.I.S.*, p. 396; Heist, *V.S.H.*, pp. 83–95; *Irish Saints*, pp. 261–3; *E.H.R.*, 35 (1920), pp. 71–8; *O.D.S.*, p. 343; M. Esposito, 'The Sources of Conchubranus' Life of St Monnena', *E.H.R.*, 35 (1920), pp. 71–8.

Senan: Whitley Stokes (ed.), *Lives of Saints from the Book of Lismore* (1890), pp. 219–20; Heist, *V.S.H.*, pp. 301–24; Kenney, pp. 304–6; P. Grosjean in *Anal. Boll.*, 66 (1948), pp. 199–230; *Irish Saints*, pp. 285–7. There is a metrical Life, said to have been written by Colman of Cloyne.

3   Ireland: the Consolidators

Introduction: as for Chapter 2. For the *Ceíli Dé*, see W. Reeves, *The Culdees of the British Isles* (Dublin, 1864); *D.A.C.L.*, 3, pt 2, cols. 3186–90; Kenney, pp. 68–85; for the Paschal Controversy, see Bede, *H.E.*, bk 2, chs. 4 and 19; Kenney, pp. 99–100, 210–23; for the provenance and published versions of Irish chronicles, see Kenney's index for entries under 'Annals', 'Chronicles', 'Martyrologies', etc.

Aedh Mac Brice: *AA.SS.*, Nov., 4; Heist, *V.S.H.*, pp. 118–31; Plummer, *V.S.H.*, 1, pp. 34–43; *Irish Saints*, pp. 22–5; Kenney, p. 393: *O.D.S.*, pp. 5–6; *Butler 2000*, Nov., p. 79.

Brendan of Birr: Adamnan, *Columba*, pp. 119, 162–3, 222; *Irish Saints*, pp. 35–6; *O.D.S.*, p. 68–9; *D.N.B.*, 2, p. 1167.

Cainnech: *AA.SS.*, Oct., 5; Adamnan, *Columba*, p. 24, bk 1, ch. 4, bk 2, chs. 13–14, bk 3, chs. 13–14, nn. 145–6; *K.S.S.*, pp. 295–7; Heist, *V.S.H.*, pp. 182–98; Plummer, *V.S.H.*, 1, pp. 152–69; *Irish Saints*, pp. 52–7; *D.N.B.*, 3, pp. 665–7; *O.D.S.*, p. 82–3.

Colman of Cloyne: *Irish Saints*, pp. 85–6; *O.D.S.*, p. 105; *Butler 2000*, Nov., pp. 197–8; *D.N.B.*, 4, pp. 842–3; *N.C.E.*, 3, p. 1013.

Colman of Kilmacduagh: *AA.SS.*, Oct., 12; *Irish Saints*, pp. 91–2; *O.D.S.*, p. 106; *N.C.E.*, 3, p. 1013.

Colman of Llan Elo: Plummer, *Lives*, pp. 162–76; *Irish Saints*, pp. 86–9; *D.N.B.*, 4, pp. 843–5; *N.C.E.*, 3, p. 1013; John Carey, *King of Mysteries: early Irish religious worship* (1988), pp. 231–45, includes *The Alphabet of Devotion*.

Cumian Fota: Bieler, pp. 108–35; Adamnan, *Columba*, pp. 37; Kenney, pp. 220–1, 242, 324–5; L. Gougaud, *Christianity in Celtic Lands* (1932), p. 285; *Butler 2000*, Nov., pp. 97–8; *K.S.S.*, pp. 316–17.

Cumine: *K.S.S.*, pp. 316–17; Kenney, pp. 220–1, 324–6.

Diarmaid: *Irish Saints*, pp. 142–3; *O.D.S.*, p. 132.

Fechin: *AA.SS.*, Jan., 2; Heist, *V.S.H.*, 2, pp. 76–86; Whitley Stokes (ed.), 'The Life of St Fechin of Foss', *Révue Celtique*, 12 (1891), pp. 318–53. The Latin Life includes two hymns for his feast day. *Butler 2000*, Jan., p. 134.

Finan Cam: Plummer, *V.S.H.*, 2, pp. 87–95; *Irish Saints*, pp. 158–9; *N.C.E.*, 5, pp. 919–20.

Finan Lobur: Plummer, *V.S.H.*, 2, pp. 96–106; *Irish Saints*, pp. 159–60; *B.T.A.*, 1, pp. 606–7.

Finbar: Adamnan, *Columba*, pp. 317–18; *AA.SS.*, Sept., 7; Plummer, *Lives*, pp. 65–74; *Irish Saints*, pp. 160–4; *Anal. Boll.*, 69 (1951), pp. 324–47; *Butler 2000*, Sept., pp. 275–6.

Fintan Munnu: *AA.SS.*, Oct., 9; Adamnan, *Columba*, pp. 254–5, n. 53; Plummer, *V.S.H.*, 2, pp. 226–39; *Irish Saints*, pp. 184–7; *D.N.B.*, 7, pp. 42–3.

Flannan of Killaloe: Heist, *V.S.H.*, pp. 280–301; *Irish Saints*, pp. 177–30; P. Grosjean in *Anal. Boll.*, 46 (1928), pp. 122–4; *D.H.G.E.*, 17, cols. 365–7; Life by S. Malone (Dublin, 1902); *D.N.B.*, 7, pp. 250–1; *Butler 2000*, Dec., p. 151; Kenney, p. 405.

Kevin (Coemgen) of Glendalough: *AA.SS.*, June, 1; Plummer, *Lives*, pp. 121–61; *Irish Saints*, pp. 79–83; *Anal. Boll.*, 63 (1945), pp. 122–9 and *Anal. Boll.*, 70 (1952), pp. 313–15; *D.N.B.*, 4, pp. 667–8; *Butler 2000*, June, pp. 28–9; Kenney, pp. 403–4.

Maedoc of Ferns: *AA.SS.*, Jan., 2; *O.D.S.*, p. 311; *Irish Saints*, pp. 214–18; Plummer, *Lives*, pp. 177–281; Kenney, p. 449.

Maelruain of Tallaght: E. J. Gwynn and W. J. Purton (trans. and ed.), *The Monastery of Tallaght*, Proceedings of the Royal Irish Academy, 29c (1911), pp. 115–79; E. J. Gwynn and W. J. Purton (trans. and eds.), *The Rule of Tallaght* (1927); R. I. Best and J. Lawler (trans. and eds.), *The Martyrology of Tallaght* (1931); P. Grosjean, 'Le Martyrologie de Tallaght', *Anal. Boll.*, 51 (1933), pp. 117–30; *O.D.S.*, pp. 311–12; *Irish Saints*, pp. 228–41; John Carey, *King of Mysteries: early Irish religious writings* (1998), pp. 246–58.

Mochua of Timahoe: *Irish Saints*, pp. 248–9; *O.D.S.*, pp. 341–2; *Butler 2000*, Dec., p. 185; Plummer, *V.S.H.*, 2, pp. 184–9, and editor's comments in 1, pp. lxxix-xi.

Mo-Chuta: P. Power (trans. and ed.), *The Life of St Declán of Ardmore and the Life of St Mo-Chuda* (1914); P. Sheridan (ed.), *The Rule of St Carthage*, Irish

Ecclesiastical Records, 27 (Jan./June 1910), pp. 495–517; Plummer, *Lives*, pp. 282–302; *Irish Saints*, pp. 57–61 under 'Carthach'; *D.N.B.*, 3, pp. 1126–7; Kenney, pp. 452–3.

Modomnoc: J. W. James (trans. and ed.), *Rhigyfarch's Life of St David* (Cardiff, 1967), pp. 41–2; B.T.A., 1, p. 322; *O.D.S.*, p. 341.

Molaise: *AA.SS.*, April, 2; *K.S.S.*, pp. 407–9; Plummer, *V.S.H.*, 2, pp. 131–40; *Irish Saints*, p. 252; *Irish Ecclesiastical Records*, 79, 7, p. 318; *O.D.S.*, p. 288; Kenney, pp. 387–8.

Moling: *AA.SS.*, June, 4; Plummer, *V.S.H.*, 2, pp. 190–205 and notes in 1, pp. lxxxi–iii; Heist, *V.S.H.*, pp. 353–6; H. J. Lawlor, *Chapters in the Book of Mulling* (1897); *Irish Saints*, pp. 252–7; *O.D.S.*, pp. 342–3; *Butler 2000*, June, pp. 128–9; Kenney, pp. 462–3.

Molua: *AA.SS.*, Aug., 1; Plummer, *V.S.H.*, 2, pp. 206–25; *Irish Saints*, pp. 257–9; *D.N.B.*, 12, pp. 263–4 under 'Lugid'; Kenney, pp. 398–9.

Munchin: *Irish Saints*, pp. 263–4; *O.D.S.*, p. 349; *Butler 2000*, Jan., pp. 20–1; Kenney, p. 276.

Mura: *O.D.S.*, p. 349.

Murtagh: *Irish Saints*, pp. 264–5; *O.D.S.*, pp. 349–50.

Oengus: *AA.SS.*, March, 2; *Butler 2000*, March, pp. 116–17; *Irish Saints*, pp. 239–41 (subsumed under 'Maelruain'); *Félire*.

Ruadhan: *AA.SS.*, April, 2; Plummer, *Lives*, pp. 308–20; *Irish Saints*, pp. 280–1; *O.D.S.*, p. 423; Kenney, pp. 392–3.

Samthann: *Irish Saints*, pp. 282–4; *Butler 2000*, Dec., p. 153; Plummer, *V.S.H.*, 1, pp. xvi, lxxxvii–viii, *V.S.H.*, 2, pp. 253–61.

Tigernach of Clones: *AA.SS.*, April, 1; Kenney, pp. 386–7.

Ultan: There is a long notice in the *Félire* of Oengus, and a Latin poem in E. Dummler, *Poetae Latini medii aevi Carolini*, 1 (1881), p. 589; *Butler 2000*, Sept., p. 33.

4 The Western Isles and Scotland

Introduction: Bede, *H.E.*, bk 3, ch. 4; A. O. Anderson, *Early Sources of Scottish History* (1922); F. T. Wainwright, *The Problem of the Picts* (1955); R. P. C. Hanson, *St Patrick* (1968); W. D. Simpson, *St Ninian and the Origins of the Christian Church in Scotland* (1940); Adamnan, *Columba*; *Butler 2000* entry on Ninian, Sept., pp. 144–5; *K.S.S.*, pp. 351 and 389.

Baldred: *K.S.S.*, pp. 273–4; B.T.A., 1, p. 502; *O.D.S.*, p. 36; *D.N.B.*, 1, p. 950.

Brendan the Navigator: *Anal. Boll.*, 48 (1930), pp. 99–123; J. F. Webb and D. H. Farmer (eds.), *The Age of Bede* (1988), pp. 233–67; T. Severin (1978); G. A. Little (1947); Kenney, pp. 410–17. 'The Voyage of St Brendan' in J. F. Webb's *Lives of the Saints* (1965), pp. 33–68 gives the text of the *Navigatione Sancti Brendani* in full.

Chattan and **Blane:** *K.S.S.*, pp. 180–1; *Butler* 2000, May, p. 82; E. G. Howell, 'The Travels of the Celtic Saints', *Antiquity*, 8 (1944), pp. 16–18.

Columba: *AA.SS.*, June, 2; Adamnan's Life is the most valuable source on Columba, and this is available in several editions, including translations by A. O. Anderson and O. M. Anderson (1961, repr. 1990); and Richard Sharpe (1995), which has a good commentary. See also Bede, *H.E.*, bk 3, chs. 4 and 25, bk 5, ch. 9; *K.S.S.*, pp. 46–174; *D.N.B.*, 4, pp. 865–9; K. Hughes, *Early Christian Ireland* (1972) and *Early Christianity in Pictland* (Jarrow Lecture, 1970); N. Chadwick, *The Age of the Saints in the Early Celtic Church* (1961); Máire Herbert, *Iona, Kells and Derry* (Oxford, 1988); Kenney, pp. 263–5; Findbar McCormick, 'Iona: the Archaeology of the Early Monastery', in Cormac Bourke, pp. 45–68; Ben Mackworth-Praed, *The Book of Kells*, 1993, see especially comments of J. O. Westwood opposite Plate II. For Columba's poems, see the Irish *Liber Hymnorum* (1898), 1, pp. 62–89; 2, pp. 23–8 and 140–57.

Comgan: *AA.SS.*, Oct., 6; *K.S.S.*, pp. 110–11; *O.D.S.*, pp. 109–10.

Conan: *K.S.S.*, pp. 307–8; *Butler* 2000, Jan., pp. 180–1.

Donald: *K.S.S.*, pp. 324–5, 395–6; *Butler* 2000, July, p. 115.

Donan and his Companions: *AA.SS.*, April, 1; *K.S.S.*, p. 325; A. B. Scott, 'St Donan the Great', *Transactions of the Scottish Ecclesiological Society*, 1 (1906), pp. 256–67; D. Pochin Mould, *Scotland of the Saints* (1952), pp. 142–9; *D.H.G.E.*, 14, pp. 662–4; *Butler* 2000, April, p. 117.

Drostan: *AA.SS.*, July, 3; *K.S.S.*, pp. 326–7; *Butler* 2000, July, p. 80.

Fergus: *K.S.S.*, pp. 336–8; *O.D.S.*, p. 177; *Butler* 2000, Nov., pp. 213–14.

Fillan of Glendochart: *K.S.S.*, pp. 341–2; *Butler* 2000, Aug., pp. 258–9; *D.N.B.*, 6, pp. 1302–3; *O.D.S.*, p. 178.

Kentigern: A. P. Forbes (ed.), *Lives of St Ninian and St Kentigern* (Edinburgh, 1874); *N.L.A.*, 2, pp. 114–27; K. H. Jackson, 'The Sources for the Life of St Kentigern', in N. K. Chadwick (ed.), *Studies in the Early British Church* (1958), pp. 273–357; *Saints, Seaways*, pp. 83–92; *D.N.B.*, 9, pp. 26–7; *O.D.S.*, pp. 180–1; *Butler* 2000, Jan., p. 91.

Kentigerna: *K.S.S.*, p. 373; *B.T.A.*, 1, p. 120; *O.D.S.*, p. 281.

Kessog: *K.S.S.*, p. 373–4; *B.T.A.*, 1, p. 546.

Machan: *K.S.S.*, pp. 380–1; *O.D.S.*, p. 309.

Machar: *K.S.S.*, pp. 393–4; Plummer, *V.S.H.*, 2, pp. 164–83 (Mochoemog); *O.D.S.*, p. 309.

Maelrubba: W. Reeves, 'St Maelrubba, his History and his Church', *Proceedings of the Society of Antiquaries of Scotland*, 3 (1861), pp. 285–96; A. B. Scott, 'St Maelrubba', *Scottish Historical Review*, 6 (1909), pp. 260–80; Douglas Simpson, *The Celtic Church in Scotland* (1935); *Irish Saints*, p. 312; *K.S.S.*, pp. 382–4; *Butler 2000*, April, p. 156.

Maughold: Stanton, pp. 609–10; *O.D.S.*, p. 309, under 'Machallus'; *Butler 2000*, April, p. 191.

Modan: *AA.SS.*, Feb., 1; *K.S.S.*, pp. 401–3; *Butler 2000*, Feb., p. 45.

Moluag of Lismore: *K.S.S.*, pp. 408–11; *AA.SS.*, June, 7; *Irish Saints*, pp. 259–60; *O.D.S.*, p. 343; *Butler 2000*, June, pp. 190–1; personal information from Alastair Livingstone, Baron of Bachuill.

Ninian: Bede, *H.E.*, bk 3, ch. 4; W. Levison, 'An Eighth Century Poem on St Ninian', *Antiquity*, 14 (1940), pp. 280–91; Aelred's Life in A. P. Forbes (ed.), *The Lives of St Ninian and St Kentigern* (1874); *K.S.S.*, pp. 421–5; Haddan and Stubbs, 1 (1964), pp. 120–1; W. D. Simpson, *Saint Ninian and the Origins of the Christian Church in Scotland* (1940); F. T. Wainwright, *The Problem of the Picts* (1955); *Butler 2000*, Sept., pp. 144–5; *D.N.B.*, 14, pp. 513–14; Peter Hill, *Whithorn and Ninian: the excavation of a monastic town 1984–91* (Whithorn Trust, 1987) and *Whithorn 3: Excavations 1988–90* (Whithorn Trust, 1991).

Ronan of Kilmaronen: Bede, *H.E.*, bk 3, ch. 25; *K.S.S.*, pp. 441–2; *O.D.S.*, pp. 422–3.

Rule: *AA.SS.*, Oct., 8; W. F. Skene, *Celtic Scotland: a history of ancient Albion*, 1, (1876), pp. 296–9; *K.S.S.*, pp. 445–7; *O.D.S.*, p. 424; *D.N.B.*, 16, p. 867.

5 Wales: the Founders

Introduction: Nennius: *British History and the Welsh Annals* (1980), pp. 87, 145, 147–9; Bede, *H.E.*, bk 2, chs. 2–4; J. Gwenoguryn Evans and John Rhys (trans. and eds.), *The Book of Llan Dav*, (Oxford, 1893); A. W. Wade-Evans, *The Emergence of England and Wales* (1959); E. G. Bowen, *The Settlements of the*

Celtic Saints in Wales (1956); Doble, *Welsh Saints*; John Davies, *A History of Wales* (1995), p. 69.

Asaph: *AA.SS.*, 1, May; B.G.F., 1, pp. 177–85; Wade-Evans, *V.S.B.*, pp. 191–4; *O.D.S.*, p. 40; *Butler 2000*, May, p. 4.

Barry: B.G.F., 1, pp. 194–6; Worcestre, p. 107; Stanton, pp. 460, 671; *O.D.S.*, p. 39.

Beuno: The *Buchedd Beuno*, a Life in Welsh, is printed in *Cambro-British Saints*, pp. 13–21 (in Welsh) and pp. 299–308 (in English). See Winifred, for further sources.

Brychan: Roscarrock, pp. 58–60; Worcestre, pp. 63–5; Doble, *Welsh Saints*, pp. 151 and n.; B.G.F., 1, pp. 303–31 gives a number of genealogies in somewhat bewildering detail. Wade-Evans, *V.S.B.*, pp. 314–15.

Cadfan: B.G.F., 2, pp. 1–9; A. W. Wade-Evans, *Welsh Christian Origins* (1934), pp. 161–4; *Butler 2000*, Nov., p. 7.

Cadoc: Wade-Evans, *V.S.B.*, pp. 24–141; *N.L.A.*, 1, pp. 167–73; P. Grosjean in *Anal. Boll.*, 60 (1932), pp. 35–67; C. N. L. Brooke, 'St Peter of Gloucester and St Cadoc of Llancarfan', in *Celt and Saxon*, pp. 258–322; B.G.F., 2, pp. 14–42; Doble, *Cornish Saints*, 4, pp. 55–66; *O.D.S.*, p. 77; *Butler 2000*, Sept., pp. 200–1; Kenney, pp. 179–80.

Collen: B.G.F., 2, pp. 157–61; *O.D.S.*, p. 105.

Congar of Wales: *AA.SS.*, Nov., 3; Stanton, p. 158; Doble, *Cornish Saints*, 5, pp. 3–29; P. Grosjean, 'Cyngar, Sant', *Anal. Boll.*, 42 (1924), pp. 100–20; *O.D.S.*, p. 110; *Butler 2000*, Nov., pp. 211–12.

Cybi: *Cambro-British Saints*, pp. 183–7 (Latin) and pp. 496–501 (English); Wade-Evans, *V.S.B.*, pp. 234–51; Roscarrock, pp. 82–3; E. G. Bowen, *The Settlement of the Celtic Saints in Wales* (1956), pp. 118–20; Doble, *Cornish Saints*, 3, pp. 105–52; *O.D.S.*, pp. 118–19; *Butler 2000*, Nov., pp. 65–6; *The Poems of Matthew Arnold*, ed. Kenneth Allott (1965), pp. 492–3.

David: The Life by Rhygyfarch is published as *Buched Dewi*, ed. D. S. Evans (Cardiff, 1959), and in translation as *The Life of St David*, trans. and ed. A. W. Wade-Evans (1914, repr. 1923, 1927) and J. W. James (1967). See also E. Rhys (1927), S. M. Harris, *St David in the Liturgy* (Cardiff, 1927); J. Dixon (1948); D. Crowley (1954); *N.C.E.*, 4, p. 660; *O.D.S.*, pp. 127–8; *B.T.A.*, 1, p. 450; *Butler 2000*, March, pp. 1–2; Kenney, pp. 178–9. For the Synod of Brefi, see Haddan and Stubbs (1964), 1, pp. 116–20.

Deiniol: There is no contemporary or ancient Life of Deiniol, though he is referred to in the Lives of other saints. B.G.F., 2, pp. 325–31; *D.N.B.*, 5, pp. 408–9 (under 'Daniel' in an account that seems to confuse father and son); *D.C.B.*, 1, p. 302; *O.D.S.*, p. 130; *Butler 2000*, Sept., pp. 100–1.

Derfel: B.G.F., 2, pp. 33–6; *O.D.S.*, p. 31.

Dinwydd: Bede, *H.E.*, bk 2 ch. 2; *K.S.S.*, p. 362; Nora Chadwick, 'The Battle of Chester: a study of sources', in *Celt and Saxon*, pp. 167–85.

Dubricius: The main source for Dubricius's life is the Life of Teilo in the *Book of Llan Dav*. See also the Life of Samson of Dol, trans. and ed. T. Taylor (1925), pp. 19, 37, 44–5, 67–8; *N.L.A.*, 1, pp. 267–72. Haddan and Stubbs (1964), 1, pp. 146–8, deals with his participation in the Synod of Brefi. B.G.F., 2, pp. 359–82; Doble, *Welsh Saints*, pp. 56–87; *O.D.S.*, pp. 140–1; *Butler 2000*, Nov., pp. 114–15.

Dwyn: Worcestre, p. 60; B.G.F., 2, pp. 387–92; *O.D.S.*, p. 140.

Germanus of Man: *Nennius*, pp. 34–5, 55–8, 69; B.G.F., 3, pp. 60–79; Haddan and Stubbs (1964), 1, pp. 19–21; *O.D.S.*, p. 201.

Gildas: Le Grand, 1, pp. 17–29; *D.N.B.*, 7, pp. 1223–5; J. L. N. Myres, *The English Settlements*, Oxford History of England (1986), pp. 8–15; M. Winterbottom (ed.), *Gildas: the Ruin of Britain and Other Works* (1978); M. Miller, 'Bede's Use of Gildas', *E.H.R.*, 90 (1975), pp. 241–61; M. Lapidge and D. Dumville (eds.), *Gildas: New Approaches* (1984); *O.D.S.*, p. 205; *Butler 2000*, Nov., pp. 206–7; Kenney, pp. 176–7.

Gwladys and Gwynllyw: *Cambro-British Saints*, pp. 145–57 (Latin) and pp. 449–54 (English); B.G.F., 3, pp. 202–3, 234; Roscarrock, pp. 77–8; *D.N.B.*, 8, pp. 847–8; *Butler 2000*, March, pp. 269–70.

Hwyn: B.G.F., 3, pp. 163–5.

Illtud: *Cambro-British Saints*, pp. 158–82 (Latin) and pp. 465–94 (English); *N.L.A.*, 2, pp. 52–6; Wade-Evans, *V.S.B.*, pp. 194–233; Doble, *Welsh Saints*, pp. 88–145; B.G.F., 3, pp. 303–17.

Non: Rhygyfarch, pp. 3–5; B.G.F., 4, pp. 22–5; Roscarrock, p. 97; G. H. Doble, *St Nonna* (1928); *O.D.S.*, pp. 127, 358–9.

Oudoceus: *AA.SS.*, July, 1; B.G.F., 4, pp. 28–36; Doble, *Welsh Saints*, pp. 207–29; *O.D.S.*, p. 372.

Padarn of Wales: *Cambro-British Saints*, pp. 189–97 (Latin) and pp. 502–14 (English); Wade-Evans, *V.S.B.*, pp. 252–69; B.G.F., 4, pp. 39–41; G. H. Doble, *St Padarn* (1940); E. G. Bowen, *The Settlements of the Celtic Saints in Wales*, pp. 50–6; *Anal. Boll.*, 67 (1949), pp. 384–400.

Paulinus of Wales: Life by Wrmonoc (tenth century) in *Revue Celtique*, 5 (1883), pp. 417–58; eleventh century Life in *Anal. Boll.*, 1 (1882), pp. 209–58 and 2 (1883) pp. 191–4. There is evidence in the Lives of other saints, including *David, *Cadoc, *Gildas, *Samson and *Teilo, all of whom were students of Paulinus. See also Doble, *Welsh Saints*, pp. 146–61; *D.N.B.*, 15, p. 514; *O.D.S.*, p. 382; *Butler 2000*, March, pp. 122–3.

Pyr: T. Taylor (trans. and ed.), *The Life of St Samson of Dol* (1925), pp. 26, 27, 29, 38; Le Grand, 1, p. 315; B.G.F., 4, pp. 85–90; *O.D.S.*, pp. 409–10.

Seiriol: B.G.F., 4, pp. 177–80; *O.D.S.*, pp. 429–30. See also references for *Cybi.

Tathai: *N.L.A.*, 2, pp. 361–3; *Cambro-British Saints*, pp. 255–64 (Latin) and pp. 589–91 (English); Stanton, p. 609; Wade-Evans, *V.S.B.*, pp. 270–87; B.G.F., 4, pp. 211–14.

Teilo: G. H. Doble, *Welsh Saints*, pp. 162–206, and *St Teilo* (pamphlet, 1942); J. Loth in *Annales de Bretagne*, 9 (1893), pp. 81–5, 277–86, 438–46 and 10 (1894), pp. 66–77; B.G.F., 4, pp. 226–42; *O.D.S.*, pp. 449–50; *Butler 2000*, Feb., pp. 87–9.

Theodoric: B.G.F., 4, pp. 252–4; Stanton, p. 638.

Trillo: B.G.F., 4, pp. 263–4.

Tydfil: B.G.F., 4, pp. 286–7; *O.D.S.*, p. 471.

Tysilio: *AA.SS.*, Oct., 1; B.G.F., 4, pp. 296–305; G. H. Doble, *St Suliau and St Tysilio* (1936) and *Cornish Saints*, 5, pp. 104–26; *O.D.S.*, pp. 470–1.

Winifred: *AA.SS.*, Nov., 3; *Cambro-British Saints*, pp. 198–209 (Latin) and pp. 515–29 (English); *N.L.A.*, 2, pp. 415–22; B.G.F., 4, pp. 185–96; *O.D.S.*, p. 500. See also *Beuno.

6 Cornwall: the Travellers

Introduction: B.G.F., 1, pp. 189–90; Doble, *Cornish Saints*, 5, pp. 35–8; Roscarrock, introduction by Nicholas Orme, pp. 1–52; Orme, pp. 1–44.

Breage: Leland, 1, p. 187; Worcestre, pp. 28–9; B.G.F., 3, pp. 80–1; *O.D.S.*, pp. 67–8; Doble, *Cornish Saints*, 1, pp. 97–8; Doble, *Welsh Saints*, p. 151n.; Kenney, p. 18; Orme, pp. 71–2.

Clether: B.G.F., 1, pp. 149–51 includes a photograph of the well; Doble, *St Clether* (pamphlet, 1930); *O.D.S.*, p. 103.

Constantine: Gildas, chs. 28, 29; *AA.SS.*, June, 1; Roscarrock, pp. 68–9; Doble,

Cornish Saints, 2, pp. 15–24; B.G.F., 2, pp. 170–3; O.D.S., p. 112; Orme, pp. 94–6. The *Aberdeen Breviary* story is in *K.S.S.*, pp. 311–14.

Crowan: Leland, 1, p. 187; G. H. Doble, *Cornish Parish Histories*, no. 5 (1939); but cf. *Anal. Boll.*, 59 (1941), pp. 523–4; O.D.S., p. 115; Orme, pp. 98–9.

Endellion: Roscarrock, pp. 71–3; B.G.F., 2, pp. 452–5; O.D.S., p. 158; Orme, pp. 113–14.

Erc of Cornwall: Worcestre, pp. 114–15; B.G.F., 2. pp. 459–63; Doble, *Cornish Saints*, 1, pp. 95–6; O.D.S., p. 160; Orme, pp. 116–17.

Euny: Worcestre, p. 115; B.G.F., 2, pp. 470–4; *Cornish Saints*, 1, pp. 79–88; O.D.S., p. 170; Orme, pp. 118–19.

German of Cornwall: Haddan and Stubbs (1964), 1, pp. 19–21; W. M. M. Picken, 'St German of Cornwall's Day', *Devon and Cornwall Notes and Queries*, 27 (1956–8), pp. 103–7, 110; O.D.S., pp. 100–1; Orme, pp. 127–9.

Germoc: Leland, 1, p. 187; Worcestre, pp. 28–9; B.G.F., 3, pp. 80–1; Orme, p. 129.

Glywys Cernyw: Doble, *Cornish Saints*, 3, pp. 15–19; B.G.F., 3, pp. 131–2; O.D.S., p. 207.

Goran: Worcestre, p. 88; B.G.F., 3, pp. 157–8; O.D.S., pp. 209–10; Doble, *Cornish Saints*, 5, pp. 128–31; Orme, p. 121.

Gwinear: For Gwinear, see *AA.SS.*, March, 3; Doble, *Cornish Saints*, 1, pp. 100–10; O.D.S., p. 222; Orme, pp. 136–8. There is a unique Life in the Bibliothèque Nationale in Paris, according to Orme. For Fingar and Piala, see J. P. Migne (ed.), *Patrologia Latina* (Paris, 1844–64), vol. 159, cols. 323–4; B.G.F., 3, pp. 24–30; Stanton, p. 600; O.D.S., p. 179. For the attribution of the Life of Fingar to St Anselm, see T. S. Hardy, 'Catalogue of Materials, History of Great Britain and Ireland', R.S., 26, 1, p. 59.

Helen: Leland, 1, p. 187; B.G.F., 3, pp. 253–4; O.D.S., p. 226; Orme, p. 312.

Ia: Doble, *Cornish Saints*, 1, pp. 89–94; Worcestre, p. 115; Roscarrock, p. 78; *Butler 2000*, Aug., p. 33; Orme, pp. 144–5.

Kea: B.G.F., 2, pp. 224–8; Doble, *Cornish Saints*, 3, pp. 89–104; O.D.S., p. 279; Le Grand, 2, pp. 561–7; Orme, pp. 156–7.

Kew: Doble, *Cornish Saints*, 1, pp. 105–9; B.G.F., 2, pp. 139–46; Orme, p. 161.

Keyne: N.L.A., 2, pp. 102–4; Roscarrock, pp. 84–5; G. H. Doble, *St Nectan, St Keyne and the children of Brychan*, Cornish Saints Series, no. 25 (1930); O.D.S., p. 282; *Butler 2000*, Oct., p. 51; Orme, pp. 162–3.

Lide: Leland, 1, p. 190; H. E. O'Neill, 'Excavation of a Celtic hermitage on St Helen's, Isles of Scilly', *Archaeological Journal*, 121 (1964), pp. 46–69; O.D.S., p. 299; Orme, pp. 111–12.

Madron: B.G.F., 3, pp. 396–8; B.T.A., pp. 337–9; O.D.S., pp. 310–11; Orme, pp. 169–71.

Mawnan: B.G.F., 3, pp. 453–7; O.D.S., p. 333; Orme, p. 184.

Meriadoc: Doble, *Cornish Saints*, 1, pp. 111–45; W. Stokes, *Beunans Meriasek* (1879): extracts from this edition are included in R. M. Nance and A. S. D. Smith's version of the play (1946); Le Grand, 1, pp. 219–22; O.D.S., pp. 337–8.

Nectan: Worcestre, pp. 33, 63, 65, 83, 89; Roscarrock, pp. 93–4; B.G.F., 4, pp. 1–2; Doble, *Cornish Saints*, 5, pp. 59–79; P. Grosjean in *Anal. Boll.*, 71 (1953), pp. 359–414; *Butler 2000*, June, pp. 125–6; Orme, pp. 197–200.

Neot: Asser, *Life of King Alfred*, trans. and intro. Simon Keynes and Michael Lapidge (1983), p. 55; N.L.A., pp. 213–18; AA.SS., July, 7; Leland, pp. 94–7; O.D.S., p. 352; Orme, pp. 200–3.

Petroc: AA.SS., June, 1, contains a '*vita suspecta*' by John of Tynmouth; N.L.A., 2, pp. 317–20; O.D.S., p. 112; Worcestre, pp. 87, 89, 103, 113; Roscarrock, pp. 101–4, 164–5; Doble, *Cornish Saints*, 4, pp. 132–66; P. Grosjean in *Anal. Boll.*, 74 (1956), pp. 131–88; R. H. Pinder-Wilson and C. N. L. Brooke, 'The Reliquary of St Petroc and the Ivories of Norman Sicily', *Archaeologia*, 104 (1973), pp. 261–306; Stanton, pp. 254–5; D.N.B., 15, pp. 651–2; O.D.S., pp. 395–6; *Butler 2000*, June, pp. 33–4; Orme, pp. 214–18.

Perran: N.L.A., 2, pp. 320–7; Doble, *Cornish Saints*, 4, pp. 3–30; Worcestre, p. 83n.; Roscarrock, pp. 105–8; P. Grosjean in *Anal. Boll.*, 109 (1941), p. 221; O.D.S., p. 400; Orme, pp. 220–3.

Probus: B.G.F., 4, p. 107; Stanton, p. 75; Orme, pp. 223–4.

Rumon: William of Malmesbury, *Gesta Pontificum*, R.S. 52, pp. 202–3; P. Grosjean in *Anal. Boll.*, 71 (1953), pp. 359–414; Doble, *Cornish Saints*, 2, pp. 120–34; Worcestre, pp. 113, 115; O.D.S., p. 424.

Selevan: Doble, *Cornish Saints*, 1, pp. 3–9; O.D.S., p. 430; Orme, pp. 227–8.

Sithney: Doble, *Cornish Saints*, 2, pp. 3–14: cf. *Anal. Boll.*, 59 (1941), pp. 220–1; O.D.S., pp. 438–9; Orme, pp. 236–7.

7 Brittany: the Settlers

Introduction: H. Waquet, *Histoire de la Bretagne* (Paris, 1943, repr. 1964); A. de La Borderie, *Histoire de la Bretagne Armorique* (Paris, 1906); J. Loth,

L'Émigration Bretonne en Armorique (Rennes, 1883); T. Taylor, introduction to *The Life of St Samson of Dol* (1925), pp. xxiii–xxx; for the letter on *conhospitae*, see Doble, *Cornish Saints*, 2, p. 111, quoting La Borderie, 2, pp. 526–7.

Armel: Le Grand, pp. 383–7; J. Macé, *Histoire merveilleuse de S. Armel* (Quimper, 1909); B.G.F., 1, pp. 170–3; *Butler* 2000, Aug., p. 161.

Austell: B.G.F., 1, pp. 189–90; Doble, *Cornish Saints*, 5, pp. 35–58; O.D.S., p. 35; Roscarrock, p. 56; Orme, p. 67.

Brieuc: A. de La Borderie, *Histoire de la Bretagne Armorique* (Paris, 1906), 1, pp. 359–61; Le Grand, 1, p. 150; Doble, *Cornish Saints*, 4, pp. 67–104; *Butler* 2000, May, pp. 2–3.

Budoc: Doble, *Cornish Saints*, 3, pp. 3–14; Le Grand, 2, pp. 613–50; Roscarrock, p. 61; O.D.S., p. 74; *Butler* 2000, Dec., p. 75.

Carantoc: *AA.SS.*, May, 3; Wade-Evans, *V.S.B.*, pp. 142–50; *N.L.A.*, 1, pp. 177–80; Worcestre, p. 73; Roscarrock, pp. 65–6; A. de La Borderie, *Les Deux Saints Caradoc* (Paris, 1883); B.G.F., pp. 78–9; Doble, *Cornish Saints*, 4, pp. 31–52; *D.N.B.*, 3, p. 459; *Butler* 2000, May, p. 88.

Congar of Brittany: *AA.SS.*, Nov., 3; P. Grosjean in *Anal. Boll.*, 42 (1924), pp. 100–20; Doble, *Cornish Saints*, 5, pp. 5–29; G. H. Doble, 'St Congar', *Antiquity* 19, (1945), pp. 32–43, 82–95; O.D.S., p. 110; *Butler* 2000, Nov., p. 211.

Corentin: Le Grand, 2, pp. 683–99; L. Duchesne, *Fastes épiscopaux de l'ancienne Gaul* (3 vols., 4th edn, Paris, 1908), 2, pp. 242 and 371–5; Doble, *Cornish Saints*, 2, pp. 45–53; *Butler* 2000, Dec., p. 107.

Dogmael: *AA.SS.*, June, 3; B.G.F., 2, pp. 349–51; O.D.S., p. 133; *Butler* 2000, June, p. 106.

Ernin: B.G.F., 2, pp. 464–5; O.D.S., p. 152.

Gudwal: The Lives of Gudwal in *AA.SS.*, June, 1 are twelfth century. N.L.A., 1, pp. 501–4; Le Grand, 1, pp. 216–19; Doble, *Cornish Saints*, 1, pp. 61–70; Stanton, pp. 258–9; *D.N.B.*, 8, p. 759; *Butler* 2000, June, pp. 53–4; *D.H.G.E.*, fasc. 128, 645–6.

Gwen Teirbron: Roscarrock, pp. 62, 77; Le Grand, 1, pp. 454–78; B.G.F., 3, pp. 166–71 (Gwen) and 3, pp. 37–42 (Fracan); O.D.S., p. 22.

Judicaël: Orderic Vitalis, *The Ecclesiastical History*, trans. and ed. M. Chibnall (1969), 2, pp. 156–7; Le Grand, 2, pp. 711–13; *Butler* 2000, Dec., p. 145.

Judoc: Orderic Vitalis, *The Ecclesiastical History*, trans. and ed. M. Chibnall, (1969), 2, pp. 156–66, 366–7; Worcestre, pp. 147, 149, 151n.; Le Grand, 2, pp. 699–702; *D.C.B.*, 3, pp. 467–8; *Butler* 2000, Dec., pp. 114–15.

Maelor (Maglorius): *AA.SS.*, Oct., 10; *N.L.A.*, 1, pp. 501–4; *D.N.B.*, 10, p. 5; Le Grand, 2, pp. 534–40; *O.D.S.*, p. 313; *Butler 2000*, Oct., pp. 170–1.

Malo: *AA.SS.*, June, 3; L. Duchesne, 'La Vie de S. Malo: étude critique', *Revue Celtique*, 9 (1890), pp. 1–22; A. Poncelet, 'Une source de la vie de S. Malo par Bili', *Anal. Boll.*, 24 (1905), pp. 483–6; Le Grand, 2, pp. 693–6.

Mawes: Roscarrock, p. 87; *B.G.F.*, 3, pp. 441–9; Doble, *Cornish Saints*, 3, pp. 57–73; *Butler 2000*, Nov., p. 166.

Mewan: *AA.SS.*, June, 5; *Anal. Boll.*, 3 (1884), pp. 141–58; Roscarrock, pp. 103, 157; Doble, *Cornish Saints*, 5, pp. 35–58; Le Grand, 1, pp. 246–8; T. Taylor (trans. and ed.), *The Life of St Samson of Dol* (1925), pp. 30–3, 37.

Padarn of Vannes: *N.L.A.*, 2, pp. 274–9; P. Grosjean in *Anal. Boll.*, 67 (1949), pp. 384–400; *O.D.S.*, p. 379; *Butler 2000*, May, p. 114.

Paul Aurelian: There is an early copy of the Life by Wrmonoc in the public library at Orléans, and more accessible copies are in *Anal. Boll.*, 1 (1882), pp. 209–36 and 2 (1883), pp. 191–4. Le Grand, 2, pp. 98–114; Roscarrock, pp. 98–101; *B.G.F.*, 4, pp. 75–86; Doble, *Cornish Saints*, 1, pp. 10–60 and Doble, *Welsh Saints*, pp. 146–61; *D.N.B.*, 15, p. 541; *O.D.S.*, p. 382; *Butler 2000*, March, pp. 122–3; Kenney, p. 176. See also *Paulinus of Wales, p. 273.

Ronan of Locronan: *B.G.F.*, 4, p. 123; *O.D.S.* p. 423. There is another description of *La Grande Troménie* in L. Gougaud, *Christianity in Celtic Lands* (trans. M. Joynt) (1932), pp. 159–62.

Samson of Dol: T. Taylor (trans. and ed.), *The Life of St Samson of Dol* (1925); *AA.SS.*, July, 6; *N.L.A.*, 2, pp. 350–5; Roscarrock, pp. 109–12; A. Plaine in *Anal. Boll.*, 6 (1887), pp. 77–150; R. Fawtier (1912); Le Grand, 1, pp. 314–16; Doble, *Cornish Saints*, 5 (1970), pp. 80–103; *Butler 2000*, July, pp. 203–4; Kenney, pp. 173–5.

Tudwal: A. de La Borderie, *Les trois anciennes vies de S. Tudwal* (Paris, 1887); Worcestre, pp. 156–7; Leland, 3, p. 88; *Anal. Boll.*, 8 (1889), pp. 158–63; Le Grand, 2, pp. 667–9; *B.G.F.*, 4, pp. 271–4; *O.D.S.*, p. 469; *Butler 2000*, Dec., p. 5.

Tudy: Doble, *Cornish Saints*, 4, pp. 110–15; Le Grand, p. 809; *B.G.F.*, 4, pp. 276–9; *O.D.S.*, p. 469.

Winwaloe: *Anal. Boll.*, 7 (1888), pp. 167–264 has the Life written by Wrdisten, who was abbot of Landévennes about a century later. There is a manuscript copy in the public library at Quimper. *N.L.A.*, 2, pp. 460–5, 558–73; Le Grand, 1, pp. 54–78; Doble, *Cornish Saints*, 2, pp. 59–108; *O.D.S.*, p. 501; *Butler 2000*, March, pp. 23–4; Kenney, pp. 175–6.

8 Travellers in Europe

Introduction: Tommasini; Menzies; Gougaud.

Cathaldus of Taranto: J. Hennig, 'Cathaldus Rachau', *Mediaeval Studies*, 8 (1946), pp. 217–44; *Irish Saints*, pp. 61–2; Menzies, p. 89; *Butler 2000*, May, p. 54.

Columbanus: D. C. Monro, *The Life of St Columbanus by the monk Jonas* (1993); Kenney, pp. 186–205; P. Grosjean in *Anal. Boll.*, 46 (1955), pp. 200–15, 231–6; *Irish Saints*, pp. 105–24 includes a rather hearty translation of the poem; Gougaud, pp. 51–62; Bieler, pp. 96–107; G. Metlake, *The Life and Writings of St Columbanus* (1914); Menzies, pp. 117–18, G. M. S. Walker (trans. and ed.), *Sancti Columbani opera* (Dublin Institute for Advanced Studies, 1957), has an extensive bibliography.

Donat: *AA.SS.*, Oct., 9; *Irish Saints*, pp. 143–5; Gougaud, pp. 76–7; *O.D.S.*, pp. 135–6; *Butler 2000*, Oct., p. 154.

Ferghil of Salzburg: Alcuin, *Monumenta Germaniae Historiae: Poetae*, 1, p. 340; P. Grosjean in *Anal. Boll.*, 78 (1960), pp. 92–123; Tommasini, pp. 170–2; *Irish Saints*, pp. 154–6; Gougaud, pp. 170–2; *Butler 2000*, Nov., pp. 212–13.

Fiacre of Breuil: Gougaud, pp. 86–92; *Irish Saints*, pp. 156–7; *O.D.S.*, p. 177; *Butler 2000*, Aug., p. 315.

Fintan of Rheinau: Tommasini, pp. 95–6; Gougaud, pp. 173–4; *O.D.S.*, p. 180, *Butler 2000*, Nov., p. 122.

Gall: *AA.SS.*, Oct., 7; M. Joynt (trans. and eds.) (1925); Tommasini, pp. 114–19; *Irish Saints*, pp.186–90; Menzies, p. 190; Gougaud, pp. 114–19; *O.D.S.*, p. 194; *Butler 2000*, Oct., pp. 108–9, Kenney, pp. 206–8.

Gunifort of Pavia: *AA.SS.*, Aug., 4; Tommasini, pp. 220–8.

Kilian of Würzburg: *AA.SS.*, July, 2; *Irish Saints*, pp. 200–2; Gougaud, pp. 125–9; *Butler 2000*, July, pp. 56–7; Kenney, pp. 512–13.

Pellegrino: *AA.SS.*, Aug, 1; Tommasini, pp. 346–59.

Ursus of Aosta: *AA.SS.*, Feb., 1 (appendix); Tommasini, pp. 265–74.

9 Northumbria and Anglo-Saxon England

Introduction: Bede, *H.E.*, bk 2, chs. 4, 9–20; bk 3, chs. 1–3, 5–6, 9, 11–13, 14, 21–3; Mayr-Harting, pp. 102–16.

Aidan: *AA.SS.*, Aug., 6; Bede, *H.E.*, bk 3, chs. 3–8, 14–17, 26; *N.L.A.*, 1, pp. 23–8; *D.N.B.*, 1, pp. 182–3; *N.C.E.*, 1, pp. 224; J. Godfrey, *The Church in Anglo-Saxon England* (1962), pp. 102–11; Mayr-Harting, pp. 93–113.

Begga: *AA.SS.*, Sept., 2; Bede, *H.E.*, bk 4, ch. 23; *K.S.S.*, p. 273; *D.N.B.*, 2, p. 126; *O.D.S.*, p. 44.

Boisil: Bede, *H.E.*, bk 4, chs. 27, 28, bk 5, ch. 9; Bede, *Life of Cuthbert*, chs. 6 and 8; *K.S.S.*, p. 281; *D.N.B.*, 2, p. 775; *O.D.S.*, p. 44.

Caedmon: Bede, *H.E.*, bk 4, ch. 4; *D.N.B.*, 3, pp. 647–52; *O.D.S.*, p. 78; *Butler 2000*, Feb., pp. 114–16.

Cedd: Bede, *H.E.*, bk 3, chs. 21–6, bk 4, ch. 3; *O.D.S.*, p. 92; *D.N.B.*, 3, pp. 1322–3; F. Stenton, *Anglo-Saxon England* (3rd edn, 1933, repr. 1988), p. 121.

Finan of Lindisfarne: Bede, *H.E.*, bk 3, chs. 21–2, 25; *O.D.S.*, p. 178; *Butler 2000*, Feb., p. 172.

Fursey: *AA.SS.*, Jan., 2; Bede, bk 3, ch. 19; Tommasini, pp. 108–13; *Irish Saints*, pp. 181–6; *O.D.S.*, pp. 191–2; *Butler 2000*, Jan., pp. 112–13. For Dicul, see: Bede bk 4, ch. 13; *O.D.S.*, p. 130.

Hilda: Bede, *H.E.*, bk 3, ch. 24, bk 4, chs. 25–34; *Eddius Stephanus*; A. Warren (1989); *O.D.S.*, pp. 230–1; *Butler 2000*, Nov., pp. 157–9.

Oswald: Bede, *H.E.*, bk 3, chs. 1–6 and 9–13, bk 4, ch. 14; *AA.SS.*, Aug., 2; R. Folz in *Anal. Boll.*, 98 (1980), pp. 49–94.

Oswin: Bede, *H.E.*, bk 3, ch. 14.

10 Whitby and After

Introduction: Bede, *H.E.*, bk 3, chs. 25, 28, 29, bk 4, chs. 1–5, 17, 18, 23, 24, 27–32; Mayr-Harting, pp. 102–16; P. Grosjean, 'Début de la controversie pascale chez les Celtes', *Anal. Boll.*, 64 (1940), pp. 200–44.

Adamnan: Bede, *H.E.*, bk 5, chs. 13–17, 21–2; tenth century Irish Life, ed. M. Herbert and P. O'Raian, Irish Text Society no. 54 (1988); Richard Sharpe, introduction to Adamnan, *Columba*, pp. 1–99; D. A. Bullough, 'Columba, Adamnan and the Achievement of Iona', *Scottish Historical Review*, 43 (1964), pp. 111–30 and 44 (1965), pp. 17–33; *Butler 2000*, Sept., pp. 23–4; Denis Nechan (ed.), *De Locis Sanctis* (1958).

Aebbe: Bede, *H.E.*, bk 4, chs. 19 and 25; *Eddiles Stephanus*, p. 315.

Chad: Bede, *H.E.*, bk 3, ch. 28, bk 4, ch. 3; *Eddius Stephanus*, chs. 13–15; *AA.SS.*, March, 1; *D.N.B.*, 3, pp. 1300–2; *O.D.S.*, pp. 94–5; *Butler* 2000, March, pp. 12–14.

Colman of Lindisfarne: Bede, *H.E.*, bk 3, chs. 25–6, bk 4, ch. 4; *AA.SS.*, Feb., 3; P. Grosjean in *Anal. Boll.*, 64 (1940), pp. 200–44; Mayr-Harting, pp. 94–118; *N.C.E.*, 3, p. 1013; *O.D.S.*, p. 106; *D.N.B.*, 4, pp. 845–6. For Anatolius, see *Butler* 2000, July, pp. 22–3.

Cuthbert: Bede, *H.E.*, bk 4, chs. 27–32; *N.L.A.*, 1, pp. 216–44; C. Eyre (1858); J. Raine (1828); B. Colgrave, (trans. and ed.), *Two Lives of St Cuthbert* (1940); G. Bonner, D. Rollason and C. Stancliffe (eds.), *St Cuthbert, His Cult and His Community* (1989); Eileen Power, 'St Cuthbert and St Wilfrid', in D. H. Farmer (ed.), *Benedict's Disciples* (1980, repr. 1985); Mayr-Harting, pp. 161–3, 165–7, 240–1; *O.D.S.*, pp. 116–18; *D.N.B.*, 5, pp. 358–63; Kenney, pp. 225–6.

Drithelm: Bede, *H.E.*, bk 5, ch. 21; *O.D.S.*, pp. 136–7; *Butler* 2000, Sept., pp. 4–5.

Eata: Bede, *H.E.*, bk 3, ch. 26, bk 4, chs. 12, 28, bk 5, ch. 1; *Eddius Stephanus*, ch. 24; *N.L.A.*, 1, pp. 300–2; *AA.SS.*, Oct., 11; *D.N.B.*, 6, p. 336; *O.D.S.*, pp. 142–3.

Gerald of Mayo: *AA.SS.*, March, 2; Plummer, *V.S.H.*, 2, pp. 107–15; *Irish Saints*, pp. 191–2; Nora Chadwick, 'Bede, St Colman and the Irish Abbey of Mayo', in *Celt and Saxon*, pp. 186–205.

Epilogue

Aedfrid and Aelfrid: 'Symeon of Durham', R.S., 75, pp. 57, 252, 265–94; *O.D.S.*, pp. 145–6. An illustrated book and a video on the Lindisfarne Gospels are both available from the British Library.

Ireland: W. S. Kerr, *The Independence of the Celtic Church in Ireland* (1931), pp. 86–94 and 130–48.

Iona: Bede, *H.E.*, bk 5, chs. 15–17, 21–2; *O.D.S.*, pp. 4–5, 137; *Butler* 2000, Sept., pp. 211–13; R. Sharpe, Introduction to Adamnan, *Columba*.

Wales: Haddan and Stubbs (1964), 1, pp. 203–4; *Nennius*, p. 94.

Scotland: N. K. Chadwick, *The Age of the Saints in the Early Celtic Church* (1961), pp. 134–6; J. H. S. Burleigh, *A Church History of Scotland* (1960), pp. 29–37.

Cornwall and Brittany: F. M. Stenton, *Anglo-Saxon England*, Oxford History of England, 3rd edn, repr. 1988, pp. 235, 439–40; Asser, *Life of Alfred*, ed. W. H. Stevenson (1904), p. 296; Haddan and Stubbs (1964), 1, pp. 673, 675–6; *D.N.B.*, 1, p. 688 (Athelstan).

Bede's statement on Lindisfarne: Bede, *H.E.*, bk 3, ch. 26.

Bede's Letter to Egbert: Bede, *H.E.*, pp. 337–51.

Index of Saints

(Main entries in Bold type)